RESTAURANT DEALMAKER

AN INSIDER'S TRADE SECRETS FOR BUYING A RESTAURANT, BAR OR CLUB

Steve Zimmerman

Restaurant Dealmaker

Copyright 2013 by Steve Zimmerman
First edition

International Standard Book Number
978-0-9889249-0-1

Publisher: Steve Zimmerman
Cover Design and Interior: Alan Pranke
Printed in the United States of America

Restaurant Dealmaker
(ISBN 9780988924901)

Steve Zimmerman is the consummate restaurant, bar, and club dealmaker. Fortunately, he has codified his many years of broad experience in this book, one that will serve as the "bible" for restaurant and related acquisitions. It is the ultimate guide for the industry.

— William P. Fisher, Ph.D., Darden Chair, University of Central Florida, and former Professor Cornell University School of Hotel Administration. Also CEO, National Restaurant Association, and of American Hotel & Lodging Association

Whether you already are a veteran restaurant owner, buying one, considering buying one, or even just thinking about it, Steve Zimmerman's latest book "Restaurant Dealmaker—An Insider's Trade Secrets for Buying a Restaurant, Bar, or Club," is a must.

His father owned a chain of well-known restaurants in San Francisco, and Steve began his restaurant career at age eight stacking cheese and scooping out hamburger patties. Steve has had every job possible in his 20 plus years in the restaurant business.

Today, Steve is owner of Restaurant Realty and has been personally involved in over 800 restaurant/bar transactions and has performed over 2,500 valuations of restaurants, bars and clubs. He is, indeed, an insider and this book proves it. Ten very full chapters cover every aspect of purchasing, selling and operating a successful restaurant, bar, or club. As the old saying goes: "If it's not in Steve's book, you really don't need to know it."

— Tom West, founder and past president of several large business brokerage firms, and also a founder, past president, and former executive director of the International Business Brokers Association (IBBA). He is also the founder of Business Brokerage Press, the leading publisher of educational and informational publications and services for the Business Brokerage profession.

As a long-time successful entrepreneur preparing to enter the restaurant business, I was aware that this was a very different business—and I was far from confident about how to proceed. What did I need to know as a prospective buyer? What was the smartest way to proceed? Fortunately, I must say how pleased I am that I ended up with an advanced copy of Steve's book. Every one of my questions, and much more, were answered, with great depth of information. Bottom line—If you're considering buying a restaurant, bar, or club, I highly recommend this book.

— *Ted Hunter, author and radio talk show host, www.*
moneysmartonline.com

I have been acquainted with Steve Zimmerman for 15 years. Steve knows the restaurant and related real estate business inside and out, and when I sell a restaurant, Steve is the first, and only, person I call to handle the listing. Restaurateurs are a unique breed, and Steve's intimate knowledge of the industry ensures that maximum value is achieved for his clients. His book is a must buy for the first timer, or the seasoned pro.

— *Noah Alper, founder of Noah's Bagels (a $100 million company)*
and business consultant

"I met Steve in 1995 when he represented the seller of Art & Larry's Deli in San Rafael, CA. This was one of Steve's first brokerage transactions, but his creativity and tenacity were the keys to completing this transaction. The location became our third Amici's East Coast Pizzeria, and we have operated successfully there ever since. Ten years later, Steve represented the owners of a premium San Francisco property where we were able to open another Amici's. Although this was a complex transaction, it was completed both quickly and smoothly. No one understands the restaurant brokerage business better than Steve Zimmerman. This terrific book is required reading for anyone considering buying or selling a restaurant or bar.

— *Peter Cooperstein, President, Amici's East Coast Pizzeria, one of the*
highest sales-volume-per-unit independent pizza chains in the country

I have known Steve for about 20 years, through his participation in the California Association of Business Brokers (CABB) and the International Association of Business Brokers (IBBA). Steve has created a great niche in our industry, and has been very successful in our profession. His knowledge in the restaurant and bar arena is far superior to most (if not all) of us in the Business Brokerage profession. This is due, not only his tremendous experience in selling restaurants and bars over the years, but also because of the knowledge about the restaurant and bar operations he learned as a young man while working in his father's restaurant businesses.

Steve has created a unique business model that he unselfishly shares with other business brokers in the numerous workshops that he has presented at our professional conferences over the years. A very smart businessman, he is always willing to share his ideas and knowledge at our conferences, and is the model of a successful business broker and entrepreneur. His book will be a very valuable asset to those in the restaurant and bar industry as they think about investing in, expanding, or exiting the businesses.

— *Ronald (Ron) Johnson, M&AMI, CBI, CBB, Chairman of ABI,*
Past President of the CABB, and 2007 Chairman of the IBBA

The much-referenced phrase "location, location, location" is no longer viable in the restaurant industry: there is too much competition. Today the mantra is: location, the right concept at that location, and the right sales-to-investment ratio. Contrary to popular belief, restaurants are no more prone to failure than any other business; it's just that the industry tends to attract a lot of high-level risk takers. Anyone who spends the time to read and study Steve Zimmerman's new book will get an excellent education in terms of owning and operating a successful and profitable restaurant.

— *Charles M. Perkins, President, The Boston Restaurant Group, Inc.*

I have known Steve Zimmerman for 25 years, and worked with him for the bulk of that time. I have found him to be an invaluable resource for both buying and selling restaurant real estate for my own company as well as for clients of my consulting business. Restaurant Realty's extensive listing of properties at any given time is a veritable candy store for current and would-be restaurateurs. Steve's personal commitment of time and expertise to every deal helps make most transactions and closings smooth and painless. I know of no one with more experience in the field of buying and selling restaurants than Steve Zimmerman.

— *Michael Dellar, Co-Founder, President & CEO, Lark Creek Restaurant Group, a $50 million plus sales company*

I recently purchased a large multi-million dollar café/bakery operation, and Steve handled the transaction for me, as well as the sellers. His knowledge of the business was helpful in making the due diligence process easy, and Restaurant Realty's expertise in completing hundreds of deals was evident in the smooth way the business closed escrow. I strongly recommend Steve's book to any serious buyer or seller who wants to learn the fine points in getting the deal done.

— *Sunny Bajwa, owner, Basque Boulangerie, Sonoma, CA*

I have known Steve for the past twenty years. He has done more than anyone else I know to create a robust marketplace for the purchase and sale of restaurants in the San Francisco Bay Area. I have recommended Steve's services frequently to clients due to his knowledge, integrity and work ethic. This book is a "must read" for the restaurant entrepreneur.

— *Edward N. Levine, owner & CEO at Vine Solutions Inc. (a leading restaurant accounting and consulting firm) and owner of Left Bank Brasseries & LB Steak. Previous positions were interim CEO at Gordon Biersch Brewing Company, and CFO, Il Fornaio Restaurants*

With 20 years in the bar and restaurant industry, and having opened numerous places from scratch, I know the intricacies and details involved in getting it right the first time. I have also worked with Steve as a buyer and seller of my businesses. Steve's book provides you with the guidelines you need to open your own successful business and more importantly, it provides you with the key questions you need to ask.

— Greg Medow, owner of Hobson's Choice Bar and Flanahan's Bar, and partner in many restaurant and/or bar businesses, and previously owned Indigo Restaurant/Bar and Jade Bar

A few years ago Steve conducted one of the most popular and informative webinars we've ever had on RestaurantOwner.com. Decades of experience as both a restaurant operator and business brokerage professional give Steve a depth of knowledge and experience that would greatly benefit anyone seeking to make that crucial decision of whether or not to buy a particular restaurant or bar. I will advise our members to not even consider buying a restaurant, bar. or club without first reading this book.

— Jim Laube, Founder & President, RestaurantOwner.com

I have worked with Steve Zimmerman over the years in several restaurant sales transactions. I would certainly work with him again as I respect his professionalism, knowledge, and overall integrity. He is an experienced operator of restaurants, understands the business, and has the know how to manage and close his sales transactions in a timely manner. I highly recommend Steve's book as an excellent resource and guide when seeking knowledge in selling or purchasing a restaurant.

— Ray V. Bartolomucci, Founder and President of Strizzi's and Rigatoni's Restaurants

Steve was a guest lecturer in my class for over five years, and did an excellent job teaching several hundred culinary students restaurant: valuation, site selection analysis, lease analysis, the basics on how to write a business plan, and several other pertinent business subjects. Steve's book covers many of the items he taught at the school, and his fine track record as a successful restaurateur and top restaurant broker supports the excellent material he discusses in the book. This book is a "must read" for all restaurant buyers and sellers.

— *Chef Larry Michael, Senior Chef Instructor,*
California Culinary Academy

I became acquainted with Steve over 20 years ago, and have retained him as a recognized expert on restaurant evaluation issues, as well as due diligence and standards of professional care in restaurant brokerage and sales. I have also represented him in brokerage and general business matters on a regular basis. Steve's knowledge and experience in the restaurant business, as well as his highly focused brokerage practice, has made him the top expert in California in these areas, and a highly valuable resource to the industry. His clearly superior qualifications have made him an undisputedly qualified expert in arbitration and litigation. He is uniquely qualified to share his expertise with restaurant owners, buyers, sellers, and owners, and the perfect person to author this book. I highly recommend it as an invaluable resource.

— *William G. Priest, Jr., Attorney at Law; Professor of Real Estate Law*
at Lincoln Law School; mediator, arbitrator and temporary Judge Pro-
Tem at Santa Clara County Superior Court since 1980; and a founding
member of California Association of Business Brokers

I have worked with Steve Zimmerman for over a decade on various accounting and legal matters. Steve is, undoubtedly, an expert in his field, and his background as a restaurant owner and operator, landlord and broker, is evident by the comprehensive job he has done in preparing this informative book—a must for all restaurant, bar, and club buyers and sellers.

— *Thomas Velladao, Esq, CPA, MS Tax,*
Uboldi, Heinke & Velladao LLP

Disclaimer

Because the author's business is based in California, all examples are about businesses in California. Some of the issues are relevant for California-based businesses only. However, the general information and aspects of any buyer's or seller's due diligence is relevant to anyone buying or selling a restaurant, bar or nightclub.

Because some readers will skip around to chapters that really interest them, some repetition was purposely left in as it essential for that certain section. It also makes it easier for the reader to get all the important facts in each specific area.

Dedication

This book is dedicated to my father, Arthur B. Zimmerman, who encouraged me to go into the restaurant business, and to my wife, Judy, and children, Joy, Jacob, and Joshua, who have been an inspiration to me throughout my life.

Foreword

In over six years managing the Internet's most popular and successful business-for-sale marketplace, BizBuySell.com, I have come across hundreds of business brokers, and thousands of buyers and sellers of small businesses. It was in the course of my work at BizBuySell that I first met Steve Zimmerman, President and Founder of Restaurant Realty. I quickly realized that Steve was a unique breed of business broker, at once both down to earth, and in touch with his business and his customers, and also extremely strategic and analytical in marketing restaurants for sale.

Steve has carved out a unique niche as the most successful broker of restaurants, bars and clubs in the greater San Francisco area. He built his brokerage business into a well-known name within the local restaurant and bar community, and is widely considered an expert on all things related to buying and selling a restaurant. As I got to know Steve over the last few years, I was captivated by his personal story of growing up in the restaurant business in San Francisco, evolving his career into the commercial real estate, and then business brokerage industries. I was most impressed that Steve was one of the few business brokers at the time who really had a handle on how to effectively market using the Internet, and how to use the capabilities that technology provided to track customer activity, leads, and success rates for his activities.

I can't imagine anyone more qualified to "write the book" on how to research, buy, operate, manage, and eventually sell a restaurant; Steve has done all of those things first hand over a long and storied career.

Readers of this book will benefit from Steve's great depth of knowledge in the restaurant industry, as well as from his down-to-earth manner, and his strategic and analytical approach to all elements of the restaurant business. If you're about to read this book, consider yourself lucky, you're learning from one of the best.

—Mike Handelsman, Entrepreneur, and former President of Marketplace Verticals at Loopnet, Inc.; General Manager, BizBuySell.com, BizQuest.com

Acknowledgment

I want to thank the following people who have helped me in my career, and with this book. First, my wife, Judy, who encouraged me to write a quarterly newsletter, "Restaurant Rap," which I started writing in 1999. This enterprise has resulted in close to 60 articles as of this date, many of which are the foundation for this book. Judy has also been very supportive in encouraging me to complete this project. The people who have helped in my career most have been my father, Arthur B. Zimmerman, who encouraged me to get into the restaurant business and Jacob Zimmerman, our oldest son, who developed my website when he was in high school, and subsequently has handled all of the Internet marketing development and strategy for my company. He has been an invaluable help in growing my business.

I am grateful for the opportunity to have worked with the following Restaurant Realty team members over the years: Nancy Barton, Bruce Osterlye, Keith Simpson, Jacob Zimmerman, Judy Zimmerman, Sally Packman, Julie Riboli, Lisa Mallon, Kathy Paige, Cara Crandall, Kelsey Maggiora, Emma Mesenburg and Thomas Barton. And I have most special memories related to my first associate Nicki Evatz, who unfortunately passed away a couple of years ago.

The following restaurateurs were responsible for contributing to my expertise in the restaurant business: Joe Vitale, Ken Vix, Fred Cohn, Mauro Olivieri, and Bud Springer.

Several high-producing business brokers were among my mentors, they include: Ian MacLachlan, Kathryn Scramato, Bob Brooks, Greg Carpenter, Tony Moran, George Hicks, Keith Ryan, Greg Kofman, Eldon Edwards, Charlie Perkins, and Clyth MacLeod.

I have had the opportunity over the years to work with the following attorneys and CPAs who have been helpful in my business endeavors: attorneys William Priest, William Dunn, Robert Sturges, Woody Rowland, Robert Nelson, Lawrence Jacobson, as well as Mark Rennie (ABC consultant); and Tom Velladao, CPA.

I learned a lot over the years from the primary escrow officers I worked with including Judy Hetland, Linda Chrisman, and Elizabeth McGovern.

Robert Sylvia of Liquor License Consulting has been extremely helpful in my dealing with complex alcoholic beverage control license issues over the years.

I also want to thank Connie Anderson of Words and Deeds, Inc. for helping me put all the articles I've written over a period of time together into a congruent order. She then edited it into a book designed to help prospective restaurant buyers and restaurant sellers find clear and concise answers to their questions.

Alan Pranke of AMP13 designed the cover and formatted my book. He was great to work with, and the end product far exceeded my expectation.

I would be remiss if I didn't thank the thousands of restaurant owners, buyers, and landlords, as well as the hundreds of attorneys and accountants who have contributed to the deal-making that made this endeavor possible.

Table of Contents

III: BUYERS DO'S AND DON'TS

IV: SUCCESS VS. FAILURE

V: VALUATIONS AND OTHER FINANCIAL ASPECTS

VI: IMPORTANCE OF LOCATION

VII: LEASE AND OTHER LEGAL ASPECTS

VIII: STEPS TO THE SALE

IX: IS FRANCHISING FOR YOU?

X: USING A RESTAURANT BROKER TO YOUR ADVANTAGE

Introduction

In this book you will learn my trade secrets from being a front-line restaurant, bar, and club owner/operator, as well as my extensive experience as a buyer and seller of many restaurants, bars and clubs.

For a 45-year period (1950-1996), my family owned and operated:
- Zim's Restaurants, the largest independent non-franchised restaurant chain in San Francisco
- Nearly 35 restaurants, bars and/or clubs in Northern California including Zim's Restaurants, Z's Bountiful Buffets, Kibby's Drive Ins, and Casa Carlita's Mexican Restaurants
- Miscellaneous other operations, including many cocktail lounges

Today I own Restaurant Realty Company, the largest restaurant, bar, and club business brokerage in California. I have personally sold over 800 restaurant, bar, and club businesses, and have completed over 2,500 business valuations since 1996. In addition, my current business activities include ownership interests in residential and commercial properties.

Throughout this book I will share my experiences and knowledge from my twenty-plus years of restaurant experience, and more than thirty years of real estate experience.

Why I wrote this book

Having worn many hats as a restaurant, bar, and club owner/operator, buyer, seller, landlord, and broker, I want to share my years of experience to make it easier for prospective restaurant, bar, or club buyers to learn how to effectively purchase a business.

My goal is to help a buyer understand the key things he, or she, needs to know in order to minimize mistakes, and to make a successful, well-thought-out purchase. I want this purchase to have a strong chance for success, subject to buyers operating the business properly after they take ownership.

My family's history in business

Art Zimmerman, my father, was on active duty in the Army during World War II. While eating his K rations in Europe, Dad would dream of the day he would return home, and once again be able to bite into a thick, juicy hamburger and drink a rich milkshake. This dream is where he got the idea of opening a specialty restaurant that served only high-quality broiled hamburgers, with a limited menu which included hot apple pie, milkshakes, and an assortment of other beverages.

When Dad came back from the war, he borrowed a few thousand dollars, and in 1949, he opened up a small, U-shaped, twenty-two seat counter operation at the corner of Lombard and Steiner Streets in San Francisco. He called it Zim's—his nickname, a shortened version of Zimmerman, his last name. The emphasis of his operation was quality, and he used whole, choice chucks for his hamburgers. The meat was trimmed, double-ground, and made fresh into hamburger patties daily. Dad used real ice cream for his milkshakes, and made a special hot apple pie with cinnamon sauce for his customers.

When this business became very successful, Dad opened a second unit, and then additional units, and for some 45 years Zim's Restaurants was the largest independent restaurant chain (twelve restaurants) in San

Francisco. Throughout my father's career, he owned and operated close to 35 restaurants throughout Northern California.

From the time I was a little boy, my father would encourage me to come into the business with the hope of eventually managing it. When I was eight years old, he would take me into the restaurant kitchen where I would stack cheese, cut apple pies, and double-grind hamburger meat, scooping out patties into individual portions on 6" x 6" wax papers. When I was older, I was introduced to the front of the house where I learned how to make milkshakes, floats, sundaes, and other fountain items.

As a 13-year-old boy, I wanted to attend the International Boy Scout World Jamboree. This one-week camping experience in Colorado Springs was held every four years in a different place, with Boy Scouts from around the world attending. It cost a couple hundred dollars, and when I asked my father about paying for this experience he said it would be a good idea to pay for this myself, that maybe I should consider getting a part time job. I couldn't start working at Zim's then because the law required that you be fifteen to get a work permit. My father suggested I ask my cousin David, who owned a gas station in the city, if I could get a part time job working there on weekends and on holidays. David was agreeable, and I worked very hard doing a lot of dirty jobs to earn my trip to the Boy Scout Jamboree.

Many years later, my father told me that he had actually given my cousin the money to pay me for the work I did for him. My father did this, because he felt that I would be very happy and appreciative to start working in a restaurant, when I compared it to the work I did at my cousin's gas station. I was, in fact, very appreciative when, on my fifteenth birthday, I got to work in the restaurant; cleaning the bathroom toilets and washing dishes—an upgrade compared to the work I did in the gas station. I worked inside, interfaced with customers and employees, and got to eat whatever I wanted. When I reflect on this period in my life, I tell people that I advanced from axle grease to kitchen grease. So instead of having my fingernails smell like gasoline, they smelled like onions as I always seemed to be assigned the task of peeling onions for the hamburgers.

At age fifteen, I started at Zim's as a regular employee, washing dishes on weekends, during the holidays, and during summer vacations. Throughout my high school years on weekends, holidays, and summer vacations, I worked in the restaurants cooking. Shortly after entering college in 1967, during the Vietnam War, I enlisted into the United States Air Force Reserve as I didn't want to be drafted into the Army. After completing my basic military training and returning to college, I was called to active duty for a two-year period, as a result of the invasion by the North Koreans against a United States intelligence ship, the USS Pueblo, when President Johnson activated thousands of reservists.

I spent most of that two-year period working as a cook in a mess hall at Hamilton Air Force Base in Novato, California, and continued working at Zim's on the weekends, while taking college courses in the evening. I learned a lot working in food service for the Air Force about volume cooking in that we fed several hundred Airmen daily. Also I learned a lot about maintaining high-cleanliness standards in the mess halls as the military was very strict about this.

Once I got out of the Air Force, I earned a college degree in Business Administration from the University of San Francisco in 1970. After a six-month traveling experience to Europe and Israel, I attended the School of Hotel Administration at Cornell University in Ithaca, New York in 1971. There I met my wife, Judy. We have been happily married for nearly forty years, with three grown children, all married and very successful.

Immediately after graduating from Cornell in 1973, I started working in the family business fulltime, first as a manager trainee, working my way up through the ranks from assistant manager, manager, area supervisor, vice president, executive vice president, and finally, president and chief executive officer of the company. Some of my responsibilities throughout the years included hiring and firing personnel, including management; overseeing research and development of all new food products; training cooks, food servers and managers for new store openings; site selection; purchasing, scheduling, and budgeting; negotiating leases for new locations. I also handled the acquisition of various existing restaurants we bought over the years, working with our design team in designing new units and remodeling existing units.

One of the added challenges was that our San Francisco restaurants were union operations. My father joined the union in 1950 when unions were a lot easier to deal with, and many restaurants in the city were also union. Over the years, fewer and fewer restaurants were unionized, and when I came into the business full time in 1973, less than 10% of over 4,000 restaurants in San Francisco were union. We were one of the only chain restaurants that was union. As a result of running union restaurants, our labor costs were 30% higher than our competitors, and it became very difficult to compete. It was an uneven playing field, and we could not maintain a price-value experience for our customers. In 1978, we tried to negotiate a reasonable contract with the union so we could be competitive, but we reached an impasse during negotiations, and consequently, our San Francisco employees went on strike. It lasted almost two months and resulted in our company losing over a million dollars—and alienating many of our employees and customers. As a result, we had to sign a new union contract with no material economic concessions included. Knowing that we could no longer be competitive, and frustrated with the events that occurred as a result of the labor dispute, I had second thoughts about staying in the restaurant business, and handed over the reins of the business to our chief financial officer who succeeded me as president.

In 1983, I started Goodhill Properties, a real estate syndication company. Immediately after college, I had bought and sold single-family homes and multi-residential buildings. An active real estate investor throughout his career, my father had encouraged me to invest in real estate. During my syndication career from 1983 through 1992, I was the general partner of fourteen limited partnerships, with approximately three hundred and fifty limited partners. Most of our deals were structured as deep shelter tax deals. The 1986 Tax Reform Act phased out all the tax advantages, and coupled with a very soft period for commercial real estate in the late eighties, my company experienced some difficult financial times, which ultimately resulted in Goodhill Properties winding down.

After my syndication company went out of business, I went back to Zim's and became the president again in 1992. Due to all the debt we accumulated as a result of our labor strike, I had to scale down our operation from nine to three restaurants. We sold some units, and gave some back to landlords. Ultimately the company was forced into bankruptcy and filed a reorganization plan through a Chapter 11. We had our plan of reorganization approved by the bankruptcy court, but unfortunately we could not meet the terms of the plan. Zim's was forced to go out of business in October 1995, closing our three remaining stores.

About a year before we closed our last three remaining restaurants, I knew I had to find a new career. I thought it would make sense to combine my restaurant experience with my real estate experience, and so I became a restaurant real estate broker. I worked for a local business brokerage company in the East Bay for one year, learning the basics of business brokerage before starting my own company, Restaurant Realty Company in 1996. From a small one-room office opened in Kentfield, California in February 1996, to a multi-suite multi-person staff today, Restaurant Realty Company has, in 17 years, grown into being California's largest restaurant business brokerage, completing sales of over 800 restaurants, bars, and clubs, and also completing over 2,500 restaurant valuations. In addition, I've consulted with thousands of restaurant, bar, or club owners.

As founder and president, I have utilized skills learned from 20-plus years in the restaurant business, and from my 30-plus years of real estate investing. At Zim's Restaurants, I was involved in opening over 10 restaurants and selling a number of units. This experience helped me to understand both the buyer's and seller's side of the transaction, as well as being able to use my analytical skills when evaluating financial data. As a real estate investor, I had a broad range of experience with varied properties. Using both my business experience and my education has contributed to my expertise in understanding the various aspects involved in putting together deals.

Throughout the past years, I have taught several management courses at City College of San Francisco Hotel and Restaurant School, Golden Gate University's former School of Hotel, Restaurant and Institutional Management. I have also been a guest lecturer at the California Culinary Academy (CCA) for the last several years—teaching students all aspects of purchasing a restaurant; from valuation, to putting the business plan together, and doing due diligence leading to restaurant acquisition.

I also believe strongly in continuing education, and I regularly take courses offered by the California Association of Business Brokers and the International Business Brokers Association—two organizations where I am an active member. I have earned the designation of Certified Business Broker (CBB) from the California Association of Business

Brokers, and the designation of Certified Business Intermediary (CBI) from the International Association of Business Brokers, for completing advanced education courses and passing exams. I have also led workshops and have been a featured speaker at several conferences hosted by these organizations.

I hope you'll put the material in this book to good use in purchasing your restaurant, bar, and/or club. If you would like to contact me in the future, I can best be reached best by email, which is Steve@ RestaurantRealty.com.

The Buyer

Chapter 1

MOTIVATIONS FOR BUYING A RESTAURANT, BAR, OR CLUB

If you have ever thought you'd like to own and run a restaurant, bar, or club—you are not alone. Many of us find ourselves in food service for our first job, some in franchise locations, others at a Mom and Pop café. As we get older, we may work in a bar or even a club. Sometimes the whole thing about serving people, watching people enjoy themselves and having fun—gets in your blood.

Then one day, you decide to act on that dream and say: Today I will research buying a restaurant, bar, or club. That's the easy part. Every good dream must have a sound foundation, and be built with a boatload of reality and due diligence on your part. This is not the time to do blue-sky thinking, like in "Field of Dreams,"—because, well, "If you build it, they will come" is only in the movies.

Here are some of the reasons that motivate individuals to go into the restaurant, bar, and nightclub business:

- **Make a living and become financially successful**

  This is a priority motivation of most entrepreneurs that go into business. A well-run restaurant, bar, or club can be a good vehicle for generating cash flow on an ongoing basis.

- **Provide a service to the community**

  By providing a business that is accessible to the public, you are providing goods and services to the community.

- **Express creativity**

  If you are a chef, opening a restaurant is a vehicle to demonstrate your culinary skills to the public, where you can experiment with new food and drink formulas. If you are an entertainer, owning a club gives you a vehicle for showcasing your talent.

- **Provide a job for yourself and family members**

  Many positions are required for running a restaurant, bar, or club that can be filled by the owner and family members, if desired. However, think long and hard about hiring family members for your business because in many cases, family members won't work out, which can jeopardize your future relationship with them. Remember, it is challenging enough to maintain good relationships with family members under normal circumstances.

- **Lifestyle**

  Certain types of restaurants are conducive for owners structuring desirable work hours. For example, a downtown/financial district restaurant that is open for breakfast and lunch only five days a week is desirable for the owner who want to be free every evening, and off on weekends. Most restaurant owners take the slowest weekdays off, as weekends are the busiest days for most restaurants. Some owners also prefer to take off the slow days during the week when there aren't as many people around, so they can visit and do things while avoiding big crowds. Conversely many bar or club owners prefer to not work during the normal day hours, but want to sleep in, then do their personal business during the day. They prefer working late nights when most of the bars and clubs do business. Also most clubs are only open four nights a week, Wednesday thru Saturday, which affords these operators a lot of time off during the rest of the week.

- **Control your destiny**

  By owning your own business, you are not at the whim of an employer who can eliminate your job at the snap of his finger, creating economic chaos for you and your family. This is especially true during periods of high unemployment such as the great recession we recently experienced. If you are forty years of age or older, it can be very difficult to get a new job, and by owning your own business, you can control your financial security for you and your family.

- **Personal gratification**

  Operating a restaurant, bar and/or club is a very public and visible business, giving the owner/operator much exposure to the general community as well as to friends, associates and family members. If you have a successful business, you may become well known to many people, giving you a strong sense of personal gratification.

Chapter 2

THINGS TO KNOW BEFORE YOU PURCHASE A RESTAURANT, BAR, OR CLUB BUSINESS

When you own a restaurant, the consumer judges you by the quality of service and food, and also the environment. That's your public face. But you must also understand the behind-the-scenes aspect of running this kind of business:

1. Financial
2. Operations
3. Legal and accounting
4. Marketing/Public Relations
5. Dealing with people

1. Financial

You must be able to understand how to read and analyze financial statements and reports such as:

- Monthly profit-and-loss statement, daily sales report, and monthly bank statement.

- Proper target expense percentages on the profit-and-loss statement that are acceptable for all of the major expense categories, such as food cost, pouring cost, labor cost, utility cost and occupancy cost, etc.
- The source-and-use-of-funds statement that outlines all the source of funds and uses of funds for your business to help you have better control of your cash flow.
- A balance sheet, but this is not as important as the other items mentioned above.

Inventory control is a very important aspect of running a business. Always keep the proper inventory on hand so you don't run out of product. If you're out of a product, unless it is a special of the day, when frequently only a designated amount of products are prepared, it gives the customer the wrong impression. It makes them wonder if your business is reliable, and may influence the customer's decision to return.

2. Operations

To truly understand all of the operational aspects of the business, it is helpful to have a working knowledge of each job in the business. I was taught when I was in the business that, if necessary, I should be able to fill any job that needed to be filled on a temporary basis such as cooking, waiting on tables, hosting guests, washing dishes, busing tables, seating guests or making drinks at the bar. Inevitably in running a service-oriented business, some employees get sick at the last minute or, for various other reasons, don't show up for their shift, often making it necessary for the owner to jump in and fill their shift until he has time to find a replacement employee. By having a working knowledge of all of these positions, you will be more humanistic and empathetic in dealing with employee problems and the challenges that arise in these positions, because you have experienced these situations yourself from your past experience.

3. Legal and Accounting

It is important that you follow all of the legal requirements of running a business such as:

- Making sure everyone meets the immigration requirements for being hired.
- Having the proper licenses in good standing such as business license, health department license, alcohol beverage control license, and if applicable, fire inspection approval.
- Filing the various required tax returns such as payroll tax, county tax, state tax, federal tax, etc.
- Dealing with accountants and attorneys who are experienced in working with restaurant, bar, or club businesses.

4. Marketing/Public Relations

Most small businesses cannot afford expensive advertising such as television, radio, newspaper, magazine, and billboard advertising, etc. Most marketing of a small business comes from word-of-mouth communication through customers. If a customer has had a good experience, he'll undoubtedly tell other people—and conversely, if the customer has had a bad experience, he'll spread the unpleasant news, possibly to more people than he'd tell good news. Needless to say, it is important to provide every customer with a good experience so he'll become the goodwill ambassador for your business. This will create a domino effect in reaching others who have never experienced your business, and motivate them to come and try it themselves.

Another important source of marketing your business is being reviewed by a well-known local food critic. Food critics influence many people, and a good review could draw a lot of customers into your business. However, a bad review can negatively impact a business, sometimes to the point of causing it to close. One of my clients operated a chain of well-known, up-scale restaurants nationally, and I placed them into a location in Marin County. The first couple of years they did well, and then the operation started to slip with inferior management, food, and service. At the same time they received a terrible review from the most well-known food critic at the San Francisco Chronicle. Consequently I helped them sell the business, but they lost over a million dollars on the transaction.

5. Dealing with people

As owner/operator, you should:

- Be a person that genuinely likes people, and likes to be around people.
- Realize you are dealing extensively with employees, customers, vendors, and landlords.
- Be a good communicator.
- Treat people honestly and fairly. It is very important to be objective and not favor one person over another.
- Be a role model. Employees look to the owner as the one who sets the pace for the business. Always have a smile on your face, put your best foot forward, and strive to maintain high standards in maintaining consistently good service, good food and beverage quality in a clean and safe environment.

Based on my experience as a former restaurant, bar, and club owner, it is imperative that you are proficient with all of the above items to enhance your chances for success.

Chapter 3

QUALIFICATIONS NEEDED TO PURCHASE A RESTAURANT, BAR, OR CLUB

Landlords usually have high standards for accepting a new prospective tenant for their property. Why? This is due to the high failure rate for new restaurant, bar, and club businesses. My clients know that the biggest challenge in putting together the deal is not getting the seller and buyer to agree on the price and terms of the transaction, but it is getting the landlord to approve them as the new tenant. The qualifications indicated below are not usually imposed by the seller of the business unless the seller is entering into a sublease with the buyer, but, in most cases, are required by the landlord of the business.

Operational Qualifications

On-the-Job Experience – A buyer should have a minimum of three to five years practical experience as a restaurant, bar, or club owner and/or manager. Ideally, if you are a buyer, in addition to having management experience, you should have extensive hands-on experience working in the front of the house as a food server, cashier, and host, as well as back-of-the-house experience working as a bus boy, dishwasher, and cook. By having experience in the various facets of the operation you have empathy for understanding the challenges of each job, and for whatever reasons, you can fill in anywhere as needed.

Although a solid education in the administrative, financial and marketing areas is helpful to round out your chances for success, this business is learned largely from on-the-job experience. It's a hard business to learn in a classroom situation. In some cases, in larger more-ambitious business transactions, the landlord may insist that the buyer own and operate an existing restaurant, bar, or club, where the landlord can go and see and experience the food, drink and service as a requirement for renting the premises to the prospective buyer.

Financial Qualifications

Net Worth - The net worth requirement for each deal varies, depending on the size of the deal. Usually the larger the deal, the higher the net worth requirement. Net worth is defined as a person's total assets, minus liabilities.

Let's assume that a person owns the following assets, and owes the following liabilities:

Assets	
Cash in bank	$50,000
Residence market value	300,000
Automobile	20,000
Stocks and Bonds	50,000
Business Value	100,000
Personal Items	50,000
Total Assets	**$570,000**
Liabilities	
Residence mortgage	$150,000
Credit card debt	10,000
Auto loan	10,000
Misc. other debt	10,000
Total liabilities	**$180,000**
To determine this person's net worth, subtract the total liabilities from total assets	
Assets	$570,000
Liabilities	(180,000)
Net Worth	**$390,000**

- **Cash in Bank.** The landlord usually likes to see, at least several months of working capital in the buyer's bank accounts, above and beyond the monies he needs to purchase and set up the restaurant. The rule of thumb I used personally, and what I hear from many owners today, is that working capital should be at least six months of projected payroll. So if your monthly payroll cost is $15,000, you should have $90,000 ($15,000 monthly payroll x 6 months = $90,000 working capital) set aside for working capital.

- **Good Credit Score.** Usually a landlord requires you have a good credit score to be accepted as a tenant—credit scores of at least 680. If you don't have a good credit score, the landlord may ask you for one or more or all of the following requirements:
  1) Several times the monthly rent in the form of an increased security deposit,
  2) A security agreement recorded in favor of the landlord on the fixtures and equipment of the business, and
  3) An additional guarantor with a strong financial statement to

personally guarantee the lease, should you not perform all the terms and conditions of the lease.

- **Tax Returns.** In many cases the landlord wants to review the prospective tenant's last two to three years tax returns, both personal and corporate, if applicable, to examine his income, as well as to review his balance sheet to determine his financial strength as a tenant. Also landlords may want to check tax returns to determine if the proposed tenant is honest in reporting all of his income because the proposed premises lease may have a percentage clause in it making the tenant responsible for a paying a percentage of his sales in addition to his minimum rent. If a tenant under-reports his income on his tax return, there is a good chance he'll under-report his sales to the landlord for calculating percentage rent. This could discourage the landlord from renting to the prospective tenant.

- **Bank Statements**. Frequently the landlord will want to see the prospective tenant's last three to six months bank statements to examine his inflows and outflows and determine what bank balances he maintains.

Other Requirements:

- **Business Plan.** The landlord, in most cases, will want to see the buyer's business plan to verify and, basically, explain the proposed operation in terms of menu, staffing, physical changes to the premises, and the financial projections of the new business, etc.

- **Landlord References.** In some cases, the landlord wants to speak to the proposed tenants former landlords to determine if the tenant paid his rent on time, and upheld all of the terms and conditions of his lease.

Chapter 4

THINGS TO DO BEFORE YOU PURCHASE A RESTAURANT, BAR, OR CLUB

Let's discuss a broad-brush approach—some of the major areas of experience a prospective restaurant, bar, or club buyer should have. For detailed information on how to operate a restaurant, bar, or club, I suggest you research the appropriate books. However, the ability to successfully operate a restaurant, bar, or club is achieved by actual hands-on experience, and books on this subject only supplement the knowledge that is acquired from that extensive experience.

Why should a restaurant, bar, or club buyer be experienced in that specific business before he purchases an independent non-franchised business? The reason is very simple. This business has a high failure rate, approximately 80% fail in the first five years of ownership for an independent, non-franchised operation. With specific experience, your chances for success will be higher than those who don't have it, because the experienced operator has the benefit of learning the right and wrong way of doing things, minimizing risk of not succeeding.

However, if the buyer is purchasing a franchised business, in many cases, the franchisor would prefer that the buyer had no restaurant experience so they can train and mold the buyer to specific procedures and policies unique to their franchise. Nonetheless, the items discussed below are still important to know, whether you're an independent or franchised operator.

Although an owner does not need to have strong expertise in all the positions listed below, he should have a working knowledge of these positions so he can perform any of these positions if necessary. Employees will respect the owner because he knows how to perform each position. Also, the owner won't be as vulnerable to getting jerked around by employees who think they can get away with things because the owner has no knowledge of their position.

The owner should have a knowledge of the management functions as well as both the front- and the back-of-the-house functions.

Management functions include:
1.   operational procedures,
2.   administrative and bookkeeping procedures, and
3.   marketing procedures.

1. Operational Procedures

These include all the things an owner needs to know to effectively perform and manage a restaurant, bar, or club. Some of these items are indicated below.

a.   Scheduling Procedures

Labor cost is one of the major costs in running a restaurant, bar, or club, and as such, it is imperative that a lot of thought goes into the daily schedule to assure that the customers will receive consistently good service. This business can have great fluctuations and erratic sales levels, and it is tricky to staff the business properly. Service is one of the most important priorities in a customer's mind when they visit the business. All of us have experienced having mediocre food, but excellent service that was so warm, friendly, and responsive that we would return there. In scheduling, it is a good idea to physically graph out each day of business by the hour, including the staff coverage per hour. Include the historic hourly sales indicated per hour so you can staff people appropriately. Have a special events calendar for the area of your business, so you can take into consideration any special events going on, and adjust the schedule accordingly.

As well as your regular staff, it is also a good idea to have backup employees on call. That way if you're short staff on a particular day, due to heavy employee absence, you have a source of employees to call to fill these openings, rather than have to pay a lot of overtime.

b. Hiring and Firing Employees, and Understanding the Labor Laws.

Hiring and Firing – It is extremely important to be well educated on the labor laws so you don't get involved with unnecessary legal proceedings. All employees must have the proper governmental credentials to work in this country; and if you hire employees that do not have the proper credentials, you are subject to large financial penalties. It is important to hire as many experienced employees as possible to minimize the need for excessive training. In any case, all employees, regardless of their experience, need to be trained in the particulars of your operation. All prospective employees, being considered, should have their work references checked by phone after being interviewed. Any employee required to handle money should be tested by written exam to determine if they have the basic math skills to conduct the respective transactions.

It is very important to understand labor laws so you know the proper procedures for terminating an employee. If the proper termination procedures are not enforced, the employer could be subject to reinstating the fired employee, as well as be faced with stiff financial penalties.

c. Ordering Procedures

Although the ordering of food, beverage, cleaning and paper supplies can be delegated to some extent, the owner needs to have a good working knowledge of this area to assure that the business is properly supplied, and that inventory levels are not excessive. In well-run operations, the head chef is usually charged with ordering most food items from the respective vendors, including paper and cleaning supplies. However, it is incumbent upon the manager to check the head chef's orders to make sure the proper inventory levels are maintained to meet the business needs. On all inventory items, periodically get competitive bids to assure that you are getting the best price.

d. Back-of-the-house Procedures

These functions include the various positions in the kitchen. These include the cooking positions as well as dishwashing and busboy positions. The owner should have a working knowledge of how the entire kitchen operates. Ideally the owner should know how to cook, and if necessary, be able to jump into the kitchen and perform all of the major functions of the cooking staff. Without having this knowledge, it is hard for an owner to know whether the food coming out of the kitchen is cooked properly, portioned properly, and whether the plate set-up and garnish is correct.

During the buyer's training after the close of escrow, he should spend several days in the kitchen with the head cook, learning all the plate set-ups and garnishes so he can, in turn, supervise the cooking staff, or do whatever is necessary.

The cooking responsibilities include the following:

a. Proper portion control, which includes knowing the proper weights of all the entrees on the menu as well as knowing the proper scoops and ladles to be used in portioning out all the various food items.

   1. Preparation procedures – The owner should know the formulas of all the major menu items such as pancakes, French toast, fried chicken, meatloaf, sauces, gravies, salad dressings, soups, etc. He should know the portions of all the major entrees for breakfast, lunch and dinner, including meat weights, vegetable and starch portions, etc. For consistency purposes, there should be a written formula

book in the kitchen which has pictures of all the finished menu items, as well as a written description of what goes on the plate, and how the food item is prepared. If a cook is sick, the back-up person will have a written reference to review the proper preparation and plate set up.

b. Proper receiving procedures and storage procedures. The owner should be familiar with all the proper receiving procedures, and know the responsibilities of the designated person authorized to receive product deliveries from vendors. This is a key responsibility in maintaining cost control in the kitchen. In fact, in many situations the owner actually performs this function himself rather than delegating it. All items that are received need to be counted and/or weighed, and checked against the invoice when the delivery is made. Costs can get out of line when these items are not checked properly. Delivery drivers can become aware of this and intentionally regularly short the order, resulting in the business losing money. Once items are received, especially perishable items, new items are stored behind so the old items are used first and all food products stay fresh. If some items outlive their usable life, they need to be discarded rather than to serve an inferior product to a customer. One of the key factors for a successful restaurant is serving consistently good food. The owner needs to know the side work schedule, which is a list of the side work responsibilities for each shift in the kitchen—such as which shift prepares sauces, soups, portions out meats, makes various specialty dishes, changes the oil in the deep fryer, etc. This should all be spelled out in the procedures manual so each shift knows what their side work responsibilities are, in addition to their main cooking responsibilities.

Besides the owner having a working knowledge of the cooking station, he should also be familiar with the other back-of-the-house functions, which involve all the dishwashing room procedures, as well as the side work responsibilities of the dishwashing room. These include how to change the soap, clean out the dishwashing machine, and how to troubleshoot the dishwasher and garbage disposal. The owner should also be familiar with all the side work responsibilities of the dishwashing person, which could include cleaning the dishwashing area, checking the restrooms hourly to make sure they are clean and properly stocked with supplies such as soap, paper towels, toilet seat covers and toilet paper, and bringing supplies to the various stations including the front of the house and back of the house.

The owner should know the table busboy's responsibilities including making sure each table is cleared of dirty dishes at the appropriate time during the customer's meal so no excess dirty dishes remain on the table. After the customer leaves, the busboy is responsible for clearing off and cleaning the table, and setting up the table with the proper place settings; including silverware, napkins and other appropriate items required by the specific operation. Also the busboy, in some cases, is responsible for checking the restrooms hourly to make sure they are clean and properly staffed, and is responsible for stocking the front and back of the house with the needed dining room and kitchen supplies. Have a manual for the dishwashing and busboy station stating all the procedures for these respective jobs.

e. Front-of-the-House Procedures

The owner should have a working knowledge of these various positions in the dining room including food servers, hostesses, and cashiers. He should specifically know the following:

Food servers –

- Knowing the station assignments and which are the primary stations—ones opened most of the time—and which secondary stations are only opened to handle the overflow.
- Understand balanced seating so as the dining room fills up, no single food server gets overloaded and provides inferior service to the customers.
- Customer recognition is necessary, so if customers are seated at a table, and the food server can't get to them immediately, they are welcomed by the food server and given a menu with a greeting such as, "Welcome. I'll be with you as soon I can."

- Be familiar with the pricing of all items, even if they are programmed into a point-of-sales computer system. Have a procedures' manual so each food server is familiar with the side work responsibilities, like filling salt and pepper shakers, replenishing the station with paper supplies and cloth napkins (if applicable), silverware, clean dishes, and condiments, as well as clean bus pans when busboys are not on duty.

Guest-check accountability is another important area where each of the food server's guest checks are accounted for, from issuance to completion, and the individual cash balances for each food server are reconciled at the end of each shift, (if the system is set up that way).

Host/Hostess – The host/hostess is responsible for balanced seating. It's extremely important to recognize customers immediately as they enter the restaurant. If the host/hostess can't immediately seat a customer, but he or she is recognized by the host/hostess with a greeting such as, "Hello and welcome. I'll be with you as soon as possible," the customer feels welcome and starts their experience off on a positive note.

As soon as possible, the host/hostess then proceeds to seat the customer, and gives them a menu. The host/hostess lets the food server know they have been seated so the food server can attend to them as quickly as they can.

2. Administrative Procedures

To be successful in this business, it is imperative that the proper administrative procedures are in place and utilized, which gives the owner the controls necessary to evaluate the profitability of the business. The owner needs to know his cash position daily, and whether his costs are in line, so if necessary, he can, on a timely basis, adjust his operating procedures. For example, if his costs dramatically increase on a major selling item, it might be necessary to adjust the menu price of that item immediately, rather than waiting weeks to discover that his profits have been negatively impacted due to his non-response.

Administrative procedures include banking procedures, daily sales reporting and invoice tracking systems, monthly inventories, monthly income and expense statements, and guest check accountability systems, detailed below:

- Banking procedures include daily deposits to the local bank, either by a carrier pick up or actual physical deposits by the manager.
- Daily sales reporting includes a recap of all register tapes, with a cash reconciliation per shift.
- All daily invoices are accumulated with the daily sales reports, and submitted to the bookkeeper, who enters them into the appropriate accounting records so a monthly income-and-expense statement can be generated.
- Physical inventories of all food, beverage, cleaning and janitorial supplies are taken on the first of each month, and extended on the cost basis. The cost of sales are calculated based upon the opening inventory from the prior month, plus all the invoices for the subject month, minus the closing inventory, which will give the cost of sales.
- Having accurate and timely financial statements are important for the owner to use as a tool to control costs and increase sales.

For those operators that don't use a computerized point of sales system to account for all transactions, a stringent guest check control system is necessary to assure that the food servers are reconciling their guest checks daily, and accounting for all of the checks issued to them. Guest checks are only issued by the manager to the food servers, and the food servers are to reconcile their guest checks with their cash receipts daily, turning them in to the manager before they check out from their shift.

Budgeting income and expense statements at least one year ahead is prudent, and adjusting them monthly is an effective way to monitor the financial results of the business.

3. Marketing/Public Relations Procedures

Most marketing in single-unit non-franchised restaurants occurs as a result of the customers' word of mouth experiences. If a meal is good, a guest will tell his friends about the restaurant, and they in turn, will tell their friends. This domino effect creates a basis for customers becoming aware of your restaurant, and then frequenting it. The key here is that your customers have a positive overall experience in terms of good food, good service in a clean, well-maintained environment, and a good price-value experience.

Other methods for marketing include being well positioned on search engines and websites so prospective customers can easily pull up your restaurant during a computer search. Also hiring a good public relations consultant to assure you'll be reviewed in the appropriate publications by reputable food critics could be a big impetus for customers becoming familiar with your operation.

Chapter 5

THE ADVANTAGES AND DISADVANTAGES OF BUYING AN EXISTING RESTAURANT, BAR, OR CLUB vs. STARTING ONE FROM SCRATCH

To buy an existing site or build from scratch? This is a good question, so let's discuss it.

The advantages of buying an existing business

1. **It is much less expensive.** You can purchase an existing 2,000 sq. ft. restaurant in good condition, with approximately 60 seats, a competitive premises lease, in a good location for approximately $150,000 or less. This is dependent on the quality of the location, the quality of the improvements, and the premises lease terms and conditions. If you were to build out the restaurant from scratch in the San Francisco Bay Area, it would cost somewhere between $300 to $500 a square foot, so a 2,000 square foot restaurant will cost you between $600,000 (2,000 sq. ft. times $300 sq. ft. = $600,000) and $1 million (2,000 sq. ft. time $500 = $1 million).

2. **A much-quicker timetable to get the businesses up and running.** Buying an existing restaurant, bar, or club, you can open quicker than if you need to go through a lot of red tape to build a space from scratch. This might involved hiring an architect to design the plans for the space, getting the job bid out by contractors, getting permits and approvals from the local governmental agencies, and going through a lengthy construction timetable. You can buy an existing restaurant, and remodel it to your specs in a couple of months, versus building from scratch, which can take anywhere from 6 months to a year, or longer.

3. **Take advantage of the former businesses customer base**. You get to capitalize off the former restaurant's customer base. Former customers of the prior restaurant will most likely try your new concept as many people are creatures of habit, and perhaps your restaurant is conveniently located near their home or business.

4. **Grandfathered in on various building conditions.** In some cases, you may be grandfathered in for preexisting conditions, which would be less expensive. For example, it's possible disabled retrofit laws and other physical requirements will be less stringent.

5. **Third-party financing may be available**. Financing may be available from the Small Business Administration (SBA), other lenders, or from the seller in terms of seller carry-back financing.

6. **Immediate cash flow**. If you are purchasing a going-concern business or one that is profitable, you have immediate cash flow from the day you close escrow.

7. **Less financial risk.** Buying an existing business that is profitable means there is less financial risk.

8. **The premises lease can be more competitive.** If the premises lease is assigned, the rent can be significantly less than a new market rate premise lease. An assignment of a premises lease means that the

landlord allows the seller to transfer the seller's lease to the buyer, allowing the buyer to enjoy the same lease terms and conditions as the previous seller.

And the Disadvantages Are

So what kind of things can go wrong or add risk if you buy an existing business? Buyer beware. As the new owner, you may:

1. **Have to compromise on the physical plant.** Using the former businesses' physical plant, you won't have a kitchen built specifically to meet your needs, and possibly will have to realign the kitchen equipment and modify the equipment to meet your needs. Similarly the floor plan might not meet your criteria and might need to be redesigned.

2. **Inherit the former businesses reputation to some extent.** If you are buying an assets sale, where you are changing the name and menu, you will inherit, to some extent, the prior restaurant's reputation until such time that the former customers experience your new concept.

3. **Have some extraordinary repair/maintenance bills**. If it is an older business, your maintenance and repair bills may be more expensive, because years of use has created wear and tear on the equipment.

Advantages of Building a Restaurant, Bar, or Club from Scratch

1. **Stronger definition of your concept and identity to the customer.** You can better define your new concept and image to the customer because your physical plant will have a unique feeling to it, versus being a retrofit of the former businesses physical plant. A brand-new restaurant projects a fresh, new image to the customers, and initially attracts more curiosity seekers. However, this is not necessarily always the case.

2. **A more efficient physical plant**. The kitchen, dining room, and other physical aspects of the building will be specifically designed for your concept. A more efficient plant minimizes labor cost, which can improve the profitability of the business.

3. **The landlord may make a monetary contribution to your project.** In some cases, the landlord may contribute some financial help in the form of tenant improvements since you are improving his building. The landlord may also provide some free rent for a defined number of months during construction, or until you open the business.

My recommendation is to purchase an existing restaurant, bar, or club rather than having a restaurant bar or club built to suit; as the advantages far outweigh the advantages of a build-to-suit, and most importantly the risk factors are greatly diminished.

Chapter 6

WHAT YOU ARE BUYING WHEN YOU PURCHASE A RESTAURANT, BAR, OR CLUB

When the buyer is purchasing a restaurant, bar, or club, the purchase includes:

a. Fixtures and equipment

b. Licenses

c. Leasehold improvements

d. Premises lease

e. Goodwill

f. Cash flow, and

g. Covenant not to compete

In this chapter, we will discuss all of these items in depth:.

a. Fixtures and Equipment. This includes all the fixtures and equipment which are included on the equipment lists accompanying the purchase contract at the time the offer is made. The equipment list is signed by the buyer and seller for the transaction when the offer is made. It is signed again by the seller and buyer when the buyer takes possession of the premises to assure that all of the equipment is still in place immediately before the close of escrow. In many situations, the seller has personal items such as family paintings and artifacts, unique equipment such as a pasta maker and other personal items that are not included with the sale. In this case, these items should be indicated on the fixtures and equipment list as items not included with the sale to make it perfectly clear to the buyer what is, and what is not, included.

Sometimes a piece of equipment is leased or rented. If the equipment is leased, it may be a condition of the sale that the buyer formally assumes the equipment lease at the close of escrow. If this is the case, the leased equipment list should be disclosed to the buyer before the offer is made, so the lease includes the monthly payments and the current balance on the lease. Most equipment leases are set up so at the end of the lease term, the buyer pays a fixed nominal amount (sometimes only one dollar), and then owns the equipment. Another possible situation is that some of the equipment is rented, in which case the buyer generally has the option to terminate the rental agreement if he desires and have the rented equipment removed from the premises.

In some situations all the equipment may be owned by the landlord, and the tenant is responsible for maintaining and replacing it when necessary during his tenancy. Usually attached fixtures such as duct systems and hoods, some built-ins such as the bar, counters, back bars, etc. belong to the landlord when the tenant vacates. As a rule, these items are spelled out in the premises lease with the appropriate schedules attached.

b. Licenses. Included in the sales price are the operating licenses, such as any food or bar permits necessary to operate a restaurant, bar or nightclub, and any other licenses, such as alcohol beverage control licenses, entertainment licenses or franchise licenses, etc. Although these license are included in the sale, the buyer has to go through a transfer process that requires them to qualify for these licenses, and pay transfer fees in some cases.

c. Leasehold Improvements. These include the heating, ventilating, air conditioning, plumbing, and electrical systems that the tenant has use of during his tenancy. The tenant is usually responsible for the maintenance and/or replacement of these items, although these items belong to the landlord at the end of the lease, and cannot be removed from the premises.

d. Premises Lease. The premises lease is probably the most valuable item the buyer acquires when he purchases the business. The premises lease is a legal contract between the tenant and landlord, giving the tenant the right to occupy the premises. The lease is analogous to a promissory note to the bank. It is a legal contract which obligates the tenant to make a designated number of payments for a designated number of years to the landlord. For example if the tenant has a 5-year lease, the monthly payments are as follows: year 1 - $4,000 ($48,000 per year), year 2 - $4,250 ($51,000 per year), year 3 - $4,500 ($54,000 per year), year 4 - $4,750 ($57,000 per year), and year 5 - $5,000 ($60,000 per year). This translates into the tenant being legally obligated to pay the landlord $270,000 ($48,000- year 1+$51,000-year 2 +$54,000-year 3 +$57,000-year 4 +$60,000- year 5 = $270,000) over a 5-year period. The terms and conditions of a lease include paying the rent on time, maintaining the premises in good condition, and respecting the rights of adjoining tenants and neighbors. In order to control your business destiny, you should ideally have a 5 to 10 year base term and several 5-year options, with a clear definition of your rent payments for the entire projected duration of your stay at the premises.

e. Goodwill. This term identifies the reputation of the business occupying the premises immediately before the new tenant takes possession of the premises. It consists of the trade name of the business, the menu and menu items, all the business systems—service systems, standard operating procedures, intellectual property, trademarks, phone numbers, fax numbers, email addresses, websites, etc. If you are buying a going-concern business (one that is making money), then goodwill is extremely important. A buyer purchasing this type of business will generally not change anything about the business, and will try to run the business exactly as the prior owner did. Even if you are not buying a going-concern business, but you are buying an assets sale instead, goodwill is still important as the prior business was most likely a similar business to the one you will operate, and some of their customers will be potentially your customers.

f. Cash Flow. If a buyer is buying a going-concern business, a business that is profitable, the buyer is also acquiring the cash flow or profits of the business—an important component of the purchase price. A buyer's motivation for buying a going-concern business is largely driven by the profits of the previous business. Non-franchised going-concern businesses sell for one to three-plus times the yearly adjusted cash flow—the actual cash flow benefit the owner receives from running the business.

g. Covenant not to compete. When you purchase a business, you can negotiate with the seller so that he will not compete against you within a certain radius from the business you are purchasing. He can't start a similar business for a certain number of years from the close of escrow date. This is to protect you from the seller stealing your customers; the goodwill—a major component of the price of the business you are purchasing.

Chapter 7

HOW BUYERS INITIALLY SCREEN NEW BUSINESS OPPORTUNITIES

This initial screening differs, based on whether you are doing an assets-in-place sale or a going-concern sale. These are important points you need to know to protect yourself.

Assets-in-Place Method

This method means that only the lease, leasehold improvements, licenses, and fixtures and equipment are being sold. The name, menu, concept, and goodwill are typically not included as part of the sale. Less emphasis is put on the financials of the business, and the major factors in determining the value are the lease, leasehold improvements, and the fixtures and equipment. There is no standard formula for determining value utilizing this method, and valuation is somewhat subjective, based on the broker's knowledge of the marketplace. The majority of my 800 sales of restaurants, bars or clubs since 1996 have used the Assets-in-Place Method, The main criteria was the ratio of sales to sales price on the past food and beverage businesses. I will use this method in valuing the subject business.

If the proposed business acquisition is an asset sale, the buyer will first screen the opportunity by completing the items listed below.

The buyer will initially review the sales price of the business by comparing the yearly sales to the asking price, and do a rough estimate of the ratio of the sales price to the yearly sales. For example, if the sale price of the restaurant is $150,000, and the yearly sales is $450,000, the ratio of the sales price to the yearly sales is 33.3% ($150,000 sales price / $450,000 yearly sales = 33.3%). The prospective buyer will compare this ratio to other businesses for sale to see if the price is in the ballpark.

In reviewing our transactions using asset sales over the past ten-year period, the average sales prices have been as follows:

- businesses doing between $200,000 to $500,000 in yearly sales, the average sales price has been approximately 32% of yearly sales;
- businesses doing between $501,000 to $999,999 in yearly sales, the average sales price has been approximately 29% of yearly sales;
- businesses doing between $1million to $1,999,999 in yearly sales, the average sales price has been approximately 21% of yearly sales; and
- businesses doing over $2 million in yearly sales, the average sales price has been approximately 17% of yearly sales.

The buyer will then review the total rent as a percent of yearly sales. If the total rent, which includes base rent and net-net-net (NNN) expenses, such as real estate taxes, property insurance, and common-area maintenance costs (CAM), exceeds 10% of yearly sales—then, in many cases, the buyer will immediately eliminate this business as a possible opportunity.

Once the buyer is satisfied that the price is in the ballpark, they will proceed to check out the location and walk through the business as a customer. If they like the location, they will contact us to arrange an appointment for a back-of-the-house tour of the facility. They will then review the premises lease, equipment lease, and any financials available on the business.

Going-Concern Method

This method means that the lease, leasehold improvements, licenses, fixtures and equipment, name, menu, concept, licenses, and goodwill are all included as part of the sale. The primary valuation method used for the going-concern method is the yearly adjusted cash flow method. This means that the net profit on the tax return, or on the year-to-date income and expense statement, is adjusted by adding back the following items to the net income:

- one working owner's salary,
- any personal expenses the owner is charging the business (food for consumption at home),
- life, health and disability insurance premiums,
- auto expense,
- entertainment and vacation expense, etc.,
- depreciation,
- interest expense on any loans,
- net operating loss carry forward charges, if any, and
- any other expenses that are personal and will not be applicable to the buyer.

Additionally, any extraordinary expenses and/or non-recurring expenses such as extra legal or accounting bills related to a particular lawsuit or unusual situation would be added back to the net income too.

Once the yearly adjusted cash flow is determined, a sales price multiplier is used to determine the value of the business. The sales price multiplier for independently owned, non-chain, non-franchised food service operations varies from one to three times yearly adjusted cash flow, depending on the risk factor and other factors listed below.

The risk factor is determined by the following criteria:

- The degree of difficulty in operating the business, i.e., an espresso operation has a low degree of difficulty as it is an easy operation to run, but an upscale dinner house operation has a high degree of difficulty because it requires a high degree of expertise and sophistication to run this type of business successfully.
- How long the business has been in operation, and the past history of the business, in terms of profitability and sales growth. A business with an easy-to-operate format, coupled with a well-seasoned profitable earnings history, will utilize a higher sales price multiplier when compared to a business with a high degree of difficulty and no track record.

The other factors which determine the sale price multiplier are as follows:

- The lease value (whether the lease is at market, below market or above market, and the length of the lease).
- The potential upside of the business (i.e., a business currently only serves dinner, and has only a beer and wine license, and there is potential for a strong lunch and/or brunch business and liquor sales).
- The future growth opportunities of a particular location (i.e., if there is some major new development(s) that will add potential customers to the area without a lot of extraordinary new competition).

Today, an additional factor considered in valuing businesses is the current economic condition of the market. A large number of restaurant, bar, and nightclub business are currently experiencing negative customer counts, increased expenses and, consequently, decreased profits. Today, the buying market requires that businesses be priced more competitively than during normal economic periods. Many transactions today are being sold at lower multipliers than in the past, and in some cases, seller carry-back financing is required.

If the proposed business acquisition is a going-concern sale, the buyer will first screen the opportunity by completing the items listed below.

The buyer will review:

- the business profile to analyze the sales, cash flow, and sales price.
- the location, and will walk through the business as a customer.
- the premises lease and other written documents in detail, and set up an appointment for a back-of-the-house tour of the facility.
- the financials of the business, in detail, including:
- the past three years of tax returns, and corresponding year-end income and expense statements,
- the year-to-date income and expense statement for the current year, and current year's sales tax returns,
- buyer's discretionary cash-flow statements for past couple of years, and current year to date numbers.

What Do You Need?

Chapter 8

THE ESSENTIALS FOR PREPARING A BUSINESS PLAN FOR FUTURE GROWTH OPPORTUNITIES

If you plan on opening a new restaurant, bar, nightclub, or other business, it is essential that you prepare a comprehensive business plan. A business plan is necessary for raising money from investors, getting third-party financing, and/or getting approval from a prospective new landlord to lease a site.

The essentials of a business plan include the items listed below:

1) A Summary of the Concept

This includes a definition of the physical characteristics for the operation discussing the format of the operations (full service, self service, take out, etc.) and the type of operation (i.e., breakfast/lunch, Italian, Mexican, deli, etc.). Whether alcohol will be included and, if so, the projected sales of alcohol compared to food sales. Other items include a definition of who the customers are, number of seats, square footage, hours of operation, licenses needed, a copy of the menu including pricing, and sketches and floor plans for the business.

2) A Demographic Study

This includes a definition of the trade area of the business, which is the distance the customer will travel to come to the business. For example, the trade area draw for a neighborhood breakfast-and-lunch operation may be only a one-mile radius,-whereas a popular dinner house operation may have a trade area draw of up to a 30 mile radius or more. The demographic study will give you the following statistical information within the trade area you are studying: total population, population broken down by age, household income, per capita income, ethnic mix, education levels, and how much money is spent for food away from home, etc.

STEVE ZIMMERMAN

Demographic Comparison Report
Sample Study Area

	1 MI RING		3 MI RING		5 MI RING	
Population						
2016 Projection	29,399		332,283		662,835	
2011 Estimate	28,544		321,394		639,961	
2000 Census	27,391		317,433		618,262	
1990 Census	26,093		302,691		599,776	
% Change 2011-2016	3.0%		3.4%		3.6%	
% Change 2000-2011	4.2%		1.2%		3.5%	
% Change 1990-2000	5.0%		4.9%		3.1%	
Households						
2016 Projection	12,671		145,807		291,465	
2011 Estimate	12,549		143,916		287,567	
2000 Census	12,283		145,422		284,707	
1990 Census	11,475		137,641		274,119	
% Change 2011-2016	1.0%		1.3%		1.4%	
% Change 2000-2011	2.2%		-1.0%		1.0%	
% Change 1990-2000	7.0%		5.7%		3.9%	
Population by Age						
< 5 yrs	1,688	5.9%	16,614	5.2%	33,358	5.2%
5 - 9 yrs	1,396	4.9%	15,074	4.7%	30,831	4.8%
10 - 14 yrs	1,270	4.4%	14,053	4.4%	29,381	4.6%
15 - 24 yrs	3,357	11.8%	46,990	14.6%	83,492	13.0%
25 - 34 yrs	5,426	19.0%	60,329	18.8%	112,569	17.6%
35 - 44 yrs	4,233	14.8%	47,295	14.7%	96,432	15.1%
45 - 54 yrs	3,986	14.0%	45,164	14.1%	93,459	14.6%
55 - 64 yrs	3,170	11.1%	34,000	10.6%	72,430	11.3%
65 - 74 yrs	1,926	6.7%	20,061	6.2%	42,603	6.7%
75 - 84 yrs	1,372	4.8%	13,936	4.3%	29,387	4.6%
85+ yrs	720	2.5%	7,876	2.5%	16,018	2.5%
Median Age	38.6		37.5		38.6	
Male Population by Age	13,965		156,992		311,293	
< 19 yrs	2,899	20.8%	31,912	20.3%	64,989	20.9%
20 - 34 yrs	3,794	27.2%	45,698	29.1%	80,841	26.0%
35 - 44 yrs	2,166	15.5%	23,961	15.3%	48,675	15.6%
45 - 64 yrs	3,391	24.3%	37,740	24.0%	79,478	25.5%
65 - 84 yrs	1,456	10.4%	14,861	9.5%	31,589	10.1%
85+ yrs	258	1.8%	2,820	1.8%	5,719	1.8%
Median Age, Males	37.3		36.4		37.6	
Female Population by Age	14,579		164,401		328,667	
< 19 yrs	2,747	18.8%	31,047	18.9%	63,821	19.4%
20 - 34 yrs	3,696	25.4%	44,404	27.0%	79,979	24.3%
35 - 44 yrs	2,067	14.2%	23,335	14.2%	47,756	14.5%
45 - 64 yrs	3,765	25.8%	41,424	25.2%	86,410	26.3%
65 - 84 yrs	1,842	12.6%	19,136	11.6%	40,401	12.3%
85+ yrs	462	3.2%	5,056	3.1%	10,298	3.1%
Median Age, Females	39.9		38.6		39.7	

Demographic Comparison Report
Sample Study Area

	1 MI RING		3 MI RING		5 MI RING	
Total Aggregate Income ($Mil)	$1,274.1		$15,662.3		$33,809.5	
Per Capita Income	$44,636		$48,732		$52,831	
Households By Income						
< $10,000	552	4.4%	7,877	5.5%	15,096	5.2%
$10,000 - $14,999	537	4.3%	6,775	4.7%	12,855	4.5%
$15,000 - $19,999	478	3.8%	6,184	4.3%	11,886	4.1%
$20,000 - $24,999	428	3.4%	5,916	4.1%	11,298	3.9%
$25,000 - $29,999	515	4.1%	6,366	4.4%	11,784	4.1%
$30,000 - $34,999	549	4.4%	6,386	4.4%	12,197	4.2%
$35,000 - $39,999	636	5.1%	6,319	4.4%	11,668	4.1%
$40,000 - $49,999	1,033	8.2%	11,723	8.1%	22,140	7.7%
$50,000 - $59,999	834	6.6%	10,352	7.2%	20,295	7.1%
$60,000 - $74,999	1,296	10.3%	13,841	9.6%	26,699	9.3%
$75,000 - $99,999	1,577	12.6%	16,407	11.4%	32,862	11.4%
$100,000 - $124,999	1,265	10.1%	12,974	9.0%	26,305	9.1%
$125,000 - $149,999	1,029	8.2%	8,932	6.2%	18,430	6.4%
$150,000 - $199,999	944	7.5%	10,943	7.6%	23,164	8.1%
$200,000 - $249,999	287	2.3%	4,046	2.8%	9,103	3.2%
$250,000+	591	4.7%	8,872	6.2%	21,784	7.6%
Aggregate Household Income ($Mil)	$1,257.5		$15,110.4		$32,938.1	
Average Household Income	$100,203		$104,995		$114,540	
Median Household Income	$70,440		$70,040		$76,092	
Households by Disposable Income						
< $10,000	637	5.1%	8,896	6.2%	17,043	5.9%
$10,000 - $14,999	512	4.1%	6,547	4.5%	12,428	4.3%
$15,000 - $19,999	528	4.2%	6,932	4.8%	13,307	4.6%
$20,000 - $24,999	555	4.4%	7,494	5.2%	14,137	4.9%
$25,000 - $29,999	702	5.6%	8,130	5.6%	15,312	5.3%
$30,000 - $34,999	776	6.2%	7,947	5.5%	14,723	5.1%
$35,000 - $39,999	681	5.4%	7,951	5.5%	14,803	5.1%
$40,000 - $49,999	1,239	9.9%	14,477	10.1%	28,340	9.9%
$50,000 - $59,999	1,197	9.5%	12,825	8.9%	24,710	8.6%
$60,000 - $74,999	1,489	11.9%	15,495	10.8%	30,998	10.8%
$75,000 - $99,999	1,670	13.3%	16,462	11.4%	33,415	11.6%
$100,000 - $124,999	1,122	8.9%	10,718	7.4%	22,078	7.7%
$125,000 - $149,999	543	4.3%	6,722	4.7%	14,481	5.0%
$150,000 - $199,999	380	3.0%	5,411	3.8%	12,192	4.2%
$200,000 - $249,999	152	1.2%	2,274	1.6%	5,339	1.9%
$250,000+	364	2.9%	5,636	3.9%	14,261	5.0%
Aggregate Disposable Income ($Mil)	$1,039.0		$12,557.6		$27,431.9	
Average Disposable Income	$82,791		$87,256		$95,393	
Median Disposable Income	$56,625		$56,456		$61,297	
Average Family Income	$124,317		$138,074		$149,552	
Median Family Income	$89,876		$94,216		$101,517	
Average Non-family Income	$73,166		$78,549		$85,693	
Median Non-family Income	$52,644		$54,486		$58,498	

Demographic Comparison Report
Sample Study Area

	1 MI RING		3 MI RING		5 MI RING	
Population by Race/Ethnicity						
White	20,364	71.3%	240,175	74.7%	476,909	74.5%
Black	834	2.9%	12,934	4.0%	45,542	7.1%
Asian	5,209	18.2%	38,276	11.9%	60,335	9.4%
Pacific Islander	31	0.1%	565	0.2%	1,144	0.2%
American Indian	128	0.4%	2,076	0.6%	3,702	0.6%
Other/Multiple Races	1,979	6.9%	27,369	8.5%	52,329	8.2%
Hispanic Origin	6,428	22.5%	85,113	26.5%	160,016	25.0%
Education						
Population, Age 25+	20,834		228,662		462,898	
No High School Diploma	1,869	9.0%	24,445	10.7%	50,788	11.0%
High School Graduate	2,944	14.1%	36,641	16.0%	75,128	16.2%
College, No Degree	3,466	16.6%	36,446	15.9%	75,846	16.4%
Associate's Degree	1,342	6.4%	13,732	6.0%	28,240	6.1%
Bachelor's Degree	6,461	31.0%	69,407	30.4%	139,235	30.1%
Graduate/Professional Degree	4,752	22.8%	47,991	21.0%	93,660	20.2%
Labor Force						
Male Population, Age 16+	11,535		132,211		260,570	
Employed	8,053	69.8%	90,503	68.5%	177,887	68.3%
Unemployed	714	6.2%	9,648	7.3%	19,421	7.5%
In Armed Forces	4	0.0%	78	0.1%	166	0.1%
Not in Labor Force	2,764	24.0%	31,985	24.2%	63,096	24.2%
Female Population, Age 16+	12,300		140,745		279,671	
Employed	7,253	59.0%	81,094	57.6%	157,455	56.3%
Unemployed	515	4.2%	7,614	5.4%	16,357	5.8%
In Armed Forces	2	0.0%	8	0.0%	18	0.0%
Not in Labor Force	4,530	36.8%	52,029	37.0%	105,842	37.8%
White Collar Workers (2000)	12,100	82.1%	137,223	80.0%	261,010	80.2%
Blue Collar Workers (2000)	2,647	17.9%	34,200	20.0%	64,572	19.8%
Vehicles Available						
Total Vehicles	21,236		231,839		409,377	
Households with No Vehicles	820	6.5%	10,898	7.6%	22,302	7.8%
Households with 1 Vehicle	4,944	39.4%	62,032	43.1%	122,226	42.5%
Households with 2 Vehicles	4,764	38.0%	51,084	35.5%	100,839	35.1%
Households with 3 or More Vehicles	2,021	16.1%	19,903	13.8%	42,200	14.7%
Average Vehicle per Household	1.7		1.6		1.6	
Total Vehicles Owner Hshlds	11,080	52.2%	103,008	44.4%	225,139	48.0%
Total Vehicles Renter Hshlds	10,180	47.9%	129,129	55.7%	245,216	52.2%

DecisionWhere, Inc. (949)365-0125   www.demographicreports.com   Source:1990/2000 Census
2011/2016 ScanUS Est & Proj

Demographic Comparison Report
Sample Study Area

	1 MI RING		3 MI RING		5 MI RING	
Households	12,549		143,916		287,567	
Average Household Size	2.26		2.16		2.15	
Families	6,634		63,938		129,903	
Average Family Size	3.13		3.18		3.20	
Non-Families	5,915		79,978		157,664	
Average Non-Family Size	1.28		1.33		1.29	
Group Quarters	179		11,218		20,635	
Household Type						
Families						
Married Couples	4,946	74.6%	45,004	70.4%	90,809	69.9%
With Children	2,046	41.4%	18,196	40.4%	36,319	40.0%
Male Hshlder, No Wife	552	8.3%	6,022	9.4%	11,793	9.1%
With Children	213	38.6%	2,329	38.7%	4,876	41.3%
Female Hshlder, No Husband	1,136	17.1%	12,911	20.2%	27,300	21.0%
With Children	559	49.2%	6,840	53.0%	15,011	55.0%
Non-Families						
Male Hshlder, 1 Person	1,904	32.2%	27,120	33.9%	55,855	35.4%
Female Hshlder, 1 Persons	2,604	44.0%	34,118	42.7%	69,385	44.0%
Male Hshlder, 2+ Person	768	13.0%	9,864	12.3%	17,605	11.2%
Female Hshlder, 2+ Persons	639	10.8%	8,877	11.1%	14,819	9.4%
Household Size						
1 Person	4,510	35.9%	61,249	42.6%	125,210	43.5%
2 Persons	3,811	30.4%	40,416	28.1%	79,133	27.5%
3-4 Persons	3,286	26.2%	31,086	21.6%	60,110	20.9%
5+ Persons	942	7.5%	11,164	7.8%	23,112	8.0%
Households by Age of Householder						
< 25 yrs	808	6.4%	11,210	7.8%	16,914	5.9%
25 - 34 yrs	2,683	21.4%	30,910	21.5%	57,852	20.1%
35 - 44 yrs	2,402	19.1%	27,757	19.3%	56,617	19.7%
45 - 54 yrs	2,355	18.8%	27,553	19.1%	56,719	19.7%
55 - 64 yrs	1,790	14.3%	20,416	14.2%	43,833	15.2%
65 - 74 yrs	1,134	9.0%	12,147	8.4%	26,201	9.1%
75-84 yrs	919	7.3%	9,131	6.3%	19,440	6.8%
85+ yrs	458	3.6%	4,792	3.3%	9,989	3.5%
Total Housing Units	13,174		152,441		308,181	
Owned	5,485	41.6%	50,681	33.2%	108,672	35.3%
Rented	7,065	53.6%	93,235	61.2%	178,895	58.0%
Vacant	624	4.7%	8,525	5.6%	20,614	6.7%
Housing Value (2000)						
Average Home Value	$387,242		$455,634		$506,239	
Median Home Value	$372,445		$431,559		$485,671	
Average Contract Rent	$903		$930		$935	
Median Contract Rent	$860		$878		$878	

Business Comparison Report
Sample Study Area

	1 MI RING		3 MI RING		5 MI RING	
	Estab	_Emps_	_Estab_	_Emps_	_Estab_	_Emps_
TOTAL ESTABLISHMENTS/EMPLOYEES	**2,794**	**28,648**	**24,042**	**313,539**	**49,382**	**556,313**
BUSINESS BY TYPE						
Industrial	238	5,446	1,740	18,738	3,810	37,683
Mining	2	8	23	673	47	838
Construction	9	3,703	66	5,496	144	8,952
Construction, Small Firms	91	249	530	1,538	1,052	3,050
High-Tech & Research	12	377	69	1,846	137	3,506
Transportation/Communications/Utilities	19	81	155	1,705	352	3,998
Wholesale-Industrial	57	400	369	2,485	822	5,769
Warehousing	23	510	83	1,012	163	2,296
General Industrial	25	118	445	3,983	1,095	9,274
Manufacturing	91	635	553	7,594	1,165	16,141
Heavy Manufacturing	1	25	3	69	8	174
General Manufacturing	3	36	25	1,061	47	3,333
Light Manufacturing	14	314	74	4,961	153	9,335
Manufacturing, Small Module	73	260	450	1,503	957	3,299
Commercial	948	9,786	6,455	61,935	14,746	144,744
Retail Trade	409	4,860	2,492	24,023	6,203	54,366
Restaurants & Bars	174	2,618	1,092	16,393	2,339	40,176
Personal/Rent/Repair Services	149	658	1,309	6,659	2,882	14,986
Auto Repair Services	85	553	467	2,072	914	3,936
Hotels & Motels	7	46	83	3,641	206	11,869
Theaters & Retail Amusement	12	204	54	530	104	1,076
Equipment Rental	9	46	70	625	145	1,611
Wholesale-Commercial	35	206	251	1,677	605	4,246
General Commercial	70	594	639	6,316	1,347	12,478
Office	1,319	10,513	13,154	144,331	25,441	246,445
Business & Corporate Administration	8	271	56	6,627	98	9,798
Finance/Insurance/Real Estate	52	1,133	564	24,656	977	38,513
Finance/Insurance/Real Estate, Small Office	189	603	1,830	5,827	3,708	11,335
Professional Services	531	4,188	4,346	43,894	7,927	64,127
Business Services	117	1,312	1,076	13,220	2,400	25,166
General Office	164	1,351	1,441	29,550	2,964	46,411
Medical Services	259	1,656	3,041	20,556	7,368	51,096
Other	174	2,069	2,018	79,497	4,007	109,384
Schools & Colleges	22	672	220	48,235	402	56,393
Libraries	2	16	19	186	41	737
Hospitals & Related Medical Services	10	155	88	9,585	167	13,437
Museums, Art, & Gardens	1	2	23	442	55	1,494
Outdoor Recreation & Amusements	28	378	228	3,156	496	7,651
Public Administration	16	478	167	12,138	328	17,910
Churches	14	51	178	1,053	358	2,110
Other, Not Classified	83	317	1,095	4,703	2,161	9,653
Agricultural	25	199	122	1,443	213	1,915
Agricultural Production	0	0	2	2	2	2
Agriculture Services	25	199	120	1,441	211	1,913

3) Operational and Financial Information on the Principals in the Business

This includes a personal financial statement, current credit reports, two to three years of most current tax returns, and resumes on each of the principals of the business. Also included in this section are the resumes of the key management personnel for the business and their business references.

4) Financial Projections

Included in financial projections should be the items indicated below:

- The projected guest check average (per person) of each meal.
- A breakdown of the food sales based on in-house sales; take-out sales, delivery sales, and banquet and catering sales, if any.
- A projected source-and use-of-funds schedule including where the money is coming from (i.e., bank loans, investors, etc.), and a detail of the use of funds.

Make sure when allocating the use of funds you include the following categories: purchase price, remodeling costs, deposits, marketing costs, training costs, rent and other costs during remodeling period and, most important, a reserve for contingencies (at least six months payroll).

A projected income and expense statement for a 5-year period. When making projections, use conservative assumptions because so many things can go wrong when running a business. See article in Chapter 28 on that topic.

A well-put-together business plan will give you the opportunity to fine tune your business, approach investors and landlords as opportunities present themselves, and enhance your chances for success.

XYZ Restaurant

Business Plan

Company Overview

XYZ, Inc. ("the Company"), a Delaware-based company, will operate XYZ Restaurant ("the Restaurant"), a "brassiere-style" medium-size restaurant serving Asian-inspired food focused on the Bay Area's fine local ingredients. The Restaurant will serve all dishes on stoneware to achieve a nice sear and finish, and keep the dishes hot and tasty till the last bite. Beer, wine, soju and sake will also be served The Restaurant's location is to be determined.

Mission Statement

The Company's goal is that of a multi-faceted success. The first responsibility is to the financial well-being of the restaurant. The Company will meet this goal while trying to consider: 1) the effect of our unique menu and concept on the health and well-being of the customers, 2) the impact of business practices and choices on the environment, and 3) the high quality of attitude, fairness, understanding and generosity between management, staff, customers and vendors. Awareness of all these factors and the responsible actions that result will give these efforts a sense of purpose and meaning beyond basic financial goals.

Unique Concept

XYZ Restaurant utilizes the tried-and-true method of hot-stone cooking to meld new world fresh and organic ingredients with an old-world technique into an Asian-inspired New American cuisine.

Called "noo roon" in Korean and "socarrat" in Spanish, XYZ uses hot stoneware to "finish" our dishes, adding a deep golden caramelized crust. No amount of words can truly describe this comforting taste craved all over the world We hope to bring that flavor to San Francisco and accent San Francisco's rich culinary history.

Development and Status

The Company was incorporated in May of 2012 and elected sub-chapter S.

The founders are: Shareholder #1, Shareholder #2, Shareholder #3, Shareholder #4, and Shareholder #5 is the President and Shareholder #2 is the Secretary and Treasurer. A total of 1,000,000 shares of common stock were issued. Shareholder #5 owns 45%, Shareholder #2 owns 25%, Shareholder #3 owns 16.5%, Shareholder #4 owns 6.75% and Shareholder #5 owns 6.75%.

A few suitable sites for the Restaurant have been found and lease negotiations are in very early stages. The desired location will probably be in either North Beach or the Marina. When the lease is signed, there should be three to four months of free rent for construction, and in that time the balance of the start-up funds must be raised. With that phase completed, XYZ Restaurant can then open, and the operations phase of the project can begin. Expected opening is October 2012. If the Company purchases an existing restaurant, then the expected opening date would be moved up.

Future Plans

If the Restaurant is exceeding its projections by month nine, the Company will start scouting for a second location and develop plans for the next unit. Our five-year goal is to have three restaurants in the greater Bay area with a combined annual profit of between $1,000,000 and $1,500,000. After the third location is deemed successful, the Company will entertain franchising out the XYZ concept.

XYZ Restaurant

Business Plan

Industry Analysis

Although the restaurant industry is very competitive, the lifestyle changes created by modern living continue to fuel its steady growth. More and more people have less time, resources and ability to cook for themselves. Trends are very important, and XYZ Restaurant is well positioned for the current interest in unique and healthier foods at moderate prices.

The Restaurant Industry Today

The food service business is the third largest industry in the country. It accounts for over $530 billion annually in sales. The average American spends 15% of his or her income on meals away from home. This number has been increasing over the past several years, mainly driven by lifestyle changes, economic climate, and increase of product variety.

Future Trends & Strategic Opportunities

The predicated growth trend is very positive both in short- and long-term projections. As modern living creates more demands, people will be compelled to eat more meals away from home.

- Consumers will spend a greater proportion of their food dollar away from home
- Independent operators and entrepreneurs will be the main source of new restaurant concepts
- Nutritional concerns will be critical at all types of foodservice operations, and food flavors will be important.
- Environmental concerns will receive even more attention

The Menu

The XYZ Restaurant menu (see appendices) will be limited to one page and contain moderate priced items—average prices of appetizers, entrees and desserts will be around $7, $17 and $6, respectively. The menu will be a collection of Asian-inspired dishes with a common theme, served on stone or in a stone pot. Our goal is to create the image of health-conscious and unique food utilizing the Company's technique.

With an increased awareness of nutritional and health concerns in recent years, we see a growing market of people who regularly desire this style of cooking.

Production

Food production and assembly will take place in the kitchen of the Restaurant. Fresh, locally farmed produce, meat and dairy products will be used to create most of the dishes from scratch. The chef will exercise the strictest standards of sanitation, quality production and presentation over the kitchen and service staff.

Service

A customer can purchase food three ways: 1) Sit down at one of the 60 seats in the dining room and get full service from a server. 2) Sit down at one of the 10 seats at the bar and get full service from a bartender and/or server. 3) A separate take-out area will service those who wish to pick up their food. Most take-out food will be prepared to order, with orders coming from either the telephone or Internet.

Future Opportunities

A segment of this market prefers to eat this type of cooking at home although they do not have the time to cook. There are caterers and mail order companies that provide individuals and families with up to a

XYZ Restaurant

Business Plan

month's supply of pre-prepared meals. The Slanted Door, a stalwart in the Asian-Fusion scene in San Francisco, offers pre-prepared meals, and has been very successful.

This opportunity will be researched and developed on a trial basis in tandem with the retail sale of the Company's stoneware. If successful, it could become a major new source of income without creating the need for additional staff or production space.

The Target Market

The market for the Restaurant's products covers a large area of diverse and densely populated groups. Although it will be located in an urban setting, it is an area where people travel to eat out, and one that is also frequented by tourists.

Market Location and Customers

North Beach and the Marina are some of the most desirable retail locations in San Francisco.

The customer base will come from 4 major segments:

1. Local population – the neighborhoods of North Beach and the Marina has a year-round population of 28,000 and 23,000, respectively, and are centrally located in San Francisco with steady traffic all day and night
2. Greater Bay Area – North Beach and the Marina are two of the most popular areas over the weekend, attracting a large number of Bay Area residents. The lucrative demographic group (ages 25-40) frequent these areas regularly for dining and nighttime activities
3. Tourism – more than 50 hotels, motels, bed and breakfast rooms and inns are in this area, combined with general tourist foot traffic that frequent these two neighborhoods
4. Local businesses – hundreds of local businesses in these areas have both normal business hours and dinner / late night hours. Also, if a North Beach location is obtained, then the close proximity of the Financial District will add business lunches / dinners and a much sought-after demographic group for after-work happy hour and bar establishments

The food concept and product image of XYZ will attract 3 different customer profiles:

1. The "foodie" – more and more young professionals have developed unique eating habits and are willing to drive and spread the word for good food.
2. The health-conscious person of any age or sex – this includes anyone on a restricted or prescribed diet or those who have committed to a healthy diet.
3. Curious and open-minded – "if you try it, you will like it." Through marketing, publicity, and word-of-mouth, people will seek out a new experience and learn that nutritious food can be tasty, fun, convenient, and inexpensive.

Competition

Over 50 restaurants in San Francisco sell Asian-inspired food at similar or higher prices. Although this presents an obvious challenge in terms of market share, it also indicates the presence of a large, strong potential. The newest competitors have made their successful entry based on an innovative concept or novelty. XYZ Restaurant will offer an innovative product in a familiar style at a competitive price. Aggressive plans of marketing, both traditional and Web 2.0, and targeting charitable and corporate events, will also give us an advantage to create a good market share before the competition can adjust or similar concepts appear.

Competing with XYZ Restaurant for the target market are these categories of food providers:

Page | 3

XYZ Restaurant

Business Plan

- Independent table service restaurants of similar menu and price structure
- Traditional Asian cuisine restaurants

Some of the independent operators include The House, Isa, Rohan, Ana Mandara and The Slanted Door. Most are ethnic based and will carry at least 5 similar menu items. The House and The Slanted Door are long-standing businesses while the others are fairly new. They all are doing very well.

Competitive Strategy
We will create an advantage over our competitors in three major ways:

1. Product identity, quality, and novelty
2. High employee motivation and good sales attitude
3. Innovative and aggressive service options

XYZ Restaurant will be the only restaurant among all the competition that focuses the entire menu on hot stone cooking. Some of the competitors may offer a similar item (most likely an appetizer) that utilizes a hot stone.

Once customers have tried the restaurant, their experience will be reinforced by friendly, efficient, and knowledgeable service. Return and repeat business will be facilitated by accessible take-out and late-night dining.

Market Penetration
Entry into the market should not be a problem. The Restaurant will have high visibility with steady-to-heavy foot traffic all day and night. Local residents always support new restaurants, and tourists do not have fixed preferences. In addition, $10,000 has been budgeted for a pre-opening advertising and public relations campaign.

Marketing Strategy
Focusing on the unique aspect of the product theme (healthy, tasty foods), a mix of marketing vehicles will be created to convey the Restaurant's presence, image and message:

- Print media – local newspapers, magazines and neighborhood publications
- Broadcast media – local programming and special interest shows / websites
- Internet – find a domain name that makes it easy for people to find your restaurant and is an asset to your specific concept) is obtained and a Web 2.0 website is currently being planned and built; grassroots campaign via Yelp and other social networking sites
- Hotel guides, concierge relations, Chamber of Commerce brochures
- Direct mail – subscriber lists, offices for delivery
- Leverage local institutions and advertise on their premises websites, i.e.. Beach Blanket Babylon in North Beach, is the longest running musical revue in theatre history with over 12,000 performances in San Francisco. If the Company can leverage this by offering pre-show specials and after-show drink / appetizer specials, XYZ Restaurant could garner numerous customers from the shows
- Misc. – yellow pages, charity events, corporate events, networking, etc.

A public relations firm may be retained to create special events and solicit print and broadcast coverage, especially at the start-up.

The marketing effort will be split into 3 phases:

XYZ Restaurant

Business Plan

1. Opening – An advanced notice (press packet) sent out by the PR firm to all media and printed announcement ads in key places. Budget: $10,000
2. Ongoing – A flexible campaign (using the above media), assessed regularly for effectiveness. Budget: $10,000
3. Point of sale – A well-trained staff can increase the average check as well as enhancing the customer's overall experience. Word-of-mouth referral is very important in building a customer base

Future Plans and Strategic Opportunities
Catering to offices (even outside of our local area) may become a large part of gross sales. At that point a sales agent would be hired to directly market our products for daily delivery or catered functions. Also, franchise opportunities, new concepts, such as a steakhouse and expansion into stoneware sales, will be carefully considered.

Facilities and Offices
The ideal establishment will be around 2,500 square foot. Offices of the Company are presently at Shareholders #1 home but will be moved to the restaurant after opening.

Hours of Operation
The restaurant will be open for lunch and dinner 7 days a week. Service will begin at 11:00 AM and end at 11:00 PM Sunday through Wednesday, and end at 3:00 AM Thursday through Saturday. Holidays should be a lucrative market and the Company will consider having the Restaurant open on those days.

Employee Training and Education
Employees will be trained not only in their specific operational duties but in the philosophy and applications of the Restaurant's concept. They will receive extensive information from the chef and be kept informed of the latest information on healthy eating and locally available ingredients.

Systems and Controls
A strong emphasis will be placed on extensive research into the quality and integrity of all products. The products will constantly be tested on high standards of freshness and purity. Food costs and inventory control will be handled by a computer system and checked daily by management.

Food Production
Most food will be prepared on the premises. The kitchen will be designed for high standards of sanitary efficiency and cleaned daily. Food will be made mostly to order and stored in large coolers in the basement.

Compensation and Incentives
XYZ Restaurant will offer competitive wages and salaries to all employees with benefit packages available to key personnel only.

Long-Term Development
XYZ Restaurant is an innovative concept that targets a new, growing market. We assume that the market will respond, and grow quickly in the next 5 years. The Company's goals are to create a reputation of quality, consistency and security (safety of food) that will make XYZ Restaurant the leader of a new style of dining.

XYZ Restaurant

Business Plan

Milestones

After the Restaurant opens, management will keep a close eye on sales and profit. If the Restaurant is on target after nine months, the Company will look to expand to a second unit.

Risk Evaluation

With any new venture, there is risk involved. The success of our project hinges on the strength and acceptance of a fairly new market. After Year 1, the Company expects some copycat competition in the form of other independent units. Chain competition could come much later.

Financials

	Q4 2012	FY 2013	FY 2014	FY 2015	FY 2016	CAGR '12 - '16
Total Sales	$ 351,381	$ 1,405,523	$ 1,546,076	$ 1,700,683	$ 1,870,731	
Net Credit Card Discount Fee	7,028	28,110	30,922	34,014	37,415	
Net CA Sales Tax	29,867	119,469	131,416	144,558	159,014	
Net Sales	$ 314,486	$ 1,257,943	$ 1,383,738	$ 1,522,111	$ 1,674,322	10.0%
Cost of Goods Sold	100,804	403,214	443,535	487,889	536,678	
Gross Profit	$ 213,682	$ 854,729	$ 940,202	$ 1,034,222	$ 1,137,645	
Fixed Costs	36,900	147,600	154,980	162,729	170,865	
Selling Expenses	20,760	83,040	87,192	91,552	96,129	
Administrative Expenses	25,000	100,000	100,000	100,000	100,000	
Depreciation	7,500	30,000	30,000	30,000	30,000	
Income from Operations	$ 123,522	$ 494,089	$ 568,030	$ 649,942	$ 740,650	14.4%
Other Income / Expenses	5,000	20,000	20,000	20,000	20,000	
Income Before Taxes	$ 118,522	$ 474,089	$ 548,030	$ 629,942	$ 720,650	
Income Tax Expense	41,483	165,931	191,811	220,480	252,227	
Net Income	$ 77,039	$ 308,158	$ 356,220	$ 409,462	$ 468,422	15.0%

Margin Analysis

	Q4 2012	FY 2013	FY 2014	FY 2015	FY 2016	
Gross Margin	67.9%	67.9%	67.9%	67.9%	67.9%	
Occupancy Costs Ratio	11.7%	11.7%	11.2%	10.7%	10.2%	
Selling Expenses Ratio	6.6%	6.6%	6.3%	6.0%	5.7%	
Administrative Expenses Ratio	7.9%	7.9%	7.2%	6.6%	6.0%	
Operating Margin	39.3%	39.3%	41.1%	42.7%	44.2%	
Tax Rate	35.0%	35.0%	35.0%	35.0%	35.0%	
Net Margin	24.5%	24.5%	25.7%	26.9%	28.0%	

Note: Net Sales does not include gratuity.

Ownership

The stockholders will retain ownership, with the possibility of offering stock to key employees, if deemed appropriate.

XYZ Restaurant

Business Plan

Uses of Proceeds

The Company will aim to raise $500,000 from investors and founders. The preliminary use of proceeds for the first year will be as follows:

Capital Equipment - $100,000

Leasing and Store Improvements - $150,000

Administrative Salaries for Managing Director - $100,000

Other general operating costs will be funded through first year sales using a normal Working Capital cycle.

Management

Shareholder #1, Managing Director

Shareholder #1 food service experience has spanned from high school through college, and most recently, 2010 and 2011, where he worked as a line cook and prep cook at Fiji Restaurant, Danny Singles and Jens Restaurant. Previously, he has worked and managed numerous restaurants ranging from family restaurants to country clubs to upscale dining. Since college, Shareholder #1 has catered events for friends and family focusing on California and Asian cuisines.

Prior to joining XYZ, Shareholder #1 was at Lehman Brothers as an investment banker in the Healthcare Group. He has extensive experience in both private and public companies, and has been involved in over $2 billion of debt and equity capital raising transactions and domestic and international mergers and acquisitions transactions.

Additionally, Shareholder #1 was a key member within the Corporate Finance Group at Levi Strauss focusing on the company's $5 billion supply chain. There he was involved in the launch of Levi's new distribution relationship with Wal-Mart, Levi Strauss Signature.

Shareholder #1 received a B.S. degree in Economics and Accounting from University of San Francisco.

Shareholder #2, Founding Partner

Shareholder #2 is currently the owner of Jones Wessen, a large apparel chain in Philadelphia. The flagship store has over 6 0,000 square feet of retail space. The newest store is in the up-and-coming district with over 15,000 square feet of retail space. Shareholder #2 founded Jones Wessen over 20 years ago.

Shareholder #3, Founding Partner

Shareholder #3 is currently the SVP, Finance and Corporate Development at Jones Newsom New Media, a mobile advertising company. He was previously the CFO at Alexis, a Software Service company. Prior to Aldopha, Shareholder #3 co-founded Maximus, a leading Internet insurance brokerage firm, which was acquired.

Shareholder #3 has also worked on numerous technology financings and acquisitions as an investment banker at Merrill Lynch's Technology Investment Banking Group and with Epoch Partners, a technology focused investment bank that was acquired by Goldman Sachs.

Shareholder #3 earned his M.B.A. at the Haas School of Business at the University of California, Berkeley, and graduated with a Business Administration degree from Georgetown University.

XYZ Restaurant

Business Plan

Shareholder #4, Founding Partner

Shareholder #4 is currently obtaining her M.A. in Communication Studies at San Francisco State University.

Previously, Shareholder #4 owned and managed two QSRs in the greater New York area for over 5 years. Shareholder #4 comes from a family with both restaurant and retail gas station properties in the greater New York area.

Shareholder #4 has significant experience in retail and sales. Previously, Shareholder #4 worked as a Sales Associate at Benetton. Shareholder #4 also has prior experience managing all aspects of several gas stations from accounting, training, purchasing and inventory management. She also has experience as a sales coordinator at Hilton International's headquarters.

Shareholder #4 earned her B.S. in Communication Studies at University of Chicago.

Shareholder #5, Founding Partner

Shareholder #5 is currently at Melanga as a Director in the Network division, overseeing Melanga's category-leading consumer web products. Previously, Shareholder #5 was an investment banker with Merrill Lynch and Johnstown Partners, solely focusing on Internet and Media.

Shareholder #5 received a B.A. from the Haas School of Business at the University of California, Berkeley.

Appendices – Menu Concept #1

APPETIZERS

Arugula and Toasted Walnuts
Goat cheese and pomegranate seeds with lemon Wasabi vinaigrette warmed on stone

Spinach and Poached Egg
Newsom Farms country ham with Miso vinaigrette wilted over stone

Spicy Yellowfin Tuna
Asian chili spiced on top of crispy rice seared on stone   our signature appetizer

Rock Wings
Fulton Valley chicken wings and sweet spices finished on stone

Tiger Prawns
Thai spiced served on hot stone

ENTREES

Dol Sot Bi Bim Bap
Fresh, seasonal vegetables, Niman Ranch rib-eye steak and an organic fried egg served over rice "finishing" in a sizzling hot stone pot   our signature dish and inspiration

Pad Thai
Tiger prawns, deep-fried Thai basil and local, organic vegetables "finished" in a hot stone pot

Misoyaki Butterfish
Edamame seaweed salad and kitsune udon served on hot stone

Kashmir Lamb
East Asian spices and mint with heirloom tomatoes and rosemary potato gratin served on hot stone

Page | 8

XYZ Restaurant

Business Plan

Beef - Parts I, II and III
3 different cuts, cheek, filet mignon, bone marrow "finished" on a sizzling hot stone

Bo Ssam
Grilled Berkshire pork belly finished on hot stone, 6 oysters on the half shell, Bibb lettuce and accompaniments...the rest is up to you

Roasted Fulton Valley Chicken
Sautéed garlic pea sprouts and fingerling potatoes served on hot stone

Appendices – Menu Concept #2

A P P E T I Z E R S

StoneStickers
Pork, ginger and leeks dumplings caramelized on sizzling hot Stone

Tour of the Worldly Curries
Japanese, Indian and Thai curries served with crispy rice skewers in hot Stone mini pots

Seaweed Salad
Sweet marinated seaweed served warm on Stone

Mushroom Dobinmushi
Oyster, enoki and shitake mushrooms with dashi broth served in a Stone teapot

Unagi Yaki
Broiled unagi with scallions and sweet sauce "finished" on hot Stone

Jalapeno Hamachi Sashimi
Chiso soy glaze served on top of sliced jalapenos searing over hot Stone

E N T R E E S

Niman Ranch Skirt Steak
Bibb lettuce, wide rice noodle wrappers and accompaniments served on sizzling hot Stone

Asian Paella
Chinese sausage, scallops and halibut served "soccarat" on hot Stone

Black Bean Skate
Bak choy and parsnip purée "finished" over hot Stone

Chilean Sea Bass
Saikyo miso served with soba noodles and edamame "seared" on hot Stone

Duck - Parts I, II and III
3 different cuts crispy skin, tongue, breast "finished" on a sizzling hot Stone

Fulton Valley Chicken for 2
Singaporean style with sautéed baby carrots and polenta seared on sizzling hot Stone

Appendices – Menu Concept #3

A P P E T I Z E R S

XYZ Restaurant

Business Plan

Hog Island Oysters
Seafood-infused kimchi sautéed on hot Stone

Prince Edward Island Mussels and Razor Clams
Clear sake-infused miso soup served hot in a Stone pot

Warm Napa Cabbage Salad
Blue cheese, blood oranges and glazed walnuts with a longyan honey dressing in a warm Stone pot

Glass Noodle Salad
Jahp chae style noodles with seasonal vegetables and Thai chicken "finished" on hot Stone

Ishiyaki Wagyu Beef
Simplify, simplify, simplify sliced wagyu beef sashimi you can sear on your own hot Stone

Grilled Baby Octopus
Frisee salad and sliced fingerling potatoes finished over hot Stone

ENTREES

White Miso Salmon
Sweet wine miso, mirin and sake infused served with sliced asparagus and enoki mushrooms "finished" on hot Stone

Spicy Tofu Bouillabaisse
Tiger prawns, halibut and razor clams served hot in a Stone pot

Diver Scallops
Kimchi risotto served "noo roon" style over hot Stone

Niman Ranch Rib Eye
Wasabi smashed potatoes and grilled scallions served sizzling hot on Stone

Pig - Parts I, II and III
3 different cuts, cheeks, shoulder, belly "finished" on a sizzling hot Stone

Black Sesame Chicken
Pan seared then oven roasted with tiger lily and edamame stir-fry "finished" over hot Stone

Chapter 9

HOW MUCH MONEY DO YOU NEED TO OPEN AND OPERATE A RESTAURANT, BAR, OR CLUB?

If you are purchasing a restaurant, bar, or club business, you need to have adequate money on hand (as indicated below) before you move forward with the acquisition. Let's assume, for illustrative purposes, you will be purchasing a business for $150,000, which includes an alcohol license.

Purchase Price. In addition to $150,000 cash that you need to purchase the business, you will need additional cash per the items indicated below:

- **Saleable Inventory**. This includes the food, beverage, paper and cleaning supplies inventory the buyer purchases from the seller at the seller's cost, based on a physical inventory to be taken between buyer and seller immediately before the close of escrow. There is usually a not-to-exceed amount for this inventory that is written in the Asset

Purchase Agreement. It is stated that the buyer will not be obligated to buy any additional inventory above this "not-to-exceed" amount. For purposes of this exercise, lets assume the saleable inventory will be $5,000.

- **Escrow Fees and Closing Costs.** To purchase a business in California, you need to use an escrow to assure you get a title that is free and clear of all liens and encumbrances. If the buyer does not use an escrow, he is liable for the seller's past tax liabilities, including State Franchise Taxes (FTB), State Board of Equalization Taxes (SBE), Employment Development Department Taxes (EDD), and county taxes, as well as any vendor debt that the seller owed. Escrow fees and closing costs are split 50/50 between buyer and seller, and in general, they run approximately $1,500 per party. However, the escrow fees will increase if the deal size goes up.

- **Deposits.** You will need the deposits indicated below:
  - Premises Lease Deposit. Usually 1 to 2 times the monthly rent is required as a security deposit to make sure the buyer returns the premises at the end of his lease in the same condition they received it, with normal wear and tear. If the rent is $5,000 a month, the buyer will need to put up a security deposit of somewhere between $5,000 to $10,000.
  - Utility Deposit. Usually the gas and electric vendors require a sum equal to one to two months of the business's monthly utility bill as a security deposit. Assuming your monthly utility bill will be $2,500, you'll have to come up with a utility deposit of somewhere between $2,500 to $5,000.
  - State Board of Equalization Deposit. In California the State Board of Equalization (SBE) may require a security deposit ranging between $2,000 to $50,0000 to act as collateral against any potential future State sales tax liabilities. The State will release the security deposit after the business has had a history of three years of perfect tax payments. For illustrative purposes, the State Board of Equalization security deposit will be $10,000.

- **Fees and Permits**. These will vary in different cities, counties and states.
  - Department of Alcoholic Beverage Fee. In California, if you are transferring a beer and wine license, the transfer cost is approximately $600, and if you are transferring a hard-liquor license, the transfer fee is approximately $2,000. In addition to these upfront fees, there are yearly renewal fees.
  - Health Department Fee. In California, in order to get a change-of-ownership health department clearance, the buyer is responsible for paying for the inspection report. This is approximately $300, and the seller is responsible to correct all the items on the report and get signed off by the health department. This is true unless it is an "AS IS" sale, which means the buyer is buying the business AS IS, and is responsible for all governmental clearances, including the change-of-ownership health department clearance.
  - Business License Fee. In California, this will vary from several hundred dollars to a couple of thousand of dollars, depending on the county.

- **Remodeling Costs.** If you plan to do major remodeling, you could spend money on an architect, food-facility engineer (who design kitchens and the other mechanical systems in the business), general contractor, and various sub-contractors. You'll pay all kind of fees associated with engaging these individuals, in addition to building permit fees and other miscellaneous construction fees.

- **Training Costs**. You might hire some of the employees from the prior operation, but undoubtedly, you will be hiring new employees who will need to be trained prior to opening the business. You'll incur advertising costs for finding these employees as well as costs for training employees prior to the opening.

- **Pre-Opening Marketing Costs.** Typically not much is spent here because most marketing for independent, non-franchised businesses comes primarily from the word-of-mouth advertising of customers. However, it is common for a business to have a couple of preview openings before the restaurant is open to the public, where selected guests are invited to have a meal for free. These guests usually include vendors, management of the business and their spouses, and selected customers and friends. Sometimes these preview openings are tied in to a sponsorship by a non-profit organization, where the invited guests pay to come to the preview opening, and the proceeds go to the non-profit. These preview openings are good practice for the employees to get some of the kinks out of the operation, and help assure a smoother first day when the business opens to the public. Frequently, adjustments are made to the menu and service procedures as a result of these preview openings.

- **Rent and Other Costs During Remodel**. Unless you can negotiate free rent from the landlord before you open for business—which is unlikely in the San Francisco Bay area—you will have to start paying rent and other operating expenses when you take possession of the premises. These expenses include utilities, insurance, of course, payroll, and some food costs for training purposes and possible preview opening events.

- **Working-Capital Reserve.** The rule of thumb here is that you should have at least six months of projected payroll set aside for unanticipated expenses, which include the items indicated below:

1) Your operating results to be far less than expected, and you need this reserve to pay the negative cash flow generated from an underperforming business. The restaurant business is a cash business in that you need to pay your employees and vendors regularly if you want to stay in business.

   If you don't pay your bills (food, beverage, insurance, utilities, etc.), you won't receive products or services. If you don't pay your employees, you won't have employees to serve your customers, and if you don't pay your rent, you will be evicted.

2) Unusual unforeseen events might include extremely poor weather conditions, such as excessive rain and earthquakes, as well as major downward turns in the economy. Assuming your monthly payroll

is averaging $15,000, you should have $90,000 ($15,000 monthly payroll times 6 months = $90,000) set aside as a working capital reserve.

Summary of Cash Needed to Open and Operate a Restaurant, Bar, or Club

If you are buying an existing business and keeping the same name, menu and concept, and not making any major changes to the business (using the assumptions indicated above), you will need:

Purchase Price	$150,000
Saleable Inventory	5,000
Escrow Fees and Closing Costs	1,500
Premises Security Deposit	10,000
Utility Deposit	5,000
State Board of Equalization Deposit	10,000
Department of Alcoholic Beverage Control Fees	2,000
Health Department Fees	300
Business License	500
Working Capital Reserves	90,000
Total Cash Needed	$274,300

Summary of Cash Needed to Open and Operate a Restaurant, Bar, or Club If You're Changing the Name & Doing Remodeling, etc.

Using the assumptions indicated above, and assuming you'll spend $100,000 for remodeling, $10,000 in training costs, $10,000 in pre-opening marketing costs, and you'll be closed for three months for remodeling before you open for business, the summary of this scenario is indicated below. For this scenario we will remove saleable inventory, as it is assumed if a buyer is changing the menu, he does not want the seller's saleable inventory.

The costs indicated above	$274,300
Remodeling costs	100,000
Training costs	10,000
Rent costs during remodeling	15,000
Saleable inventory	(5,000)
Total cash needed	$394,300

From the information above, you see you need cash on hand in addition to the initial money needed to purchase the business. Unfortunately a lot of businesses fail because they don't anticipate all the start-up expenses as indicated above. In many transactions I have worked on, owners were forced to sell because they were undercapitalized. Many of these businesses would still be successful businesses today if they had initially raised the proper money. Unless you have enough money to start your business, I would strongly recommend that you do not purchase a business.

Chapter 10

METHODS FOR RAISING MONEY FOR A RESTAURANT, BAR, OR CLUB ACQUISITION

Methods for raising money for a restaurant, bar and/or club acquisition are divided into these four topics:

1. Raising you own money,
2. Seller financing,
3. Third-party financing, and
4. Investor financing.

1. Raising Your Own Money

If you are fortunate to have your own financial resources, this is usually the easiest way to raise money for your investment. A good source for creating liquidity for an investment is to take an equity line of credit from your home since the interest expense is tax deductible. Make sure that you can easily pay back this loan should a worse-case scenario occur, and your investment fails.

Other sources for raising cash yourself include selling your stocks and bonds, or cashing in your retirement fund, although there could be stiff penalties for doing so.

Try not to request/accept investment money from family members or close friends. The risk factor is so high in the restaurant, bar, and club business that there is a strong possibility that they could lose their money, and you might not be able to pay them back, which will most likely damage your future relationship.

2. Seller Financing (also called seller carry-back promissory note).

In this case, the seller carries back a negotiated amount of the purchase price in the form of a seller carry-back promissory note that is secured by the assets of the business, and personally guaranteed by the buyer. In California, this lien against the business assets is in the form a UCC1 security agreement recorded with the Secretary of State. It will appear as a cloud against the title of the business should the business owner decide to sell the business before he pays off the lien. This means that if the business fails, the seller can take legal action against the buyers, and regain control of the business and its assets. For example, let's assume that the selling price of the business is $250,000 with $100,000 cash down at the close of escrow. The seller agrees that he'll carry back the $150,000 balance in a seller carry-back note. Furthermore, the terms of the seller carry-back note are 8% interest per annum. This is computed from change of possession of the business so as to fully amortize, over 60 months (i.e., $3,041.96 per month), payments to begin one month from change of possession. This is secured by a security agreement on the assets of the business, and personally guaranteed by the buyer, with the right to prepay without penalty.

Many of my business broker associates in California who sell businesses other than restaurants, bar, and clubs, tell me that seller financing is a common technique used in selling businesses. However, from my experience in selling restaurants, bars, and clubs, few sellers are willing to carry back a portion of the purchase price using a seller carry-back note, due to the high risk factor in this industry. Most sellers I have dealt with would rather get a lower all-cash price than provide seller financing. In the limited transactions where the sellers were willing to finance a portion of the price in the form of a seller carry-back note—the seller, in many cases, required the note to be secured by real property owned by the buyer. This was, in addition to securing the note with a UCC1 security agreement against the business and assets being sold, and having the note personally guaranteed by the buyer. In these cases, where real property was being used to secure the seller's note, the seller usually specifies that the total debt on the real property being secured, including the seller carry-back note, does not exceed 70% of the fair-market value. A current appraisal is usually requested by the seller to approve the buyer's real property as additional security. The sellers insist on this conservative loan-to-value ratio to assure themselves that if the buyer fails, there is enough equity in the property to handle the foreclosure costs, legal costs, etc., required for the seller to take title of the property in default.

3. Third-Party Financing

- SBA Loans. SBA stands for Small Business Administration, a United States government program, whereby the government guarantees loans made by banks to small businesses. The major SBA program for small businesses is called 7(a) loans, which are the most-basic and most-used type loans of SBA's business loan programs. All 7(a) loans are provided by lenders who are called "participants" because they participate with SBA in the 7 (a) program. Not all lenders choose to participate, but most American banks do. Some non-bank lenders also participate with SBA in the 7(a) loans. The lender and SBA share the risk that a borrower may not be able to repay the loan in full. Repayment ability from the cash flow of the business is a primary consideration in the SBA loan decision process, but good character, management capability, collateral, and owner's equity contribution are also important considerations.

  All owners of 20% or more are required to personally guarantee SBA loans—a guarantee against payment default. Eligibility factors for all 7(s) loans include: size, type of business, use of proceeds, and the availability of funds from other sources. The maximum loan available in this program is $2 million, of which the government will guarantee 75% of the amount borrowed. For more information on SBA loans, look up SBA on the internet, and, in particular, check out the following websites: www.sba.gov and www.sba.org.

- Minority- and Woman-Owned Business Loans – Numerous loan programs are available for small, minority-owned, and woman-owned businesses. To get information for the particular loan program you are looking for go to the internet and search Minority- and Woman-Owned Business Loans.

- Bank Loans – If you have had a pre-existing relationship with a bank, you may be able to have the bank provide the necessary financing to purchase the business. Usually the bank will want to secure the loan with other tangible property, such as real estate and securities.

Learn the various ways investors can be helpful by investing into your business, and the various formulas that I have seen used by owner/operators to raise money for their business.

4. Investor Financing

A common source of raising money for one's business is from third-party investors. These are people, other than family members or close friends, who know of your track record, either as a customer, or because of your reputation with those who have seen you in operation, or have read reviews about you. Since this is a high-risk business I recommend you accept investments only from individuals who are financially strong and can afford to lose their investment. Many investors are driven to restaurant, bar, or club investments for ego gratification, so, hopefully, they can brag to their friends that they own a piece of a well-known business. Usually the investor's principal is returned to him, over a number of years, from the cash flow of the business. After the investor recovers his initial capital back, then profits are split on a pre-negotiated formula between the investor partners and the managing partner. Various economic structures exist for investors coming into deals, but in most cases, they limit their financial and overall liability exposure by becoming involved in a limited partnership, as a shareholder in a corporation, or as a member in a limited liability company. In these entities, usually the managing partner gets a salary for running the business before there is any return of original capital or profit to the partner.

Examples of Formulas to Use for Investors Investing Money for Purchase of a Business

Formula 1 – This is a situation where 100% of the money needed for the purchase of the business is provided by the investor(s), and the managing partner does not make an investment, but receives a market-rate salary for running the business, and the opportunity to share in the profits in the future, after the investor(s) get their investment back. In this situation, it is agreed that the profits will be split 50% to the investor(s) and 50% to the managing partner after the investor(s) get back their original investment. In reviewing the profit-and-loss statement, and after the managing partner of the business gets a market-rate salary as a working owner, the remaining money is distributed to the investor(s).

Below is an example of Formula 1. At the end of the fiscal year there is a profit of $250,000 after the managing partner received a salary of $60,0000 for running the business. In some cases, included with the salary for the managing partner will be health insurance, a food allowance, plus a car allowance for business purposes, etc. The total investment made by the investor(s) was $200,000, so after the first $200,000 is distributed to the investors(s), a remaining $50,000 is split 50/50, or $25,000 of the profits distributed to the managing partner, and $25,000 distributed to the investor(s). In this given fiscal year, the total compensation paid to the managing partner was $85,000 ($60,000 salary + $25,000 profit distribution = $85,000 total compensation). In subsequent years, since the investor(s) investment has been paid back, any future profits would be split 50% to the managing partner and 50% to the investor(s). Let assume the next year's profits were $150,000. The distribution of these profits would be $75,000 to the managing partner, and $75,000 to the investor(s), so the total compensation to the managing partner would be $135,000 ($60,000 salary + $75,000 profit distribution = $135,000 total compensation). If an additional investment is required by the investor(s) in the future, the same formula indicated above will apply.

The summary of the above is as follows:

First Operating Year Calculation

$250,000   profit
(200,000)   return of investor(s) investment
  $50,000   remaining profit
  (25,000)   to managing partner
  (25,000)   to investor(s)
      $0   remaining balance

Second Operating Year Calculation

$150,000   Profit
  (75,000)   to managing partner
  (75,000)   to investor(s)
      $0   remaining balance

Formula 2 – This situation is similar to Formula 1 above. However the investor(s) receives a yearly preferred return on their investment until their investment is paid back in full before profits are split between the managing partner and the investor(s).

A preferred return is a pre-negotiated percentage return on the investor(s) investment when the deal is put together. Let's assume that the preferred return is 10% of the investor(s) investment. The investor(s) investment is $200,000, so the yearly preferred return to the investor(s) would be $20,000 ($200,000 original investment x 10% = $20,000 preferred return). If there was a $250,000 profit after the managing partner received his salary of $60,000, the profit distribution would be as follows: the original investor(s) investment of $200,000 + $20,000 preferred return or $220,000 would go the investor(s) first, so the remaining profit to be distributed is $30,000 ($200,000 investor(s) investment + $20,000 preferred return = $220,000 less $250,000 profit = $30,000 remaining profit to be distributed). This remaining profit would go 50% or $15,000 to the managing partner and 50% or $15,000 to the investor(s).

The summary of the above situation would be as follows: the managing member would receive $75,000 ($60,000 salary for running the business + $15,000 profit =$75,000) and the investor(s) would receive $235,000 ($200,000 investment + $20,000 preferred return + $15,000 profits = $235,000 investor(s) return).

The summary of the above is as follows:

  $250,000 profit
   (20,000) preferred return to investor
 (200,000) return of investor(s) original investment
   $30,000 remaining profit to be distributed
   (15,000) distributed to managing partner (50%)
   (15,000) distributed to investor(s) (50%)
        $0 remaining balance

Formula 3 – In this situation the managing partner makes an investment in the business, as well as the investor(s). In this situation the deal is structured as follows:

The total investment is $300,000, and the managing partner puts in $150,000, and the investor(s) puts in $150,000.

The managing partner receives a $60,000 yearly salary, which is adjusted annually for cost of living, for running the business. This comes out of the business, before profits are divided.

The agreed profit split after the partners receive a 10% preferred return on their investment is 60% to the managing partner and 40% to the investor(s).

Here is an example of the third formula. The profits of the business are $150,000 after the managing partner receives his yearly salary of $60,000. The $150,000 yearly profit would be split as follows: preferred return to partners of $15,000 each ($150,000 investment x 10% = $15,000 preferred return), then remaining profits would be split 60% to the managing partner, and 40% to the investor(s).

The summary of the above is as follows:

   $150,000 profit
   (15,000) preferred return to managing partner
   (15,000) preferred return to investor(s)
   $120,000 remaining profit
   (72,000) distributed to managing member (60% profit)
   (48,000) distributed to investor(s) (40% profit)
       $0 remaining balance

Other Formulas – There can be many other variations of the above formulas, depending on the priorities of the parties involved. Below are some common variations for profit distribution. In a situation where the managing partner puts no money up, and the investor(s) wants to give the managing partner an extra incentive to increase profits, a formula can be set up as follows: after the managing partner gets his salary, he also gets a performance bonus that can be set up in a number of ways. One common method is to have part of the bonus tied to increased sales rather than budgeted sales, and a larger part of the bonus is tied to increased profits versus budgeted profits.

Let's assume the bonus formula is that the managing partner receives 5% of increased sales versus budgeted sales, and receives 10% of increased profit versus budgeted profit. For example, if the budgeted sales were $1 million, and the actual sales were $1.1 million, and the budgeted profit was $150,000, and the actual profit was $200,000, the yearly incentive bonus to the managing partner is as follows: a) he gets a $5,000 sales bonus ($100,000 increased sales versus budgeted sales x 5% = $5,000), and b) he gets a $5,000 profit bonus ($50,000 increased profit versus budgeted profit x 10% = $5,000). In the above example, we will assume that after the managing partner receives a yearly $60,000 salary adjusted annually for inflation, and receives a performance bonus, if applicable, then the investor(s) gets their original investment back, and profits are split 50/50 between the managing partner and the investor(s). Furthermore, we will assume that the investor(s) invested $250,000 and that the profits of the business are $200,000.

The summary of the above is as follows:

$200,000	yearly profit
(10,000)	performance bonus paid to managing partner
	($5,000 sales bonus + $5,000 profit bonus)
(190,000)	profit paid to investor(s)
$0	remaining balance

In the second year of operation the profits are $250,000 and the managing partner's performance bonus is $15,000, and the summary is as follows:

$250,000	yearly profit
(15,000)	performance bonus paid to managing partner
<u>(60,000)</u>	profit to investor(s) to get 100% of their original investment back (the investors' investment is $250,000, and they have previously received $190,000 back of their original investment, so their remaining investment is $60,000
$175,000	profit to be split
(87,500)	50% paid to managing partner
<u>(87,500)</u>	50% paid to investor(s)
$0	remaining balance

In the previous example, the managing partner would receive, in addition to his $60,000 yearly salary, a $15,000 performance bonus, plus 50% of the remaining profits or $87,500. His total compensation would be $162,500 ($60,000 salary + $15,000 performance bonus + $87,500 profit split = $162,500). The investor(s) would receive $147,500 made up of $60,000, which is the remaining return of their original capital, plus 50% of the remaining profits or $87,500 ($60,000, the remaining return of their original capital + $87,500 profit split = $147,500).

These methods are just a few of the many formulas that can be used to raise money for a new investment opportunity.

Buyers Dos and Don'ts

Chapter 11

THE BUYER'S THREE-STAGE CHECKLIST

The following list is broken down as follows:

Stage 1 – Items you need to do before you sign a purchase contract.

Stage 2 – Items you need to complete after you sign a purchase contract.

Stage 3 – Items you need to do in order to close escrow.

Many other items are important, but this is an outline of the major items that need to be covered.

Stage 1: Items you need to do before you sign a purchase contract

- Use a specialized restaurant broker to ensure that you are not overpaying for the business. Follow his expertise and let it guide you through all the proper steps in the transaction to make sure the transaction gets closed properly without any surprises.

- In doing your due diligence on the business being purchased, make sure the location and surrounding area is built out, so there is little room for a head-on competitor to come into the immediate area.

- Make sure to be adequately capitalized to fund, not only, the purchase of the business, but to have adequate monies for marketing expenses, training costs, remodeling costs, plus reserves set aside for unforeseen circumstances.

- Do conservative projections of income and expenses for several years when evaluating the potential future of the business.

- Conduct an extensive review of the competition in the area to assure yourself that your operation will be competitive.

- Be prepared for the unexpected.

- Be prepared to be an active, hands-on working owner in the business, unless you are purchasing a large-scale operation and you can afford to hire a high-powered general manager.

- Complete a comprehensive business plan before you get into the contract.

- Set up the proper entity, such as corporation or limited liability company, to take title to the business.

Stage 2: Items you need to complete after you have signed a purchase contract

- Conduct a detailed review of the physical aspects of the business, including a complete physical inspection of the premises with the appropriate contractors.

- Thoroughly review the financial records of the business—the books and records, including the tax returns for the past three years, the current year's sales tax returns, and year-to-date income and expense statement. Have your accountant help you with this process if necessary.

- Check with all city, state and federal departments including the health department, fire department, and the building and planning department's guidelines, as necessary, to make sure the physical premise is up to code, including disabled requirements. Be sure to get the proper written clearances from these agencies. Also check with the proper authorities to assure yourself that if the laws change, these changes won't have a negative impact on the operating hours and major operating conditions for your business.

- Have the premises lease negotiated properly to make sure you have enough time on the lease, with affordable rent increases in the future. Also try to negotiate a first "right of refusal" to purchase the building, and make sure you meet with the landlord before the close of escrow. Get the landlord's written consent for assignment of the premises lease or for issuance of a new lease. It is best to work closely with your broker in all matters relating to the lease.

- Have a tight, non-compete agreement with the seller for the appropriate radius from the business being purchased for a minimum 5-year period to assure yourself that the seller will not compete against you.

- Review the personnel records of all the employees with the seller to learn about the employees' strengths and weaknesses, as well as meet with the employees before the close of escrow to determine which employees you wish to keep.

- Use an attorney as necessary to review all the legal documents of the transaction, including reviewing the premises lease.

- Before the close of escrow get acquainted with all of the major tenants in the building you will occupy. These tenants will be potentially exposed to any traffic or noise factors generated by your business, and you need to make sure you'll be compatible with them.

- Check the restrictions and conditions for the premises.

- Complete the allocation of the purchase price, and have the allocation determined so it will be advantageous to you tax wise.

Stage 3: Items you need to do in order to close escrow

- Put your remaining money in escrow after the following items have been completed:

- The lien search has been completed by escrow (the escrow can assure you that you will get a title free and clear of all liens).
- All premises lease and other legal documents (equipment leases, franchise agreements, etc.) have been signed by the required parties.
- All due diligence including physical inspections, review of books and records, and other items, have been completed.
- All alcoholic beverage control forms have been properly processed, and it is certain that the alcohol license will transfer to you in the near future.

- Make sure that you receive the proper training from the seller to learn all the nuances of the business.
- Confirm that the saleable inventory is counted and properly priced out immediately before the close of escrow. Do not purchase any excess inventory per the not-to-exceed inventory limits spelled out in the purchase contract.
- Fire up all the equipment immediately before the close of escrow to make sure it works properly. Any equipment in need of repair should be repaired by the seller—or you should receive a credit in escrow for the anticipated repair costs.
- Get the seller's contact information so he can be reached after the close of escrow.
- Get the health department, fire department and other necessary clearances from these respective agencies before the close of escrow.
- If there is an equipment lease to assume, validate that it is properly assumed, including having it signed by all the required parties before the close of escrow. Either cancel or properly transfer all rental equipment accounts into your business name at the close of escrow.
- Have all your insurance policies in place, including liability, workman's compensation, and any other required insurance, immediately before the close of escrow.
- Set up all your tax accounts (in California) with the Franchise Tax Board, State Board of Equalization, and Employment Development Department, etc.
- File a fictitious name statement before you close escrow. A fictitious

name filing is for registering the use of your business name with the Secretary of State to protect use of your name for your business use.

- Get a complete set of all transaction documents signed by all parties, including the purchase agreement and addendums, if any; the equipment list, the buyer's and seller's disclosure list, premises lease documents, and copies of all the escrow papers for your transaction, including copies of tax clearances.

- Set up your accounting and bookkeeping systems before the close of escrow.

- Change over all the utility accounts to your business name at the close of escrow.

- Change over all merchants' accounts to your business name at the close of escrow.

- Transfer to your business name any other special licenses or permits you may need to operate the business, such as an entertainment license or after-hours license, before the close of escrow.

- Take physical possession of the premises at the close of escrow.

- Change all of the premise's locks, and the safe's combination, immediately upon taking possession.

Restaurant Realty Company works closely with its clients in overseeing all of the major items indicated above to assure that the escrow will close smoothly.

Chapter 12

IMPORTANT QUESTIONS AND INFORMATION TO ASK THE SELLER

The more you know in advance about the parties involved in the sale, the easier the process can be. This is no time to be shy. Ask away. What you learn may save you time, money and hassles.

1. How long has the seller owned the business?
2. What are the business's hours of operation?
3. Confirm the number of employees, and review in detail all employees histories.
4. Ask what the theoretical cost of goods should be for food sales—and for alcohol sales?
5. What is the upside for the business?
6. How many hours a week does the owner work, and what does he do in the business?
7. Does the owner have any family members working in the business? If so, who are they, what do they do, and how many hours does each of them work?

8. Are there any pieces of equipment that do not work or in need of replacement? If so, what are they?

9. How is your relationship with the landlord?, What problems have you had with the landlord, past or current?

10. Are there any lawsuits pending? If so what are they?

11. What are the neighbors like? Are there any problems with any adjacent neighbors or upstairs neighbors?

12. Are there any unusual conditions or restrictions imposed on the business by any governmental agencies, such as the building department, police department or Alcoholic Beverage Control department? If so what are they?

13. Do you comply with the disabled laws (ADA-American Disabilities Act)? And if not what are the requirements to comply?

14. Do you comply with all heath department, fire department and other governmental agencies requirements?

15. What is the guest check average per person for each meal period?

16. Why does the seller want to sell?

17. Is there any unreported income? If so, how much, and can you support the unreported income?

18. Are all bills paid current? If not, which are not current?

19. Are your employees union? If not, what is the vulnerability for the workers organizing to have a union?

20. Who are your vendors? How often do they make deliveries? How do you make sure they are competitive?

21. If I wanted to increase the size of the restaurant, is there a possibility of acquiring any contiguous space that is currently available, or may become available in the future?

22. If I want to expand the hours of operation, is there any limitation to doing so?

23. Are there separate meters for electric, gas, and water? If not, how are you charged for these utilities?

24. Is there a garbage area? How much is your monthly garbage bill?

25. Is there any possibility of an eminent domain, or condemnation proceeding that could eliminate the business?

26. Do you have a product mix breakdown for the menu? If so, may I have a copy?

27. Is there any new competition coming into the area that might affect the sales level of the business?

28. Who is the major competition in the area? Who is your head-on competition?

29. Who are your customers? What percent of your customers are regular customers? How often do the regular customers frequent the restaurant?

30. What percent of your sales are alcohol? What is the breakdown of alcohol sales between hard liquor, beer, and wine?

31. How much inventory do you keep on hand? How often do you take inventory?

32. What has been your history of your promotions? What promotions have worked best? I'd like the detail on all promotions past and present?

33. What contracts do you currently have? Could I have copies of all your contracts?

34. When you need to hire employees? What sources do you use to find them?

35. Are any of your expense categories in particular, your food and labor costs, out of line? If so, why?

36. Do you use any outside services? If so, what are they? And how much do they cost?

37. How are the daily books and records handled? Who does the daily cash reconciliation?

38. How are deposits to the bank handled? Who handles them?

39. How often do you receive income-and-expense statements? If you receive them monthly, how many days after the end of the month does it take to receive them?

40. What kind of preventative maintenance programs do you have? How often are the following items cleaned: a) duct and flu system, b) grease traps, and c) sewer drains?

41. Who handles the marketing and promotion activities for the business? How much do these services cost?

42. Who provides your liability insurance? What is the premium and amount of insurance?

43. Who provides your workman's compensation insurance? What are the premiums? What is your loss-history factor?

44. Are all your taxes current? If not, which taxes are outstanding? How much do you owe in outstanding taxes?

45. Do you have any other type of insurance?

46. Have there been any power outages or disruption of utility services for any significant amount of time?

47. Are there any gift certificates outstanding? If so, how much, and what is the redemption rate?

Chapter 13

SIGNS TO LOOK FOR TO DETERMINE IF THE SELLER'S BUSINESS IS IN TROUBLE

1. Employees comment that customers are complaining about poor service, poor maintenance conditions, and the quality and quantity of menu items.

2. Sellers owe back vendor debt, tax debt, etc.

3. Seller is having to pay all bills cash on delivery (COD) when the merchandise is delivered.

4. The employees are disgruntled, and some employees jobs have been eliminated.

5. Landlord is motivated to get new tenant as the current tenant has had a history of paying the rent late, and has serious issues with rent being in arrears/late.

6. Business has reduced its days and hours of operation.

7. Businesses owner and family members are working excessive hours in the business.

8. Lots of obvious deferred maintenance, and many pieces of the equipment are not in working order.

9. Saleable inventory (food, beverage, cleaning and paper supplies) is low, and several menu items are not available due to inventory shortages.

10. Premises are not clean.

11. Seller wants buyer to take possession of the premises before the close of escrow.

12. The ABC (alcohol) license, health department license, and business license have been suspended for delinquent renewal payments. If the business is a limited liability company (LLC) or corporation, these entities have been suspended by the state for non-payment of renewal fees.

13. The dishwasher is rented, and the vendor wants to remove this item for excessive late monthly rental payments.

14. Through a review of the books and records, it is determined that back taxes are due to various taxing agencies including the Internal Revenue Service (IRS), Franchise Tax Board (FTB) in California, State Board of Equalization (SBE) in California, and Employment Development Department (EDD) in California. In California, unless the seller can get tax clearances from these agencies during the escrow, the escrow will not be able to close, and these agencies could ultimately close the business.

15. In checking with the landlord, it is determined that the landlord is owed several months of back rent, and is the owner is on the verge of being evicted from the premises.

16. The business has been for sale for a long period, with several price reductions during this period and very little buyer activity.

If an experienced buyer looks for the above warning signs, and uses his or her negotiating skills in dealing with the seller and landlord, the buyer can turn a seller's losing business into a winning opportunity.

Success vs. Failure

Chapter 14

THE KEY INGREDIENTS OF A SUCCESSFUL RESTAURANT, BAR, OR CLUB FROM A CUSTOMER'S AND A BUYER'S PERSPECTIVE

From my many years experience in owning, operating, and selling many restaurants, bars, and nightclubs, what sets a successful operation apart from its competitors are the operator's commitment to consistently uphold certain standards. Businesses that have been around a long time have undoubtedly committed themselves to consistently maintaining the standards indicated below:

1. Serving quality food and beverages.
2. Providing good service.
3. Maintaining a clean environment.
4. Keeping all of the equipment well maintained.
5. Providing a strong price/value experience to the customer.

1. Serving quality food and beverages

When deciding whether to continue to patronize a business again, customers will always remember the quality level of the food and beverage. Today, there are many mediocre food operations. When a customer has a positive experience with good food, this encourages him to return to the business as a customer again.

2. Providing good service

Customers are very sensitive about getting good service. I know from experience as a customer, as well as from the experiences of many customers I have spoken with, that if the service is really good, a positive experience will help neutralize some of his prior negative experiences. In other words, if the food is not at its best, but the customer receives excellent service, in many cases, the customer feels that his overall dining experience is a positive one—and he will return to the business again.

3. Maintaining a clean and updated environment

Customers notice the cleanliness of a restaurant, bar, or nightclub–both in the front and back of the house. Restrooms are a key element in the whole experience of dining, since a well-maintained and updated environment helps a business to keep or enhance its value. Buyers appreciate the hard work it takes to keep a business in tiptop shape, and makes it more palatable for customers to pay a fair price if the premises are well-maintained.

4. Keeping all of the equipment well-maintained

Keeping the equipment well-maintained goes along with cleanliness. Equipment in good shape, and in good working order, almost always enhances the customer's and buyer's experience when interacting with the operation. This is especially true for buyers, as the condition of the equipment, to a large extent, sets the level of the buyer's interest in the business.

5. Providing a strong price/value experience to the customer

A strong price/value relationship is what the customer is looking for, in terms of whether or not he received value for the money spent for goods and services in the business. If the customer feels he has received value, he will most likely return. However, if a customer feels he has not received value, he will not return. Successful owner/operators have performed all of the above-mentioned services to the customer on a consistent basis. It follows that buyers are more inclined to want to buy this type of business.

Chapter 15

WHY SO MANY RESTAURANTS, BARS AND CLUBS FAIL

Many restaurant, bar, and club businesses fail due to the items indicated below:

1. Poor location.

A strong location is extremely important. Some mediocre operations survive long term due to a good location, while some better-run operations fail due to a secondary location. If your operation is not working, you can change the name, menu, concept and décor, but you can't change the location. For more information about location, see Section VI.

2. No prior restaurant, bar, or club experience.

The failure rate in this business is high as we've discussed, and without any experience, the rate is even greater. You need to be familiar with all the fundamentals of the business, including the back of the house (kitchen, prep areas, dishwashing area) and front of the house (dining room), as well as have thorough management experience. Learning from one's experience gives a better understanding of the business, and enhances one's chance for success. I found my experience of working in all of the positions in the restaurant very helpful when I ultimately supervised people in these positions because I understood the demands and challenges of these positions.

3. Lack of employee training.

All employees need to be trained to assure that all procedures are executed properly and consistently, which will contribute to the profitability of the operation and ensure that the customer will have a good experience.

4. Too much spent on capital improvements.

Frequently, I have seen situations where businesses were profitable operationally. However, they had such a high-debt service expense as a result of too much money being spent in building out the facility that they were losing money, and in many cases, went out of business. When building a restaurant from scratch, or doing a major remodeling job, make sure you have a budget, and you work with professionals who understand how to minimize the chances of over spending and incurring too much debt.

5. Inconsistent food and beverage.

It is important that the food is consistently prepared properly, and is presented tastefully to assure customer satisfaction. One of the major reasons restaurants fail is that the food is inconsistent. If the cooks are trained to prepare the food properly, the chances for inconsistent food will be minimized. Also, in a bar or club, if the drinks are not consistently made properly, this will alienate customers.

6. Inconsistent service.

One of the basic expectations that a customer has when he goes to a restaurant, bar, or club is consistent good service. It is important that the customer is acknowledged as soon as he enters the business. If there will be a delay in serving him, the food server or bartender should tell the customer he'll be with them shortly. I know of several situations where the customer had mediocre food or beverage, but, overall, had a good experience because the service was excellent.

7. Not maintaining proper cleanliness levels.

For safety and health reasons, customers are turned off by improper cleanliness levels at restaurants, bars, and clubs where food and drink are served. All public areas must be clean, including the dining room, and restrooms, as well as the back of the house areas: the kitchen, prep area, dishwashing and storage areas.

8. Not maintaining proper maintenance level.

Poorly maintained premises are a reflection of how the owner cares about the business. A professional operation has a well-maintained premises with all floors, walls, and ceilings in good condition, as well as all equipment in good working condition. Restaurants, bars, and clubs have large numbers of customers that frequent the facility, causing a lot wear and tear. Consequently, these facilities need to be maintained daily.

9.Lack of professional management.

Hiring well-trained management is imperative to assure the success of the business. Management sets the pace for the operation in terms of employee attitudes, and the customer's ultimate experience. It's helpful to hire management from both within and from outside. Hiring management from within motivates other employees because it shows there is advancement potential. Also the employees, in many cases, have respect for this individual because they know he understands the business. Hiring an individual from outside the business can also be helpful, assuming the individual comes from a professional company that is well managed. These individuals can bring more professional systems and controls to the business, which can enhance the caliber of the management of the business.

10. Lack of controls.

It's important to have the proper systems necessary for an operation's success regarding cash handling, guest check accountability, portion control, receiving procedures, and accounting systems, etc. Since the restaurant, bar, and club business handle a lot of cash, it is essential proper cash-handling procedures are in place, and require that anyone handling cash must reconcile that cash at the end of each shift.

Guest checks must be written for every order, and all food servers need to reconcile their guest checks with the cash register tapes at the end of each shift. Bartenders must also reconcile the cash with cash register tapes and the other controls put into place at the end of each shift. Portion control is a must. The customer should receive the same portion each time they frequent the business, and each item should be priced based on achieving a certain cost factor for that item. This contributes to the overall profitability of the business. There must be an accounting of all receipts by shift, and all receipts are to be accounted for and deposited daily into the bank.

Daily and weekly accounting reports, and monthly income-and-expense statements, need to be prepared so management is always aware of the business's financial position.

11. Poor price value.

Price value is the experience a customer has relative to receiving value for the money spent. A customer's expectation of price value will be different if eating in a fast-food restaurant where they paid a smaller amount for their meal. They expect fast service, and a reasonable quantity of food and beverage, but they do not have high expectations for the quality of food and beverage. However, a customer frequenting a high-end restaurant will expect excellent personal service, high-quality food, and a reasonable quantity, in an upgraded atmosphere.

12. Under-capitalized.

In several situations where the operation's concept was viable, the business was on the verge of turning the corner towards profitability. However, the owner was forced to go out of business because he didn't have enough working capital to keep the business going. It is imperative that when the owner starts the business, he has enough working capital set aside so that if the business does not perform at the projected level, money is available to keep the business going until it can be profitable.

13. Outdated concept.

Sometimes a concept is no longer viable, and needs to be changed in terms of menu selection, pricing and/or décor.

14. Partnership disputes.

This is one of the major reasons businesses fail. A partnership is like a marriage, and each prospective partner should have an extensive pre-existing relationship with the other, prior to becoming partners, so they understand each other's respective strengths, weaknesses, values, and perspectives. Frequently, two individuals who have known each other for a number of years decide to go into business together as partners. This rarely works out as one partner frequently does most of the work, the other partner does not carry his weight, and a conflict develops between the two partners. This often results in a dissolution of the partnership, and the business ends up getting sold to a third party. I strongly recommend that the only partners one should be involved within a business are investor/partners who have no control of any of the day-to-day operations.

15. No promotional activity.

No matter how successful a business is, the business must continue to promote itself. Imagine what would happen to McDonalds if they stopped advertising. Customers frequently forget about an operator's business as customers frequent new businesses from time to time, and then develop allegiances to the new businesses. The reason restaurants have daily specials is to attract and stimulate customers to frequent their business on a regular basis. Similarly, bars and nightclubs regularly have special-event nights to stimulate business.

16. Rent is too high.

Rent should not exceed 6-8% of gross sales in order to obtain a reasonable profitability. Frequently operators pay too much for rent, which can lead to their ultimate failure. In unique situations where the operator is in a high-profile location and will be generating real high-volume sales, the operator can afford to pay more for rent, assuming all of his other costs are in line.

17. Overall consistency.

It is imperative for long-term success that the operator's food, service, cleanliness, and maintenance of the premises are consistent. Specifically, the food and service should be consistently good, with a strong price/value relationship, and the premises should be consistently clean and well maintained.

18. Lack of standard operating procedures.

To have a professionally run operation, it is necessary to have written standard operating procedures for all job classifications. These are developed by the owners to assure each employee understands every aspect of his or her job, and each employee is consistent in executing that job. For example, a formula book should be in the kitchen containing a picture of each finished product that comes out of the kitchen. It should also have a detailed description explaining how to prepare the item, with specifications, including the portion size of each food item. For the dining room, the formula book should show a photo of every item, such as beverages, salads, and soups, etc., that the food server is responsible for preparing, with a detailed description explaining how to prepare each. Traditionally, you should have written details of all the side-work responsibilities for each job. Side-work responsibilities are additional responsibilities each job must perform, such as the kitchen staff responsibilities to clean certain pieces of equipment and maintain par stocks of food inventories for each shift.

19. Getting into business with family members and friends.

It is challenging enough to get along with family members, and maintain good relationships with friends, without having the challenges of running a successful business potentially get in the way of these relationships. We have seen on many occasions where families and friends have become alienated as a result of being involved in business relationships that didn't work out. To keep peace in your family, and maintain long-term reasonable relationships with friends, it best not to have family members or good friends be involved in business relationships.

20. Working with professional consultants when necessary.

The operator needs to work with an attorney to review all legal matters, such as reviewing the premises lease and all legal contracts of the business, to help assure the operator will do everything legally correct. A major legal problem could result in a legal action that can put the owner out of business. Similarly, it is important that the operator hire an accountant and bookkeeper to maintain the business books and records. This will make the operator comply with all the laws regarding paying accurate and timely taxes, wages, and all other business expenses.

From time to time, it may be necessary to hire other outside consultants, such as a human relations specialist if the operator wants to set up any kind of employee benefit program, such as a retirement plan or health plan. If the menu needs a major overhaul, it may be necessary to hire a food consultant who can work with the operator in developing new menu items, or hire an architect, a designer, or a food facilities engineer if remodeling or redesign of the kitchen or other area of the premises is needed.

Chapter 16

TURNING A LOSING BUSINESS INTO A WINNING BUSINESS OPPORTUNITY

Many buyers are interested in buying businesses in trouble that can be turned around and made profitable. In general, the buyers that focus on this type of business opportunity are experienced operators, with a successful track record of operating a profitable restaurant, bar, or club. The major benefits these buyers seek in this type of turnaround situation are indicated below:

Advantages in dealing with the landlord.
The buyer will in many cases have the ability to negotiate a more favorable lease than the current lease, and perhaps be able to negotiate some free rent from the landlord in the initial stages of operation, as well as a first right of refusal to purchase the building. Frequently, when a tenant is financially in trouble, he has a history of late rent or excessive delinquent rent payments, and the landlord is frustrated and highly motivated to

replace the existing problem tenant with an experienced new operator. In many cases, the new tenant can negotiate a lower rent and more favorable terms than the current tenant. Additionally, the landlord may contribute either some free rent so the new tenant can close the business and make improvements to the business, or the landlord may make a cash contribution toward the new tenant's remodeling project

Advantages in dealing with the seller.

The buyer will, in many cases, be able to purchase the business more reasonably, for well below the replacement cost. A seller in a troubled business is motivated to sell the business quickly, and will frequently reduce the sales price far below the asking price, enabling the buyer to get a very good deal. In some situations, the buyers pay very little cash, and have the seller carry back the balance of the purchase price, in the form of a seller carry-back note paid over several years, with no interest, or at a very low interest rate. In other situations, the seller would rather get an all-cash price, and not carry a seller carry-back note, in which case, the seller will discount the price even further to get all cash.

In some cases, the seller will include, at no extra cost to the buyer, the alcohol inventory or other saleable inventory, such as food, paper products or cleaning supplies, to help sweeten the deal for the buyer. In some situations, little or no cash is paid to the seller, and the buyer merely assumes the seller's debt, which may include the buyer assuming the seller's accounts payable, and/or assuming the seller's equipment lease, etc.

Chapter 17

WHY DO SELLERS SELL?

1. **Retirement** – This is a common reason why sellers sell. They, simply grow too old to properly run and manage the affairs of their business. If a seller does not have heirs interested in coming into the business, it is best that they take a proactive approach in planning the sale of their business so they have plenty of time to sell their business before they become physically and mentally unable to do so.

2. **Boredom/burnout** – At times, sellers get so immersed in the day-to-day events of running their business that they tend to get burned out, and are no longer effective in managing their business. When they get burned out, their thinking may get blurred, they lose perspective in making the right decisions, and it becomes difficult for them to run a profitable and competitive business.

3. **Undercapitalization** – This is a common reason why businesses must sell, and is especially true in the restaurant, bar, and nightclub business. These businesses are very cash intense in that the payables

need to made on a timely basis—such as payroll, and food and beverage bills, plus bills for utility, rent, taxes, etc. Employees generally have to be paid every two weeks, most vendors need to be paid weekly or monthly, and the rent needs to be paid monthly. If these bills mentioned are not paid on time, you will not have the supplies necessary to serve your guests, you will not have the employees you need to make the products and serve the guests, and you will not have a premises to operate in because you'll be evicted. Frequently, operators get into business without having the proper level of cash reserves set aside to deal with unexpected events. For example, the operator may have projected that he would do $40,000 a month in sales, which is his breakeven point, and in fact he does only $30,000 a month in sales. Where is the shortfall of $10,000 going to come from if the operator did not establish the proper cash reserve account when he purchased the business?

What typically happens if he can't raise the cash is he'll defer making his sales tax payment and/or payroll tax payment, which will mean steep interest and penalty charges. For example, in California if you do not make your sales tax payment timely, there is a 10% penalty on the amount owed, plus a steep monthly interest charge. If you don't make your payroll tax payment timely, there is a 50% penalty on the amount owed, plus a steep monthly interest rate. If you don't keep your vendor bills current, you will quickly find yourself in a C.O.D. position, which means that vendors will not leave the merchandise ordered unless you pay them cash on the spot.

4. **Health/death of the owner** – The restaurant, bar, and nightclub business, in most cases, requires the owner to be hands-on in operating the business. These businesses are usually physically demanding, and frequently the owner is working the front of the house as a host, waiter or bartender, or in the back of the house cooking. If the owner gets sick, the business will suffer. Most owners of independently run restaurant, bar, and nightclub businesses are immersed in the operations, and they generally control them, set the pace for their employees, and control the cash flow. When the owner/operator is out of the picture due to health reasons, the consistency of the food quality and service could suffer. Also since these businesses are largely

cash-oriented, there is a strong chance of cash shortages as the owner is not around to oversee the management of the cash.

Also if the owner dies suddenly, and no other family members are available to step into the business, it is almost certain to fail due to the items indicated above. This is why it is so important that if no family members will take over the operation of the business—in case of a prolonged sickness or death of the owner operator—that a plan is in place to quickly sell the business and/or liquidate the assets to minimize any loss of value of the business to the owner's heirs. If an owner operator dies without warning, and you are a family member trying to keep the business operating, I would suggest calling a reputable restaurant, bar, and/or nightclub consultant to help you find an interim manager to keep the business running until it is sold. Also, have a trustworthy bookkeeper that you know will monitor the business's daily cash flow. And also consider a long-term key employee or employees (one for the front of the house and one for the back of the house) that you could interact with who could keep the business running under your supervision. A business that is operating usually has much more value than one is closed, so I would encourage you to keep the business running until it is sold.

5. **Partnership disputes** – This is another common reason why many businesses fail, and I am asked to come in and sell the business.

Too many times there are situations with partners where each partner has made a 50% investment in the partnership, and one partner contributes 70% or more of his time to the success of the business, while the other partner contributes 30% of his time or less. As a result, the partner contributing more to the success of the business gets upset with the other partner who is not carrying his share of the load. Consequently, ill feelings develop between the partners, making the work situation intolerable, which can damage or ultimately destroy a business. Owners frequently ask me to find them a partner to help them run the business, in which case, I respond that this situation will most likely not work out. This is because people having different values and standards, and frequently it is difficult to match people's operating standards with one another.

I have always maintained that the only partner you want in your life is your spouse.

This is based on my own experience over the years of having several partners involved in several operating restaurant businesses that did not work out. I even had a pre-existing relationship with several of these people, many of whom worked for years in our business in management and non-management positions before they became partners with us. In most cases, these partnerships were not effective. Although these people were good managers, they lacked the entrepreneurial qualities necessary to be good managing partners, and they became too independent in their thinking. Most of these managing partners put up little cash. Most of their equity was developed through sweat equity, which they received as a result of their physical contributions and the profits of the business.

They felt now that they were part owners, they could make radical changes to the operation without discussing their recommendations with us. Specifically, they had a difficult time changing their past role from employee to owner, and it became difficult for them to relate to employees from an owner's point of view, after working with them as peers for so many years.

6. **Insufficient profits** – A business's primary goal is to make money, and without an adequate profit, it will ultimately go out of the business. As mentioned elsewhere in this book, only approximately 20% of independent, non-franchised restaurants succeed. If the owner cannot make a reasonable living from the business, he will ultimately sell, or go out of business. Unfortunately, many sellers in financial trouble wait too long before they put the business up for sale, and consequently, they have to close the doors. In a lot of cases, the landlord takes back physical possession of the premises before the seller has a chance to recover any of his losses. In the case where the seller has to close down and return the premises to the landlord, the seller may still have continued lease liability until his lease expires. The landlord has to make a reasonable effort to release the space. But until the space is released, the seller is still liable for monthly lease payments unless he works out a deal with the landlord to give the

landlord possession of the premises, in exchange for a relief of any future lease liability.

7. **Divorce** – Unfortunately, many businesses are forced to be sold, even if they are doing well, in order to satisfy a divorce settlement issued by the court. Although the business may be doing well, and both the husband and wife want to keep the business, they simply cannot work the business together. In this situation, they may be forced to sell to a third party at a lower price than they would have ordinarily received if they could sell it at time that was more advantageous to getting a higher price. This means that they have to sell the business that they formerly both worked together, because to settle the divorce everything has to be split 50/50.

8. **Greed** – Some sellers have an excessive desire to acquire or possess more money and power than they need, and they will sell strictly to make more money

Valuations and Other Financial Aspects

Chapter 18

HOW TO EVALUATE AN EXISTING BUSINESS TO DETERMINE ITS WORTH

Assets-in-Place Method of Valuation

We use this method of valuation for businesses that fall in the following categories, and are:

1) marginally profitable,

2) not making money, and

3) losing money, and on the verge of going out of business.

This valuation method is used to determine the value of a built-out business that has all of the major physical components in place for a restaurant, bar, or club operation.

In the case of a fully equipped restaurant, this would mean the kitchen would be fully intact, including the hood-and-duct system, all the major cooking equipment including grills, stoves, fryers, burners, refrigeration, etc. The back of the house would include the prep, dishwashing, storage, and office areas. And the front of the house would have all refrigeration, service stands, restrooms, tables and chairs, etc. in place. In addition to the above, all of the leasehold improvements would be in place. These are all of the improvements made either by the former tenant(s) or possibly by the landlord contributing to some of these leasehold improvements. This includes the mechanical systems (heating, ventilating and air conditioning systems), as well as the plumbing and electrical systems. In summary, a fully equipped restaurant, bar, or club is the prerequisite for approaching this type of valuation.

In addition, this type of valuation also considers goodwill, the premises lease, and licenses. Although the buyer for this type of business usually plans to change the name, menu and other proprietary aspects of the former business, things which usually makes up the goodwill of the business, there is still some goodwill value to the buyer. We call this residual goodwill because a certain percentage of the customers of the previous operation will try the new business because they have developed a habit of frequenting the former operation, and it is geographically convenient for them to continue to patronize this location.

With this method of valuation, very little emphasis is put on the former operation's financial results. However, the buyer is concerned about the past sales history, and some of the past operating expenses, including utilities, insurance and occupancy costs. The buyer's concern with the past sales history is that this data gives the buyer a foundation to build upon in projecting his future sales levels. Additionally, the buyer can evaluate the average menu prices and guest check averages per person, to determine how the buyer's projected new-menu pricing will compare to the former operator's pricing structure. This is an important factor to the buyer because it ensures he can recapture a large percent of the former operator's customer base and build upon it. The buyer is also concerned with the past history of utility, insurance and other occupancy costs, as these costs will be similar to his projected costs in preparing his proforma (projected) income and expense statement for his new operation.

The licenses, also referred to as entitlements, are also of great value to the buyer purchasing an assets-in-place business. The licenses usually include a food service-use permit, giving the operator the right to operate a restaurant at the given site for designated days and hours of operation, and an alcoholic beverage license, giving the operator the right to serve alcoholic beverages at the site.

These licenses are valuable, and sometimes unavailable in certain locations. For example, in San Francisco many districts have a moratorium in place prohibiting new food-and-beverage operations from opening. These moratoriums come into being as a result of neighborhood residents and businesses complaining that there are too many existing food-and-beverage operations in place, and arguing that any new operations will exacerbate the existing noise, litter, loiter, and parking problems. The only way some operations can get into a given area is to buy an existing business that has these licenses in place, even though these buyers have no interest in any other aspects of the business, including the fixtures and equipment and leasehold improvements.

No standard formula exists for determining an assets-in-place valuation. This method is somewhat subjective, and is based largely on the broker's experience in selling assets-in-place businesses. The majority of the sales my company has completed over the years have been assets-in-place transactions rather than going-concern transactions, discussed in Section Five.

In tracking the history of my assets-in-place transactions sold, they can best be characterized based upon their yearly sales levels (relative to their sales price), and are categorized as indicated below.

In reviewing our transactions using asset sales over the past 10-year period, the average sales prices have been as follows for businesses doing:

1. between $200,000 to $500,000 in yearly sales, the average sales price has been approximately 32% of yearly sales;

2. between $501,000 to $999,999 in yearly sales, the average sales price has been approximately 29% of yearly sales;

3. between $1million to $1,999,999 in yearly sales, the average sales price has been approximately 21% of yearly sales; and

4. over $2 million in yearly sales; the average sales price has been approximately 17% of yearly sales.

Chapter 19

EXTRAORDINARY CIRCUMSTANCES THAT DETERMINE ASSETS-IN-PLACE VALUATIONS

The assets-in-place transactions indicated above are summaries of past transactions, and extraordinary circumstances exist in almost every transaction. Some of these extraordinary circumstances include the situations indicated below.

a. **The buyer is on the verge of going out of business, and is being evicted.** He is desperate to sell. In this situation, the seller may sell for any price he can get, and if he doesn't move quickly, he'll get nothing, and will be stuck with thousands of dollars of bills owed. In this case, the seller may get as little as 5-10% of the yearly sales of his business as his price.

b. **The buyer gets nothing for his business other than release of lease liability**. In numerous situations, the buyer had personally guaranteed the premises lease, and had several years of lease liability left. Rather than risk that the landlord could not release the space on a timely basis, and the operator would be responsible for thousands of dollars of lease liability, he agreed to give his business to a buyer for no monetary consideration other than to be released from any future lease liability, making the buyer responsible for any future lease liability.

c. **The business had to close**. In several situations, the business had been closed, and the seller owed thousands of dollars of past bills including rent, vendor debt, and tax liability. In some of these circumstances, the buyer merely paid these past bills and took over the space with a new lease. In several other circumstances, the buyer told the landlord that he would enter into a new lease with him— once the landlord went through an eviction process and got legal possession of the premises, and went through the necessary time period to claim possession of the fixtures and equipment. In this case, the buyer gets into the space for no cost, and although the equipment and fixtures are legally owed by the landlord, the tenant gets use of the equipment and fixtures for either a nominal monthly cost, or for no cost. They have the understanding that in both of these circumstances, the buyer is responsible to maintain all the equipment, and replace it with comparable equipment as necessary during the life of the lease. He is also responsible for returning the equipment to the landlord at the end of the lease with reasonable wear and tear.

d. **The business filed for bankruptcy.** In some situations, the buyer has filed bankruptcy during the sales period. In these cases, the bankruptcy court has appointed us as the broker representing the debtor or seller, and has solicited offers from third parties. Once a bona fide offer is accepted between debtor and buyer, it is submitted to the bankruptcy court for approval. Proper bankruptcy procedure requires that once an accepted offer is placed in the bankruptcy court, the court gives a 30-day notice to the public to announce that an offer has been accepted, subject to any future better offers to be made to the court within that 30-day period. The best offer made to the court within that 30-day period gets to be the ultimate buyer of the business, subject to approval of the bankruptcy court. We have been involved in one situation where the business cost over $2.5

million to build—only three years before. Ultimately we sold it for $250,000, or 10% of the original cost, to a third party buyer in the bankruptcy court.

e.   **The business has a below-market lease, and a discounted cash flow analysis of the below-market lease is used to determine the value of the business.** In some cases, the buyer of this type of business is only interested in the premises lease, which may be a long-term, below-market lease that is assignable from the buyer to the seller. In this case, the buyer is not interested in the fixtures and equipment. He may plan to totally demolish the existing premises, and/or remodel the entire space to meet his criteria for the new proposed operation. The discounted cash-flow method is a calculation taking the existing below-market rent structure for the ensuing years, and comparing it to the current market rent for the same years. To calculate this, you take the difference in rent savings of the current rent structure for the life of the lease, compared to the existing and projected market rent, and calculate these differences to determine the value of those cash-flow savings over the projected years to today's value.

NOTE: In finance, the discounted cash flow (or DCF) approach describes a method to value a project, company, or financial asset using the concept of the time value of money. All future cash flows are estimated and discounted to give them a present value. The discount rate used is generally the appropriate cost of capital, and incorporates judgments of the uncertainty (riskiness) of the future cash flows.

Discounted cash flow analysis is widely used in investment finance, real estate development, and corporate financial management. The discounted cash-flow formula is derived from the future value formula for calculating the time value of money and compounding returns.

$FV = PV \cdot (1 + i)^n$ The simplified version of the discounted cash flow equation (for one cash flow in one future period) is expressed as:

$$DPV = \frac{FV}{(1 + d)^n}$$ where Discounted Present Value (DPV) is the discounted present value of the future cash flow (FV) adjusted for the opportunity cost of future receipts and risk of loss. *FV* is the nominal value of a cash flow amount in a future period; *d* is the discount rate, which is the opportunity cost plus risk factor (or the time value of money) and *i* is the future-value equation).

    – *Wikipedia Internet Source under Discounted Cash Flow.*

In a deal we completed, the buyer paid $240,000 for the restaurant, then totally demolished it, and spent an additional $700,000 building a new restaurant in this space. His basis for spending the $240,000 for the space was the below-market value of the lease, which had a value (using the above mentioned formula) of $240,000.

Explanation of the Discounted Cash Flow Valuation (DFF) Lease Equity Chart

This chart relates to a fully built-out 8,332 square foot restaurant we were working on that had 14 years left on its lease. The rent was 84¢ a sq. ft. /$6998.80 per month/$83,987 per year, and the market rent was $1.25 a sq. ft. /$10,415 per month/$124,980 per year. The yearly rent increased 3.5 % per year versus the market increase of 3% per year. In calculating the difference between the existing rent and the market rent for the 14-year remaining lease term, the difference was $650,820.

    To determine the value of this below-market lease, we use the Discounted Cash Flow Valuation Method (see chart below). This method brings the future cash benefits of the lease to today's value using various discount factors, depending upon the degree of risk for the operator. A strong AAA tenant, such as McDonald's or some other well-established chain, would have a lower degree of risk and, therefore, a lower discount factor than a independent newer restaurant. If you assume the tenant is going to be a AAA tenant, one would use a lower discount factor of 20% as shown in Scenario 1. So if you were buying this lease, and had a low-risk tenant, the discounted cash value of the lease would be worth $189,003. If the lease was going to be with an independent non-chain tenant, one would use a higher discount factor of perhaps 30% per the chart, and the lease would be worth $133,174 per the chart.

California's Largest Restaurant Business Brokerage
*Specializing in Sales, Acquisitions and
Leasing of Restaurants, Bars and Clubs*

Discounted Cash Flow Valuation (DCF) - Lease Equity

DCF Lease Valuation Parameters	
Square Feet	8,332
Years Left on Lease	14
Montly Rent/Sq. Ft.	0.84
Monthly Market Rent/Sq. Ft.	1.25
Lease Yearly Increase	3.50%
Market Yearly Increase	3.00%

DCF Scenarios	
Risk Level	Discount Rate
Scenario 1: Lower	20%
Scenario 2: Medium	25%
Scenario 3: Higher	30%

DCF Value Conclusions		
Risk Level	Discount Rate	Discounted Value
Lower	20%	$189,003
Medium	25%	$156,762
Higher	30%	$133,174

Fiscal Year	Yearly Total Rent	Yearly Market Rent	Lease Equity Prior to Discount	Scenario 1	Scenario 2	Scenario 3
2005/06	$83,987	$124,980	$40,993	$34,161	$32,795	$31,533
2006/07	$86,926	$128,729	$41,803	$28,468	$26,236	$24,256
2007/08	$89,969	$132,591	$42,623	$23,723	$20,989	$18,659
2008/09	$93,117	$136,569	$43,452	$19,769	$16,791	$14,353
2009/10	$96,377	$140,666	$44,290	$16,474	$13,433	$11,041
2010/11	$99,750	$144,886	$45,136	$13,729	$10,746	$8,493
2011/12	$103,241	$149,233	$45,992	$11,441	$8,597	$6,533
2012/13	$106,854	$153,710	$46,855	$9,534	$6,878	$5,025
2013/14	$110,594	$158,321	$47,727	$7,945	$5,502	$3,866
2014/15	$114,465	$163,071	$48,605	$6,621	$4,402	$2,974
2015/16	$118,471	$167,963	$49,491	$5,517	$3,521	$2,287
2016/17	$122,618	$173,002	$50,384	$4,598	$2,817	$1,760
2017/18	$126,909	$178,192	$51,282	$3,831	$2,254	$1,353
2018/19	$131,351	$183,537	$52,186	$3,193	$1,803	$1,041
TOTALS	**$1,484,629**	**$2,135,449**	**$650,820**	**$189,003**	**$156,762**	**$133,174**

In summary, a buyer can get a very good deal on an assets-in-place transaction, and will usually end up spending cents on the dollar on the initial purchase, compared to the replacement cost of this purchase. Timing is everything, and if the buyer's timing is right, he can get into some assets-in-place transactions for little or no initial cash.

Chapter 20

SAMPLE OF
ASSETS-IN-PLACE VALUATION

In this chapter, I am showing you a sample letter of valuation for the XYZ Restaurant & Bar, 1234 America Way, Anywhere, California.

Dear John:

I have prepared the following letter of valuation based on the following: 1) my recent tour of your business, 2) my review of the premises lease, 3) my review of the Profit and Loss Statements for 2010, and 4) our discussions regarding various other aspects of the business.

The two basic methods for valuing a restaurant are discussed below:

I. **Going-Concern Method** – This method means that the lease, leasehold improvements, fixtures and equipment, name, menu, concept, goodwill, licenses and cash flow are all included as part of the sale. The primary valuation method utilized for the going concern method is the yearly adjusted cash flow method. Since the subject business is not profitable, I will not discuss this method of valuation further, but will use the Assets-in-Place Method as described below.

II. **Assets-in-Place Method** – This method means that only the lease, leasehold improvements, licenses, fixtures and equipment are being sold. The name, menu, concept and goodwill are usually not included as part of the sale. With this method, less emphasis is put on the financials of the business; the major factors in determining the value are the lease, leasehold improvements, licenses and the fixtures and equipment. There is no standard formula for determining value utilizing this method, and valuation is somewhat subjective based on the broker's knowledge of the market place. I have sold over 800 restaurants, bars or clubs, and completed over 2,500 valuations on restaurants, bars and clubs since 1996. The majority of these sales have been sold by the Assets-in-Place Method. I will use this method in valuing this business. The main criteria I will use in this method to determine the sales price is the ratio of sales to sales price on the past restaurants that we have sold using the Assets-in-Place Method.

The following is a partial list (most recent first) of the restaurants we have sold using the Assets-in-Place Method:

Restaurant 1, San Francisco – 1500 sq. ft. $1 million sales; lease terms – 6/11/12- 3/31/17, $6,000 monthly flat + 5-year option at $7200 monthly flat. COE 6/2012; sales price $230,000.

Restaurant 2, San Francisco – 1850 sq. ft. + mezzanine; $800,000 sales, but closed when sold; lease terms – 9/20/11- 9/19/21, monthly rent of $6643 plus 2.5% yearly increase + two 5-year options at market. COE 2/2012; sales price $176,000.

Restaurant 3, San Anselmo – 2,000 sq. ft. $600,000 sales, but closed when sold; lease terms – monthly rent year 1 - $3250, year 2 - $3500; then CPI yearly with a minimum of 2% and maximum of 6%, + 5-year option with CPI yearly with a minimum of 2%, and maximum of 6%. COE 1/2012; sales price $90,000.

Restaurant 4, Novato – 3,000 sq. ft. + patio, $875,000 sales; years 1-2, $4,167 per month; years 3-4, $5,000 per month; year 5, $5416 per month; and two 5-year options at market. COE 12/11; sales price $160,000.

Restaurant 5, San Francisco – 2500 sq. ft., $227,000 sales; $8,000 monthly rent years 1-3; then CPI increases yearly through 3/31/17, plus a 5-year option at market, the net rent is $5,500 as the tenant subleases the upstairs space for $2,500 month. COE 10/11; sales price $44,000.

Restaurant 6, Vallejo – 1400 sq. ft., $216,000 sales; $2644 all inclusive monthly rent and expires 9/30/16, with yearly CPI increases with a minimum of 3% yearly, and a maximum of 6% yearly, plus a 5-year option at market with the same yearly increases as indicated. COE 10/11; sales price $45,000.

Restaurant 7, San Francisco – 2,000 sq. ft. + full useable basement, $300,000 sales; yearly rent is $6,010 plus yearly fixed increases, and expires 2016, with one 5-year option at market. COE 9/11; sales price $120,000.

Restaurant 8, San Francisco – 1500 sq. ft., $240,000 sales; $3,035 monthly rent with yearly CPI increases, and expires 3/31/15, with one 5-year option at market. COE 9/11; sales price $94,000 with $70,000 down and $24,000 seller carry back note at 8% interest, fully amortized over 24 months from close of escrow.

Restaurant 9, Oakland (Montclair) – 1800 sq. ft., $500,000 sales; $6125 monthly rent all inclusive, with yearly CPI increases, with 3% minimum yearly increases, and 10% maximum yearly increases, and expires 2020 with one 5-year option at market rent. COE 8/11; sales price $135,000.

Restaurant 10, San Jose – 3,000 sq. ft., $360,000 sales, although closed when sold; 5-year lease with two 5-year options, $4,500 monthly rent year 1 + NNN, with yearly 3% increases, plus two 5-year options at market with 3% yearly increases. COE 8/11; sales price $109,000.

Restaurant 11, Redwood City – 5,800 sq. ft., $240,000 sales; 10-year lease with first year rent at $4,000 + NNN with fixed increases yearly, and two 5-year options at market. COE 7/11; sales price $78,000 with $60,000 down and seller carry back note for $18,000 at 7% interest, with two balloon payments 6 months and 12 months from the close of escrow.

Restaurant 12, Berkeley – 800 sq. ft., $225,000 sales, although closed when sold; $1500 monthly rent fixed for 3 years, the CPI in years 4 & 5, not to exceed 3% year. COE 7/11; sales price $60,000.

Restaurant 13, Berkeley – 1350 sq. ft., $196,000 sales, although closed when sold; $4,310 monthly rent all inclusive, 3% yearly increases, expires 2015, plus two 5-year options at market. COE 6/11; sales price $40,000.

Restaurant 14, Larkspur – 1,200 sq. ft. + enclosed outdoor seating area; $276,000 sales; $3,200 gross monthly rent with fixed increases, and expires 12/2015, with 5-year option at market rent. COE 5/2011; sales price $84,000.

Restaurant 15, San Francisco – 1,200 sq. ft., $300,000 sales; $2,500 monthly gross rent fixed for 2 years, then steps up to $3,000 month, with yearly CPI increases for 5 years, with two, 5-year options with yearly CPI adjustments. COE 5/2011, sales price $105,000.

Restaurant 16, Berkeley – 4,300 sq. ft. + large outdoor unfinished seating area, $440,000 sales, although closed when sold; $10,181 month + NNN, and expires 4/30/1016, with yearly CPI increases, and one 5-year option at market. COE 5/11; sales price $225,000.

Restaurant 17, San Francisco – 1,500 sq. ft., $240,000 sales; $3,075 monthly rent all inclusive, with yearly CPI, increases with a minimum of 2.5% yearly, with lease expiring 5/31/2017, plus a 5-year option at market rent. COE 4/2011; sales price $65,000.

Restaurant 18, San Francisco – 1,500 sq. ft., $240,000 sales; $3,400 + NNN, with yearly CPI increases, with 4 year term and two 5-year options at a continuation of CPI adjustments yearly. COE 4/2011; sales price $100,000.

Restaurant 19, San Francisco – 2,000 sq. ft., $297,000 sales; $4,800 monthly rent with yearly CPI increases, with 5-year term with 5-year option at market rent. COE 4/2011; sales price $75,000.

Restaurant 20, San Francisco – 1,000 sq. ft. + full basement; $300,000 sales; $6,500 all inclusive monthly rent, CPI yearly with 5-year term and 5-year option at market. COE 3/2011, sales price $85,000.

Restaurant 21, San Francisco – 2,500 sq. ft., $455,000 sales; $6,000 month rent with yearly CPI increases, with 5-year term and 5-year option at market rent. COE 1/2011, sales price $155,000.

Restaurant 22, Walnut Creek – 1,900 sq. ft., $336,000 sales; $6,200 month rent all-inclusive, with yearly CPI increases, 7-year term. COE 11/2010, sales price $79,000.

Restaurant 23, San Mateo – 2,100 sq. ft., $120,000 sales; $4,000 month rent with yearly CPI increases for 5-year term, with 5-year option. COE 10/2010; sales price $79,000.

Restaurant 24, San Leandro – 1,000 sq. ft., $90,000 sales; $2300 monthly rent with 2% yearly increases with 5-year term and 5-year option at market rent. COE 9/2010; sales price $47,000.

Restaurant 25, Berkeley – 5,000 sq. ft., $420,000 sales; $10,500 all inclusive monthly rent with 3% yearly increases, with 5-year term and 5-year option continues with 3% yearly increases. COE 9/2010; sales price $175,000.

Restaurant 26, San Francisco – 3,358 sq. ft. + outdoor seating, $630,000 sales; $6835 all inclusive monthly rent, with CPI increases yearly, with 8-year term remaining, plus 5-year option at market. COE 8/2010; sales price $145,000.

Restaurant 27, San Francisco – 1,652 sq. ft., $288,000 sales; $3490 all-inclusive rent with 3% yearly increases, with 5-year term and one 5-year option at market. COE 8/2010; sales price $100,000.

Restaurant 28, Berkeley – 900 sq. ft., $220,000 sales; rent $4,138 all inclusive, 5-year lease with 5-year option, rent increases 3% per year, and option is at market. COE 8/2010; sales price $80,000.

Restaurant 29, Petaluma – 1,600 square feet plus large outdoor seating area, $672,000 sales; rent was $2,400 month with yearly CPI increases, with 5-year term with 5-year option at market; restaurant was converted to a totally different food concept. COE 6/4/2010; sales price $130,000.

Restaurant 30, San Francisco – 2,200 sq. ft., $800,000 sales; $10,000 month rent with fixed yearly increases, with 5 year term and 5-year option at market rent; restaurant was sold through the US Bankruptcy Court; and restaurant was closed at the time of sale. COE 3/2010; sales price $120,000.

Restaurant 31, Palo Alto – 2,100 sq. ft. + 1,000 sq. ft. upstairs for service space, $600,000 sales; $8,750 month rent with yearly CPI increases, and lease expires in 2013 with 5-year option at market; restaurant was closed at time of sale. COE 3/2010; sales price $150,000.

Restaurant 32, San Francisco, CA – 3,000 sq. ft., $1 million sales; $10,000 month with yearly CPI increases, with 5-year term with 5-year option at market; name and menu were not included with the sale. COE 2/2/010; sales price $150,000.

Restaurant 33, San Anselmo, CA – 2,000 sq. ft., $420,000 sales; lease terms $4,700 month with 5% yearly increases, expires 2011, + 5-year option at market rent. COE 1/2010; sales price $160,000.

Restaurant 34, Mill Valley, CA – 2,400 sq. ft., closed at time of sale but previously did $1million sales yearly; lease terms - $6,000 month with yearly CPI, expires 3/2011 + 5-year option at market rent. COE 6/09; sale price $105,000.

Restaurant 35, Pleasanton, CA – 2,500 sq. ft. + 564 sq. ft. covered patio, closed at time of sale, but prior owner was doing $140K sales yearly; lease terms - $4,947 all inclusive, yearly CPI with 5 year term + 5-year option at market rent. COE 5/09; sales price $60,000.

Restaurant 36, San Jose, CA – 5,000 sq. ft., $1.8 million sales; lease terms - $18,000 month + NNN, but restaurant was sold back to the landlord so don't know lease terms. COE 4/09; sales price $200,000.

Restaurant 37, Novato, CA – 1,860 sq. ft. + large outdoor seating area, $420K sales; lease terms - $6,866 all inclusive, expires 2010, yearly CPI + 5-year option at market. COE 4/09; sales price $140,000.

Restaurant 38, San Rafael, CA – 1,500 sq. ft. + outdoor seating area, closed when sold but previously was doing $15K a month or $180K year; lease terms - $4,500 month all inclusive + yearly CPI with new 5 year term plus 5-year option at market rent. COE 3/09; sale price $69,000.

Restaurant 39, San Francisco, CA – 2,000 sq. ft., $264K sales; lease terms - $4,500 month all inclusive, expires 2010, + 2-3 year options. COE 2/09; sales price $75,000.

Restaurant 40, Oakland, CA – 1,500 sq. ft., $466K sales; lease terms - $3,250 monthly rent with new 5 year term and yearly CPI, + 5-year option at market rent. COE 2/09; sales price $90,000.

Restaurant 41, San Rafael, CA – 2,400 sq. ft., $360K sales; lease terms - $4,700 monthly rent all inclusive, yearly CPI, lease expires 4/30/12, + 5-year option at market rent. COE 2/09; sales price $90,000.

Restaurant 42, San Francisco, CA – 2,500 sq. ft., $720K sales before they closed; lease terms - $7,000 monthly rent with CPI yearly increases, with 5-year term plus two 5-year options at fair market rent. COE 12/15/08; sales price $200,000.

Restaurant 43, Fremont, CA – 1,485 sq. ft., $324K sales; lease terms - $4,767 per month all inclusive with yearly CPI increases, with a 5-year base term plus a 5-year option at fair market rent. COE 12/1/08; sales price $107,000.

Restaurant 44, San Rafael, CA – 2,772 sq. ft., $180,000 sales before they closed; lease terms - $3,478 per month + NNN with fixed increases in following years; the monthly rent is as follows: $3,583, $3,929, $4,047, $4,169, $4,292 and $4,423, plus NNN, plus 5-year option at fair market rent. COE 11/17/08; sales price $40,000.

Restaurant 45, Los Altos, CA – 4,200 sq. ft., $720,000 sales before they closed; lease terms - $10,800; all inclusive monthly rent with CPI adjustments yearly, with a minimum of 3% increases yearly through 9/2012, plus 5-year option at fair market rent. COE 11/08; sales price $155,000.

Restaurant 46, San Francisco, CA – 9,000 sq. ft. which includes retail space, live loft space, storage area and café of approximately 1,000 sq. ft., $180K sales + $50K rental income = $230K total income; lease terms: $5,760 monthly rent with CPI yearly through 12/31/09, with one 5-year option with a continuation of CPI yearly. COE 10/16/08; sales price $85,000.

Restaurant 47, San Francisco, CA – 2,000 sq. ft. + patio which seats 35, $600K sales; lease terms $11,000 month rent all inclusive with NNN with CPI yearly increases through 2018. COE 9/08; sales price $290,000.

Restaurant 48, Hayward, CA – 3,400 sq. ft., $216K sales; lease terms: $4,500 monthly rent, with rent going up $250 month every two years through 12/31/12, with one 5-year option with the rent $5,250 years 1 & 2, $5,500 years 3 & 4 and $5,700 year 5 of the option. COE 9/4/08; sales price $41,000.

Restaurant 49, Oakland, CA – 2,300 sq. ft., $240K sales before they closed: lease terms - $4,000 monthly rent plus yearly CPI, 5 year base lease plus 5-year option at fair market rent. COE 8/15/08; sales price $64,000.

Restaurant 50, San Francisco, CA – 8,000 sq. ft., $2 million sales before they closed; lease terms - $17,800 month all inclusive, plus yearly CPI and lease expires 2016, plus two 5-year options at fair market rent. COE 8/08; sales price $300,000.

Restaurant 51, San Carlos, CA – 3,000 sq. ft. $376,000 sales; lease terms – 6/1208-6/30/13 $7,400 all inclusive, plus yearly CPI increase, and one 5-year option at fair market rent. COE 7/10/08; sales price $100,000.

Restaurant 52, Hercules, CA – 1,300 sq. ft., $525,000 sales; lease terms 7/1/08-11/30/09 - $3,107 NNN, 12/1/09-11/30/11 - $3,575 NNN, plus 5-year option at fair market rent. COE 7/2/08; sales price $160,000.

Restaurant 53, Palo Alto, CA – 3,000 sq. ft. + large outdoor seating area, $660,000 sales; lease terms – rent 6/1/07-5/31/08 $5,500 NNN, 6/1/08-5/31/09 $5,750 NNN, 6/1/09-5/31/10 $6,000 NNN, plus two three year options as follows: 6/1/10-5/31/13 $6,250 NNN and 6/1/13-5/31/16 $6,500 NNN. COE 6/25/08; sales price $225,000.

Restaurant 54, Concord, CA – 3,655 sq. ft., $395,000 sales; lease terms - $7,300 month all inclusive with CPI yearly, and lease expires 12/31/2010, with a 5-year option at fair market rent. COE 5/8/08; sales price $180,000.

Restaurant 55, San Mateo, CA - 6,500 sq. ft., $1.1 million lease terms - $8,700 NNN with yearly CPI adjustments, and base terms expires 3/31/2012, plus a 5-year option at fair market rent. COE 5/08; sales price $425,000.

Restaurant 56, Vallejo, CA – 3,000 sq. ft., $420,000 sales; lease terms - $7,200 monthly rent flat until 12/31/08, with twp 5-year options; and first option rent is flat at $8,712 month for five years, and second option rent is flat at $9,583 for 5 years. COE 4/25/08; sales price $180,000.

Restaurant 57, Fremont, CA – 3,600 sq. ft., $425,000 sales; lease terms – expires 2011 + two 5-yearoptions, rent is $12,870 all inclusive, and options are at fair market rent, and there is CPI yearly on base rent. COE 4/17/08; sales price $149,000.

Restaurant 58, Berkeley, CA – 2,500 sq. ft., $600,000 sales; lease terms – lease expires 5/31/13, + 3 year option, + two 5-year options, and rent is flat at $4,300 per year. COE 3/24/08; sale price $195,000.

Restaurant 59, Menlo Park, CA – 4,000 sq. ft. + patio, $1.2 million sales; 5-year lease with monthly rent of $19,900, with 3% yearly adjustments, and 5-year option at market rent. COE 3/15/08; sales price $250,000.

Restaurant 60, San Francisco, CA – 3,500 sq. ft. + patio, $804,000 sales; 5-year lease through 12/31/12, with monthly rent as follows: year 1, $4,700, year 2 & 3, $5,000, year 4 & 5, $5,300 and a 5-year option with monthly rent as follows: year 1, $6,500, year 2, $6,662; year 3, $6,828; year 4, $6,999; and year 5, $7,174. COE 3/7/08; sale price $200,000.

Restaurant 61, Danville, CA – 2,200 sq. ft. + patio, $300,000 sales; lease expires 11/30/2011, and the monthly NNN rent is $3,341, and the rent is adjusted yearly by the CPI, not to exceed 5% per year, and there are two 5-year options at market. COE 3/3/08; sale price $175,000.

Restaurant 62, San Francisco, CA – 939 sq. ft., $516,000 sales; lease expires 4/30/16 and monthly NNN rent is as follows: 1-30th month–$2,817; 31st-60th month–$3,051; 61st -90th month, $3,286; and 91st month–$3,521. COE 2/15/08; sales price $180,000.

Restaurant 63, Menlo Park, CA – 4,500 sq. ft. + 500 sq. ft. upstairs, $1.6 million sales; 10-year lease with monthly NNN rent as follows: year 1, $12,500; year 2, $13,000; year 3, $13,261; year 4, $13,659; year 5, $14,068; year 6,

$14,490; year 7, $14,925; year 8, $15,373; year 9, $15,834; year 10, $16,309; and 5-year option with monthly NNN rent as follows: year 1, $16,698; year 2, $17,302; year 3, $17,821; year 4, $18,356; and year 5, $18,907. COE 1/17/08; sales price $350,000.

Restaurant 64, Alamo, CA – 1,150 sq. ft. + outdoor patio, $216,000 sales; 5 year lease expiring 12/20/12, with monthly rent as follows: year 1, $2,600; year 2, $2,700; year 3, $2,800; year 4 & 5, $2,900; and 5-year option with monthly rent as follows: year 1, $3,000; year 2, $3,100; year 3, $3,200; year 4, $3,300; and year 5, $3,400. COE 12/21/07; sales price: $97,500.

Restaurant 65, San Francisco, CA – 3,200 sq. ft., $600,000 sales; 5-year NNN lease with monthly rent as follows: year 1, $7,300; year 2, $7,600; year 3, $7,900; year 4, $8,200; and year 5, $8,500; and 5-year option at market rent. COE 11/0/07, sales price $227,500.

Restaurant 65, San Francisco, CA – 2,500 sq. ft., $850,000 sales; NNN lease with monthly rent as follows: year 1, $7,598; year 2, $8,128; year 3, $8,428; year 4, $8,728; and year 5, $8,980. COE 10/10/07, sales price $170,000.

Restaurant 67, Pleasanton, CA – 1,710 sq. ft.,$600,000 sales; 5-year lease with monthly rent at $5,800, plus yearly CPI increases with a minimum of 3% increases per year, with two 5-year options at market rent, with CPI increases yearly with a minimum of 3% per year. COE 9/28/07, sales price $285,000.

Restaurant 68, San Francisco, CA – 2,000 sq. ft. + basement, restaurant was closed at sale but prior owner's sales were $800,000; new 5-year lease with monthly rent as follows: year 1, $8,000; year 2, $8,750; year 3, $9,500; year 4, $10,250; and year 5 - $10,500 with a 5-year option as follows: year 1-110% of year 5's rent and then 3% per year increases. COE 8/15/07, sales price $300,000.

Restaurant 69, Berkeley, CA – 2,500 sq. ft., $850,000 sales; 5-year NNN lease with first year monthly rent at $7,488, and yearly increases of 3% per year; and a 5-year option with first year rent at 105% of the fifth years rent, with yearly 3% increases. COE 8/07, sales price $160,000.

Restaurant 70, Walnut Creek, CA – 3,500 sq. ft., $1,020,000 sales: lease is $8,058 all- inclusive, with yearly CPI increases, plus a 5-year option at market rent. COE 7/07, sales price $395,000.

Restaurant 71, Walnut Creek, CA – 4,750 sq. ft., $960,000 sales; Lease is $12,850 all-inclusive, with yearly CPI increases, and expires in 2014, + a 5-year option at market rent. COE 6/07, sales price $375,000.

Restaurant 72, Albany, CA – 3,200 sq. ft., $660,000 sales; Lease is 5 years with rent of $3,200 month NNN, with yearly CPI increases, with two 5-year options at market rent. COE 5/17/07, sales price $260,000.

Restaurant 73, San Francisco, CA: 3,000 sq. ft., $800,000 sales before closing; lease term is 5 years with all inclusive rent of $5,850 per month, with yearly CPI adjustments plus 5-year option at market rent. COE 4/9/07, sales price $225,000.

Restaurant 74, Menlo Park, CA: 4,500 sq. ft. + large parking lot, $1.3 million sales; lease term is 11/21/02 through 11/20/22; and monthly rent is as follows: years 1-5, $12,500 NNN; years 6-10, $14,000 NNN; year 11-15, $16,000 NNN; years 16-20, $18,000 NNN, + two 5-year options at market rent. COE: 11/06, sales price $210,000.

Restaurant 75, Berkeley, CA: 4,000 sq. ft. + patio, $625,000 sales; lease term is 6/27/02-9/30/2012 with $8,500 monthly rent NNN, with yearly CPI of 4%. COE 9/8/06; sales price $120,000.

Restaurant 76, Burlingame, CA: 2,000 sq. ft., $460,000 sales; lease term is 1/1/06-5/31/2012, + 6-year option; rent is $2,750 per month with CPI every 2 years, with a minimum of 3.5% per year. COE 7/31/06; sales price $95,000.

Restaurant 77, CA: 7,200 sq. ft., $745,000 sales; lease is for 5 years and monthly rents are as follows: year 1, $8,928; year 2, $9,216; year 3, $9,504; year 4, $9,792; and year 5, $10,080. This NNC lease has two 5-year options at fair market rent. COE 1/23/2006; sales price $195,000.

Restaurant 78, Oakland, CA: 2,500 sq. ft., $550,000 sales; Lease term is 10/15/02-9/30/07 + two 5-year options; rent is $4,200 per month with CPI every 30 months, with a 7% minimum and 15% maximum; COE 1/12/06; sales price $120,000.

Restaurant 79, San Francisco, CA: 3,500 sq. ft., $700,000 sales; Lease period is for 7 years + a 5-year option; $7,000 rent and yearly CPI, with a minimum of 3% and a maximum of 5%; and option is at market rent; and this is a NNN lease. COE 12/21/2005; sales price $225,000.

Restaurant 80, San Francisco, CA: 3,500 sq. ft., $1 million sales; Lease expires 12/31/2010 plus 2-year option; rent is $4,700 from COE-12/31/08, and $5,000 from 1/1/09-12/31/10, and $5,600 during option. COE 5/18/05; sales price $265,000.

Restaurant 81, San Francisco, CA: 6,500 square feet, $1 million sales; Lease expires 5/15/07 plus two 5-year options, $10,000 rent plus CPI yearly, first option continues at CPI and second option is at market rent, modified NN. COE 3/2005; sales price $275,000.

Restaurant 82, Sonoma, CA: 5,000 square feet, $1.5 million sales; 10-year lease, with rent in year 1 $10,000 NNN, and yearly CPI increases thereafter, plus two 5-year options at market rent with CPI increases thereafter. COE 3/2005; sales price $350,000.

Restaurant 83, San Rafael, CA: 5,000 square feet, $1.5 million sales; 10-year lease with rent in year 1 $10,500 per month NNN, and yearly CPI increases thereafter, plus one 10-year option, and the rent in the first year is market rent with yearly CPI increases thereafter. COE 8/2004; sales price $150,000

Restaurant 84, San Jose, CA: 7,500 square feet, $1.2 million sales; New l0-year lease year 1, $7,500 per month NNN with yearly CPI increases, plus a 10-year option with the rent in the first year market rent with CPI adjustments yearly thereafter. COE 6/20/04; sales price: $145,000.

Restaurant 85, San Francisco, CA: 3,500 square feet, $1.2 million yearly sales; lease terms: $27,000 per month NNN with yearly CPI increases, with a 10-year term plus two 5-year options at market rent. COE 3/1/04; sales price: $200,000.

Restaurant 86, Calistoga, CA: 5,100 square feet + large patio, $1.5 million yearly sales; current rent is $6,300, with yearly CPI increases with a minimum of 2% per year and a maximum of 7% per year, and lease expires 6/11/2016. COE 1/04; sales price: $200,000.

Restaurant 87, San Mateo, CA: 7,000 square feet, $1.5 million yearly sales, but restaurant formerly did $2.3 million sales three years ago; $7,000 NNN monthly rent versus 5% of sales, base term expires 12/31/06, and there are four 5-year options, and the rent is substantially below market until 2016. COE 1/04; sales price: $240,000.

Restaurant 88, Sausalito, CA: 2,500 square feet, $800,000 yearly sales; lease terms: monthly rent year 1 - $5,666 with 5% yearly increases, and 5-year option continues with 5% yearly increases with tenant paying a portion of real estate taxes. COE 12/11/03; sales price: $185,000.

Restaurant 89, San Rafael, CA: 8,000 square feet, over $1.5 million spent on restaurant; $2.2 million sales; lease terms: 10-year term with rent at $11,000 NNN, with yearly CPI increases plus a ten year option at market rent. COE 10/2002; sales price: $450,000.

Restaurant 90, San Francisco, CA: 11,300 square feet, over $2million was spent in building out building and brewpub, $2.2 million sales; lease terms: $6,460 month NNN with yearly CPI increases; then two 5-year options at market rent. COE 7/2002; sales price: $250,000 through the Federal Bankruptcy Court Chapter 11 proceeding.

Restaurant 91, South San Francisco, CA: 6,300 square feet, $1.4 million yearly sales but restaurant was closed a year before sale; lease terms: currently monthly rent $4,095 NNN with 5% yearly increases every 2 years until 1/31/08, plus two 5-year options at market. COE 5/13/02; sales price: $170,000 through the Federal Bankruptcy Court Chapter 11 proceeding.

Restaurant 92, San Francisco, CA; 8,000 square feet, $1.1 million yearly sales; lease terms: 6 years, monthly rent first year $4,200 fixed until 4/30/06, with 5-year option with CPI adjustment in the first year of the option period. COE 8/28/01; sales price: $285,000.

Restaurant 93, San Francisco, CA: 2,000 square feet, $950,000 yearly sales; lease terms: 5 years, $2,219 with yearly CPI with a minimum of 3% and a maximum of 7%, with a 5-year option at the ten adjusted CPI. COE 8/3/01; sales price: $262,500.

Restaurant 94, San Mateo, CA; 5,400 square feet, $1.2 million yearly sales; lease terms: $10,000 per month NNN with yearly CPI increases, and the lease expires in 11 years, and there is a 5-year option at market rent with yearly CPI increases thereafter. COE 4/27/01; sales price: $150,000.

Restaurant 95, Los Gatos: 6,200 square feet, $1.5 million sales; lease terms: $4,400 per month NNN, versus 4% of gross sales with yearly CPI increases, and expires 2016. COE 4/27/01; sales price: $500,000.

Restaurant 96, San Francisco, CA: 4,000 square feet, $1.5 million yearly sales; lease terms: 10-year terms, monthly rent first year $11,000 NNN with yearly CPI increases with minimum of 4% and maximum of 8%, 5-year option with the rent the first year of the option period not to exceed 20% of the rent in the last year of the base term. COE 3/3/00; sales price: $350,000.

Restaurant 97, San Mateo, CA; 5,000 square feet, $900,000 yearly sales; lease terms: $7,500 per month NNN with 3% yearly increases, versus 5% of yearly gross sales, lease expires 4/30/01, plus 2 ten year options at market rent. COE 2/5/99: sale price: $175,000.

Restaurant 98, Burlingame: 11,000 square feet, $2 million sales; lease terms: initial term expires 3/2004, rent is $14,000 per month NNN fixed for several years, then $15,000 per month NNN fixed for several years, then $16,000 per month NNN fixed for several years. $2.8 million invested into the building and restaurant. COE 10/1999 through the Federal Bankruptcy Court in a Chapter 11 proceeding; sales price: $700,000 through an aggressive bid process.

Restaurant 99, San Francisco, CA: 3,595 square feet, $1.3 million yearly sales; lease terms: 10 year term with monthly rent year 1, $8,500; year 2, $9,000; year 3, $10,000; then yearly CPI with a minimum increase of 3% and a maximum increase of 5%, plus two 5-year options at market. COE 6/17/98; sales price: $280,000.

Restaurant 100, Livermore, CA: 4,985 square feet, $1.3 million sales; 5-year base term lease: year 1, $4,566 per month NNN; year 2, $4,786 per month NNN; year 3, $4,985 per month NNN; year 4, $5,184 per month NNN; year 5, $5,384 per month NNN, plus two 5-year options at market. COE 10/29/97; sales price $350,000 with $200,000 cash down and $150,000 seller carry back note.

Restaurant 101, Cupertino, CA: 7,800 square feet, $2.1 million yearly sales; lease terms: $15,00 per month NNN with yearly CPI adjustments until 9/20/02, then one 5-year option at market rent. COE 3/6/96; sale price: $160,000.

Restaurant 102, San Ramon, CA: 6,000 square feet, $2.1 million sales: 15 year lease–years 1-5 $10,000 per month NNN; years 5-10 $11,000 per month NNN; years 11-15 $12,500 per month NNN, plus three 5-year options at market; and $1.2 million spent on remodel, COE 11/6/96; sales price $445,000 with $200,000 cash down and $245,000 of assumed liabilities.

Restaurant 103, Corte Madera, CA: 6,500 square feet, $2.3 million yearly sales; lease terms: 15-year lease with rent as follows: $11,677 per month years 1-5; $12,841 per month years 6-10; $14,129 per month years 11-15; all minimum rents are versus 5.5% of yearly sales, whichever is greater plus the rent is NNN. There are also three 5-year options with CPI adjustments. COE 9/27/96; sales price: $415,000.

Restaurant 104, San Francisco, CA; 3,000 square feet, $1 million yearly sales; lease terms: $5,300 month NNN with yearly increases based on the CPI, with minimum increases of 4% and maximum increases of 6%. COE 7/26/96; sales price: $139,000.

Restaurant 105, Redwood City; 10,075 square feet, $2 million sales; lease terms: 10 years with two 10-year options, $7,700 month (76 cents per sq. ft.)

years 1-5; $8,700 month (86 cents per sq. ft.) years 6-10; $9,700 month (96 cents per sq. ft.) years 11-15; $10,700 month ($1.06 per sq. ft.) years 16-20; $12,700 month ($1.26 per sq. ft.) years 21-25; $14,700 month ($1.46 per sq. ft.) years 26-30; expires 2027. COE 3/1996; sales price: $280,000.

Summary of Sales Price as a Percentage of Yearly Sales

Restaurant #	Business	Percentage
1	San Francisco	23.0%
2	San Francisco	22.0%
3	San Anselmo	18.0%
4	Novato	18.3%
5	San Francisco	19.4%
6	Vallejo	20.8%
7	San Francisco	40.0%
8	San Francisco	39.0%
9	Oakland	27.0%
10	San Jose	30.0%
11	Redwood City	32.5%
12	Berkeley	26.7%
13	Berkeley	20.4%
14	Larkspur	30.4%
15	San Francisco	35.0%
16	Berkeley	51.1%
17	San Francisco	27.1%
18	San Francisco	41.7%
19	San Francisco	25.3%
20	San Francisco	28.3%
21	San Francisco	34.1%
22	Walnut Creek	23.5%
23	San Mateo	65.8%
24	San Leandro	52.2%
25	Berkeley	41.7%
26	San Francisco	23.0%
27	San Francisco	34.7%
28	Berkeley	36.4%
29	Petaluma	19.4%
30	San Francisco	15.0%
31	Palo Alto	25.0%
32	San Francisco	15.0%
33	San Anselmo	38.7%

Restaurant #	Business	Percentage
34	Mill Valley	10.5%
35	Pleasanton	42.9%
36	San Jose	11.1%
37	Novato	33.3%
38	San Rafael	38.3%
39	San Francisco	28.4%
40	Oakland	19.3%
41	San Rafael	25.0%
42	San Francisco	27.8%
43	Fremont	33.4%
44	San Rafael	22.2%
45	Los Altos	21.5%
46	San Francisco	36.9%
47	San Francisco	48.3%
48	Hayward	19.0%
49	Oakland	26.7%
50	San Francisco	15.0%
51	San Carlos	26.6%
52	Hercules	30.5%
53	Palo Alto	37.5%
54	Concord	45.6%
55	San Mateo	38.6%
56	Vallejo	42.8%
57	Fremont	35.1%
58	Berkeley	32.5%
59	Menlo Park	20.8%
60	San Francisco	24.9%
61	Danville	58.3%
62	San Francisco	34.9%
63	Menlo Park	21.2%
64	Alamo	45.1%
65	San Francisco	37.9%
66	San Francisco	20.0%
67	Pleasanton	47.5%
68	San Francisco	37.5%
69	Berkeley	18.8%
70	Walnut Creek	38.7%
71	Walnut Creek	39.1%
72	Albany	39.4%
73	San Francisco	28.1%
74	Menlo Park	16.2%

Restaurant #	Business	Percentage
75	Berkeley	19.2%
76	Burlingame	20.7%
77	Livermore	26.2%
78	Oakland	21.8%
79	San Francisco	32.1%
80	San Francisco	26.5%
81	San Francisco	27.5%
82	Sonoma	23.3%
83	San Rafael	10.0%
84	San Jose	12.1%
85	San Francisco	16.7%
86	Calistoga	13.3%
87	San Mateo	16.0%
88	Sausalito	23.1%
89	San Rafael	20.5%
90	San Francisco	11.4%
91	South San Francisco	12.1%
92	San Francisco	25.9%
93	San Francisco	27.6%
94	San Mateo	12.5%
95	Los Gatos	33.3%
96	San Francisco	23.3%
97	San Mateo	19.4%
98	Burlingame	35.0%
99	San Francisco	21.5%
100	Livermore	26.9%
101	Cupertino	7.6%
102	San Ramon	21.2%
103	Corte Madera	18.0%
104	San Francisco	13.9%
105	Redwood City	14.0%

The average sales price, as a percent of yearly sales, for the above sales is 28.8%.

Valuation

If we take the first 11 months sales average of $39,177 per month and annualize them, your projected sales for 2011 will be $470,124 or round up to $500,000. If we then take the projected yearly sales of $500,000 times 28.8% (which is the average sales price as a percent of yearly sales for the restaurants as indicated above), the value of your restaurant is $144,000 ($500,000 sales x 28.8% = $144,000). I would recommend a sales price of $149,000.

If the buyer wants the salable inventory (food, alcohol, cleaning and paper supplies) they would pay additional for the inventory, at the seller's cost, based on a physical inventory to be taken at the close of escrow.

If you have any questions and would like to discuss the above further, please call me.

Thank you for the opportunity of working with you on this challenging project.

Sincerely,

Steven D. Zimmerman, CBB, CBI
President

Chapter 21

GOING-CONCERN METHOD
OF VALUATION

The going-concern method normally means that the business is making money. When the buyer purchases a going-concern business, they usually want to run the business the same way the seller did—they keep the same name, menu, operating systems, and personnel in place.

This method means that the lease, leasehold improvements, fixtures and equipment, licenses, name, menu concept, and goodwill are all included as part of the sale. The buyer is usually paying a higher price for this type of business than for a business that is not making money, or is just marginally profitable. Going-concern businesses are well-run franchises and non-franchise businesses that are profitable.

Although the name, menu, and overall concept is being well received by the customers, the operator may not be running the business properly, and consequently not making money. A new operator who does run the business properly can make it profitable. Perhaps the operator who does not make money is not spending enough time in the business, or is not attentive to controlling the costs and other details of the business necessary to make it profitable.

Yearly Adjusted Cash Flow Method/Discretionary Earnings

The primary valuation method used for a going-concern valuation is the yearly adjusted cash-flow method, also referred to as discretionary earnings. This means that the net profit on the tax return, or on the year-to-date income-and-expense statement, is adjusted by adding back the following items to the net income:

- one working owner's salary and payroll taxes,
- any personal expenses the owner is charging the business—food for consumption at home; life, health and disability insurance premiums; auto expense; entertainment and vacation expense, etc.,
- depreciation, interest and amortization expense on any loans the buyer will not be assuming,
- net operating loss carry-forward charges, and
- any other expenses that are personal, and will not be applicable to the buyer.

Once the yearly adjusted cash flow is determined, a multiple, ranging one (1) to three (3), is used to determine the value of the business. The multiple to be used is determined by several factors:

- lease value—whether the lease is at market, below market or above market,
- the potential upside of the business—that is, the current operation serves dinner only, and has only a beer and wine license, and there is potential for a strong lunch business and liquor sales,
- the quality and quantity of the leasehold improvements, and fixtures and equipment,
- whether the operation is a franchise, and
- whether the operation is a full service or self-service operation.

The sales price multiplier for independently owned, non-chain, non-franchised food service operations will vary from one to three times the yearly adjusted cash flow, depending on the risk factor and other factors listed below. The risk factor is determined by the following criteria:

1. The degree of difficulty in operating the business, i.e., an espresso

operation has a low degree of difficulty as it is an easy operation to run, but an upscale dinner house operation has a high degree of difficulty because it requires a high degree of expertise and sophistication to run this type of business successfully.

2. How long the business has been in operation, and the past history of the business in terms of profitability and sales growth. A business with an easy-to-operate format, coupled with a well-seasoned profitable earnings history, will utilize a higher sales price multiplier than a business with a high degree of difficulty without a track record.

The other factors which determine the sale price multiplier are as follows:

1. The lease value—whether the lease is at market, below market or above market and the length of the lease).

2. The potential upside of the business—a business currently serves dinner only and has only a beer and wine license, and there is potential for a strong lunch and/or brunch business and liquor sales).

3. The future growth opportunities of a particular location—if there is some major new development(s) that will add new potential customers to the area without a lot of extraordinary new competition.

For example, if the yearly adjusted cash flow of the business is $75,000, and the multiple to be used is 2.5, the value of the business would be as follows: $75,000 multiplied by 2.5, which equals $187,500 ($75,000 adjusted cash flow times 2.5 sales price = $187,500 sales price).

Chapter 22

THINGS TO REMEMBER WHEN PURCHASING A GOING-CONCERN BUSINESS

Minimizes the Risk of Purchasing a Business

Purchasing a going-concern business is less risky than buying an assets-in-place business when the buyer changes the name, menu and concept. When a buyer starts a new concept, he does not have an existing customer base because there is a strong possibility that the customer may not like the new concept, whereas the new operator in a going-concern business has an existing customer base and a positive cash flow.

Don't make changes until after you've run the business for a reasonable time period. It is prudent when a buyer takes over a going-concern operation that he runs the business as it was run before the change of ownership. He should so this for a period of time until he learns all the details of the operation. The buyer is paying a good price for a going-concern business, and any changes made prematurely to the operation may have a negative impact on the business's customer base. Remember that the customer is king, and the reason the customer is frequenting this business is his satisfaction with the existing operation. Décor, menu or service changes need to be made gradually so the buyer doesn't alienate any of the existing customers.

Keep the existing employees, and then weed out the undesirable employees. To help further maintain the continuity of the business, it is important to keep the existing employees in place, as they are largely responsible for drawing customers into the business. They are one of the most important assets of the business. Before closing escrow on the business, review all of the strengths and weaknesses of each employee with the seller to determine how best to capitalize on the employees' strengths in improving the business. If the seller indicates certain employees are marginal and are a detriment to the business, it is best to terminate them as soon as possible after taking possession of the business. It is much easier to terminate marginal employees in the early stages, rather than condoning their inferior performance, which may create difficulties in terminating them in the future.

Compulsory remodeling program for franchises

If the operator purchases a franchise, he should be aware, and have budgeted the required monies for the periodic remodeling required by franchisors. Most franchises require that every 5 to 7 years or so, a total remodeling of the premises must be completed. This is so the franchisee's operation reflects the uniform image the franchisor wants to identify for its customers. If the franchisee cannot afford to upgrade the physical aspects of the franchise per the franchisor requirements, the franchisee could jeopardize losing his franchise.

Continue using the same vendors

In a going-concern purchase, it is prudent to not risk making changes with vendors until you've operated the business for at least thirty days to maintain an orderly transition of the business. Usually you have better leverage in negotiating prices with vendors if you've had a pre-existing relationship. So once you've run the business for a period of time, you'll develop relationships with vendors, putting you in a stronger position to negotiate prices.

Usually it is cost effective for the operator to maintain the seller's existing food, beverage, cleaning and paper supply vendors. Additionally the operator should maintain the seller's other vendors—exterminators, window cleaners, landscaping, duct cleaning, security, and insurance services, etc. because these vendors are familiar with the business's past needs. However, if the vendor's quality and price level are not competitive, they should be eliminated and replaced.

In purchasing liability and workman's compensation insurance, it is usually beneficial for the buyer to keep the existing insurance companies in place, assuming the seller had a good history of minimal insurance claims with these companies. If this is the case, these insurance companies can offer more competitive insurance premiums than starting with new companies that are not familiar with your business.

Other methods to improve an existing business

In purchasing a going-concern business, it is wise, as stated earlier, to not make changes to the business until you have operated it for several months so you can develop a good understanding of the customers' likes and dislikes, which you can do from the following activities:

a. Directly interact with customers by working the floor, seating and greeting them, and going from table to table and asking the customers how they like their meal. Also ask about other aspects of the business, and what items they would like changed.

b. Distribute customer comment cards and evaluate the customer feedback.

c. Talk to food servers and get feedback from them regarding the customers' likes and dislikes.

I sold a very successful going-concern business that had been established for close to twenty years in Marin County, California. The business was known for its unique pizzas, Mediterranean entrées, full bar, and live jazz format. I cautioned the buyers that it was best not to make major changes to the business until they operated it for several months, and thoroughly understood all the nuances of the business. The owners decided within the first three months to add Thai food, as they were from Thailand— and consequently, sales dropped over 60% from the level the business at the time they purchased it The reason for this dramatic sales drop? Customers became confused, not knowing whether the restaurant was a Thai restaurant or the former well-known Mediterranean restaurant.

When you start mixing up menu concepts, many customers feel the quality of the original concepts becomes diluted. Thai restaurants serve Thai food, and not Mediterranean food, and as soon as the former operation's customers learned that, they stopped coming. As a result of this mistake in owner judgment, we ended up selling the business in less than a year for close to $100,000 less than they paid for it.

We sold another restaurant which had the reputation of being one of the most popular breakfast and lunch restaurants in San Francisco. Within six months after buying the restaurant, the buyers spent over $25,000 adding equipment, doing marketing, and hiring additional personnel in order to add dinner. Within six months, they removed dinner service as it did not develop to an adequate level to cover the additional operating expenses. This is an example of a concept that had a strong preconceived image in the customer's minds of being a great breakfast lunch operation—and no more than that.

Although the customer may feel comfortable in the business's existing environment, it is prudent to periodically freshen up the environment to make sure all the major surfaces, such as the floors, walls and ceiling, are clean and in good condition. The restrooms, in particular, should be kept well maintained, since the condition of the restrooms determines the customers' impressions regarding the operation's cleanliness. Again, all the floors, walls, and ceiling surfaces should be in good condition, as well as the toilets and sinks. In a well-run business, an employee will police the restrooms hourly to make sure they are clean, and the various dispensers—paper towel, toilet paper, toilet seat cover, and soap dispensers, always are filled. They will also check for paper towels on the floor, excess water around the sink, and see that the toilets are flushed clean.

Chapter 23

SAMPLE OF A GOING-CONCERN VALUATION

Following is an example of a letter sent to a seller detailing "going-concern valuations."

Re: Letter of Valuation for Selling XYZ Bar, 1234 America Street, Somewhere, California

Dear John:

Per your request, I have prepared the letter of valuation on your business based on the following:

1. My recent tour of your business.
2. My review of your January 1, 2008 – December 31, 2010 Profit & Loss Statement that actually covered approximately the period April 1, 2008-December 31, 2010 (as you did not open until early April 2010); the first two quarterly sales numbers of 2011; and the projected sales for the third and fourth quarters of 2011.

3. My review of the premises lease.
4. Our discussions regarding various aspects of the operation.

The two basic methods for valuing a restaurant are explained below:

1) Assets-in-Place Method – This method means that only the lease, leasehold improvements, licenses and fixtures and equipment are being sold. The name, menu, concept, and goodwill are usually not included as part of the sale. With this method, less emphasis is put on the business's financials, and the major factors in determining the value are the lease, leasehold improvements, and the fixtures and equipment. Since your business is profitable, we will use the going-concern method indicated below.

2) Going-Concern Method – This method means that the lease, leasehold improvements, licenses, fixtures and equipment, name, menu, concept and goodwill are all included as part of the sale. The primary valuation method used for the going-concern method is the yearly adjusted cash flow method. Here the net profit on the tax return, or on the year-to-date income-and-expense statement, is adjusted by adding back the following items to the net income: one working owner's salary, any personal expenses the owner is charging the business (food for consumption at home, life, health and disability insurance premiums, auto expense, entertainment and vacation expense, etc.), depreciation, interest expense on any loans the buyer will not be assuming, net operating loss carry forward charges, if any, and any other expenses which are personal and will not be applicable to the buyer. Additionally, any extraordinary expenses and/ or non-recurring expenses such as extra legal or accounting bills related to a particular lawsuit, or unusual situation, would also be added back to the net income.

Once the yearly adjusted cash flow is determined, a sales price multiplier will be used to determine the value of the business. The sales price multiplier for independently owned, non-chain, non-franchised food service operations will vary from one to three times the yearly adjusted cash flow, depending on the risk factor and other factors listed below.

The risk factor is determined by the following criteria: 1) the degree of difficulty in operating the business—an espresso operation has a low degree of difficulty as it is an easy operation to run, but an upscale dinner house operation has a high degree of difficulty because it requires extensive expertise and sophistication to run this type of business successfully., and 2) how long the business has been in operation, and the business's history in terms of profitability and sales growth. A business with an easy-to-operate format, coupled with a well-seasoned profitable earnings history, will utilize a higher sales price multiplier than a business with a high degree of difficulty without a track record.

The other factors which determine the sale price multiplier are as follows: 1) the lease value, (whether the lease is at market, below market or above market, and the length of the lease), 2) the potential upside of the business—a business currently serves dinner only, and has only a beer and wine license, but there is potential for a strong lunch and/or brunch business and liquor sales, and 3) the future growth opportunities of a particular location—if there is some major new development(s) that will add new potential customers to the area without a lot of extraordinary new competition.

An additional factor today, which is considered in valuing businesses, is the current economic condition of the market. In that a large number of restaurant, bar, and nightclub business are currently experiencing negative customer counts and increased expenses—and consequently decreased profits—the buying market is requiring that businesses be priced more competitively than in normal economic periods. Many transactions today are being sold at lower multipliers than the past, and in some cases, seller carry-back financing is required.

Based on my experience of selling nearly 700 restaurants, bars and clubs since 1996, and the current market conditions, the appropriate multiple to be used for your operation is 2.75 times the yearly adjusted cash flow.

I will be using the income and expense numbers from the nine month period April 1, 2010–December 31, 2010, and annualizing these numbers as this is the only profit-and-loss statement you provide me.

The yearly adjusted cash flow for the business based on the April 1, 2010–December 31, 2010 profit-and-loss statement I reviewed is as follows:

Net Income or (loss):	($65,746)
Add backs:	
Amortization expense	$2,538
Auto expense	6,499
Auto insurance	1,599
Closing cost	1,149
Consulting $30,500 initial set up	
$30,500 - $9,000 = $21,500 savings	21,500
Depreciation expense	43,916
Donation	214
Interest expense	324
Meals & entertainment	277
Medical expense	1,425
Start-up cost	5,000
Telephone	3,807
Unreported income, less cost of goods	
$10,000 month - $3,500 cost of goods=	
$6,500 month x 9 months =$58,500	58,500
Total add backs:	$146,748
Adjusted cash flow for the period 4/1/08-12/31/08	$81,002

Valuation

If we take the adjusted cash flow for the period 4/1/10 to 12/31/10 of $81,002 ($65,746 Net Loss + $146,748 Add backs = $81,002 adjusted cash flow), and we annualize this as follows: $81,002 adjusted cash flow for the 9-month period 4/1/10-12/31/10 / 9 months = $9,000 per month x 12 months = $108,000 adjusted cash flow for 2010. We then take the $108,000, and multiply this by 2.75 times, the value of your business is $297,000 ($108,000 x 2.75 = $297,000). I would recommend a sales price of $299,000. Saleable inventory at cost (food, beverage, cleaning and paper supplies) would be paid by buyer, in addition to the value indicated above, based on an actual inventory taken at the close of escrow.

If you have any questions and would like to discuss the above further, please call me.

Thank you for the opportunity of working with you on this challenging project.

Sincerely,

Steven D. Zimmerman, CBB, CBI
President
RESTAURANT REALTY COMPANY
California's Largest Restaurant Business Brokerage

Chapter 24

SAMPLE VALUATION USING A COMBINATION OF BOTH THE ASSETS-IN-PLACE METHOD AND THE GOING-CONCERN METHOD

Following is a sample letter I would write to a seller using the combination of the two methods to figure a valuation.

Re: Letter of Valuation for XYZ Restaurant & Bar. 1234 America Street, Somewhere, California

Dear Bob:

Per your request, I have prepared the letter of valuation on your business based on the items indicated below.

1. My recent tour of your business.

2. My review of the following financial statements:

    a. January through December 2007, 2008, and 2009 profit and loss statements,

    b.   2006, 2007 and 2008 Federal tax returns,

    c.   January–March, April–June and July–September 2009 quarterly sales tax returns, and

    d.   Financial statements for the periods December 31, 2005, 2006, 2007 and 2008 prepared by XYZ, Certified Public Accountants.

3.   My review of the premises lease.

4.   Our discussions regarding various aspects of the operation.

The two basic methods for valuing a restaurant are explained below:

   Assets-in-Place Method – This method will be discussed later in the letter.

Going-Concern Method – In this method, the lease, leasehold improvements, licenses, fixtures and equipment, name, menu, concept, and goodwill are all included as part of the sale. The primary valuation method used for the going-concern method is the yearly adjusted cash-flow method. This means that the net profit on the tax return, or on the year-to-date income-and-expense statement, is adjusted by adding back the following items to the net income: one working owner's salary, any personal expenses the owner is charging the business (food for consumption at home, life, health and disability insurance premiums, auto expense, entertainment and vacation expense, etc.), depreciation, interest expense on any loans the buyer will not be assuming, net operating loss carry-forward charges, if any, and any other expenses which are personal and will not be applicable to the buyer. Additionally, any extraordinary expenses and/or non-recurring expenses, such as extra legal or accounting bills related to a particular lawsuit or unusual situation, would also be added back to the net income.

   Once the yearly adjusted cash flow is determined, a sales price multiplier will be used to determine the value of the business. The sales price multiplier for independently owned, non-chain, non-franchised food service operations will vary from one to three times the yearly adjusted cash flow, depending on the risk factor and other factors listed below.

   The risk factor is determined by the following criteria:

1. The degree of difficulty in operating the business—an espresso operation has a low degree of difficulty as it is an easy operation to run, but an upscale dinner house operation has a high degree of difficulty because it requires an extensive degree of expertise and sophistication to run it successfully.

2. How long the business has been in operation, and its history in terms of profitability and sales growth. A business with an easy-to-operate format, coupled with a well-seasoned profitable earnings history, will utilize a higher sales price multiplier than a business with a high degree of difficulty without a track record.

The other factors which determine the sale price multiplier are as follows: 1) the lease value, (whether the lease is at market, below market or above market, and the length of the lease), 2) the potential upside of the business—a business currently serves dinner only, and has only a beer and wine license, but has potential for a strong lunch and/or brunch business and liquor sales, and 3) the future growth opportunities of a particular location—if there is some major new development(s) that will add new potential customers to the area without a lot of extraordinary new competition.

An additional factor today that is considered in valuing businesses, is the market's current economic condition. In that a large number of restaurant, bar, and nightclub business are currently experiencing negative customer counts and increased expenses, and consequently decreased profits, the buying market is requiring that businesses be priced more competitively than normal economic periods. Many transactions today are being sold at lower multipliers than the past, and in some cases, seller carry-back financing is required.

Based on my experience of selling nearly 700 restaurants, bars and clubs since 1996, completing over 2,000 valuations, as well as the current market conditions, the appropriate multiple to be used for valuing your business is two times yearly adjusted cash flow.

Valuation Method #1 The Going-Concern Valuation Method

In reviewing the January through October 2009 profit-and-loss statement, which is the business's most current financial statement, the yearly adjusted cash flow would be based on the numbers indicated below, which will be adjusted for any extraordinary items (seasonal sales fluctuations for a strong December, etc.) and then annualized to determine the yearly adjusted cash flow for 2009.

The adjusted cash flow for the period January–October 2009 is indicated below.

Net Income (Loss)	($32,541)

Add Backs:

Owner's salary ($2,500 every two weeks)	$54,166
Owner's payroll Taxes 12% x $54,166 = $6,500	6,500
Owner's cell phone	1,000
Owner's auto insurance	718
Owner's auto expense	1,797
Owner's life insurance	3,858
Owner's supplemental health insurance	1,200
Professional development	1,076
Total add backs	$70,315

Adjusted cash flow for the period Jan.–Oct. 2009	$37,774

If we take the adjusted cash flow of $37,774 for the period Jan.–Oct. 2009, and add additional amount of $25,000 for December sales, and project that the year–end net loss will be reduced to $10,000, the adjustments will be as follows for determining the yearly adjusted cash flow:

Jan.–Oct. 2009 adjusted cash flow	$37,774
Add backs above for an additional two months $70,315 /10 months = $7,031 month x 2 months = $14,062	14,062
A reduction of the Jan.–Oct. 2009 net loss by increased December sales	22,541
2009 projected yearly adjusted cash flow	$74,377

If we take the projected 2009 yearly adjusted cash flow of $74,377 times two, the value of the business is $148,754 ($74,377 x 2 = $148,754).

Since 2009 is an extraordinarily poor year compared to past years, due to the deep economic recession the country is experiencing, I think it is necessary to look at 2008 and 2007 yearly results, and factor these years into our valuation.

Based on the 2008 Federal tax return for the business, the adjusted cash flow for the period January 1–December 31, 2008 is indicated below.

Net income (loss)	$106,069
Add backs:	
Compensation of officers	$75,000
Owner's salary ($2,500 every two weeks)	65,000
Owner's payroll taxes 12% x $65,000 = $7,800	7,800
Bonus to owner	10,000
Owner's cell phone	1,200
Owner's auto insurance	850
Owner's auto expense	2,150
Owner's life insurance	4,620
Owner's supplemental health insurance	1,440
Professional development	1,324
Depreciation	5,021
Total add backs	$174,405
Adjusted cash flow for the period Jan.–Dec. 2008	$280,474

If we take the 2008 yearly adjusted cash flow of $280,474 times two, the value of the business is $560,948 ($280,474 x 2 = $560,948).

Based on the 2007 Federal tax return for the business, the adjusted cash flow for the period January 1–December 31, 2007 is indicated below:

Net income (loss)	$149,483
Add backs:	
Compensation of officers	$87,000
Owner's salary ($2,500 every two weeks)	65,000
Owners payroll taxes 12% x $65,000 = $7,800	7,800
Bonus to owner	10,000
Owner's cell phone	1,200
Owner's auto insurance	850
Owner's auto expense	2,150
Owners life insurance	4,620
Owner's supplemental health insurance	1,440
Professional development	8,372
Depreciation	5,021
Total add backs	$193,453
Adjusted cash flow for the period Jan.–Dec. 2007	$342,936

If we take the 2007 yearly adjusted cash flow of $342,936 (x 2), the value of the business is $685,872 ($342,936 x 2 = $685,872).

We next weight the past three year's adjusted cash flows. The most recent year's business performance (2009) is given more weight than the latter year's business performance (2007–2008) since the most recent year's business performance is most indicative of the business's future performance.

Year	VALUE BEFORE ADJUSTMENT	Weight factor	ADJUSTED VALUE
2009	$148,754	50%	$74,337
2008	$560,948	30%	$168,284
2007	$685,872	20%	$137,174
			$379,795

Total value based on the weighted adjusted value using the going-concern method	$379,795

Valuation Method #2 The Assets-in-Place Valuation Method

Due to the dramatic changes in the business's sales and profits from 2007 to 2009, I feel it is appropriate to further study the valuation of the business using the assets-in-place method. The current year's performance of the business is marginally profitable, and is dramatically different from the prior two years.

Assets-in-Place Method –This method means that only the lease, leasehold improvements, licenses and fixtures and equipment are being sold. The name, menu, concept, and goodwill are generally not included as part of the sale. With this method, less emphasis is put on the financials of the business, and the major factors in determining the value are the lease, leasehold improvements, and the fixtures and equipment. No standard formula exists for determining value utilizing this method, and valuation is somewhat subjective, based on the broker's knowledge of the market place. I have sold nearly 700 restaurants, bars or clubs in the Greater San Francisco Bay Area since 1996, and the majority of these sales have been sold by the assets-in-place method. I will use this method in valuing the subject business as well. The main criteria used in this method to determine the sales price is the ratio of sales to sales price on past restaurants that we have sold using the assets-in-place method.

The following is a partial list of the restaurants I have sold generating between $1 million to $2.5 million in yearly sales using the assets-in-place method:

Restaurant 1, Mill Valley, CA: 2,400 sq. ft., closed at time of sales, but previously did $1million sales yearly; lease terms–$6,000 month with yearly CPI, expires 3/2011 + 5-year option at market rent. COE 6/09; sale price $105,000.

Restaurant 2 San Jose, CA: 5,000 sq. ft., $1.8 million sales; lease terms – $18,000 month + NNN, but restaurant was sold back to the landlord so don't know lease terms. COE 4/09; sales price $200,000.

Restaurant 3, San Francisco, CA: 8,000 sq. ft., $2 million sales before they closed; Lease terms: $17,800 month all inclusive plus yearly CPI, and lease expires 2016, plus two 5-year options at fair market rent. COE 8/08; sales price $300,000.

Restaurant 4, San Mateo, CA: 6,500 sq. ft.,; $1.1 million sales; lease terms: $8,700 NNN with yearly CPI adjustments, and base terms expires 3/31/2012, plus a 5-year option at fair market rent. COE 5/08; sales price $425,000.

Restaurant 5, Menlo Park, CA: 4,000 sq. ft. + patio, $1.2 million sales; lease term: 5-year lease with monthly rent of $19,900 with 3% yearly adjustments, and 5-year option at market rent. COE 3/15/08; sales price $250,000.

Restaurant 6, Menlo Park, CA: 4,500 sq. ft. + 500 sq. ft. upstairs, $1.6 million sales; 10-year lease with monthly NNN, rent as follows: year 1, $12,500; year 2, $13,000; year 3, $13,261; year 4, $13,659; year 5, $14,068; year 6, $14,490; year 7, $14,925; year 8, $15,373; year 9, $15,834; year 10, $16,309; and 5-year option with monthly NNN, rent as follows: year 1, $16,698; year 2; $17,302; year 3; $17,821; year 4, $18,356; and year 5, $18,907. COE 1/17/08; sales price $350,000.

Restaurant 7, Walnut Creek, CA: 3,500 sq. ft., $1,020,000 sales; lease term is $8,058 all inclusive, with yearly CPI increases, plus a 5-year option at market rent. COE 7/07, sales price $395,000.

Restaurant 8, Menlo Park, CA: 4,500 sq. ft. + large parking lot, $1.3 million sales; lease terms: 11/21/02 through 11/20/22; and monthly rent is as follows: years 1–5, $12,500 NNN; years 6–10, $14,000 NNN; year 11–15, $16,000 NNN; years 16–20, $18,000 NNN + two 5-year options at market rent. COE: 11/06, sales price $210,000.

Restaurant 9, San Francisco, CA: 3,500 sq. ft., $1 million sales; lease terms: Lease expires 12/31/2010 plus 2-year option, rent is $4,700 from COE–12/31/08, and $5,000 from 1/1/09–12/31/10, and $5,600 during option. COE 5/18/05; sales price $265,000.

Restaurant 10, San Francisco, CA: 6,500 sq. ft., $1 million sales; lease terms: Lease expires 5/15/07, plus two 5-year options, $10,000 rent plus CPI yearly, first option continues at CPI, and second option is at market rent, modified NN. COE 3/2005; sales price $275,000.

Restaurant 11, Sonoma, CA: 5,000 sq. ft., $1.5 million sales; lease terms: 10-year lease with rent in year 1 $10,000, NNN and yearly CPI increases thereafter, plus two 5-year options at market rent with CPI increases thereafter. COE 3/2005; sales price $350,000.

Restaurant 12, San Rafael, CA: 5,000 sq. ft., $1.5 million sales; lease terms: 10-year lease with rent in year 1 at $10,500 per month, NNN and yearly CPI increases thereafter, plus one 10-year option, and the rent in the first year is market rent with yearly CPI increases thereafter. COE 8/2004; sales price $150,000.

Restaurant 13, San Jose, CA: 7,500 sq. ft., $1.2 million sales; lease terms: new 10-year lease with year 1, $7,500 per month, NNN with yearly CPI increases, plus a

10-year option, with the rent in the first year market rent and CPI adjustments yearly thereafter. COE 6/20/04; sales price: $145,000.

Restaurant 14, San Francisco, CA: 3,500 sq. ft., $1.2 million yearly sales; lease terms: $27,000 per month NNN with yearly CPI increases, with a 10-years term plus two 5-year options at market rent. COE 3/1/04; sales price: $200,000.

Restaurant 15, Calistoga, CA: 5,100 sq. ft. + large patio, $1.5 million yearly sales; current rent is $6,300 with yearly CPI increases, with a minimum of 2% per year and a maximum of 7% per year, and lease expires 6/11/2016. COE: 1/04; sales price: $200,000.

Restaurant 16, San Mateo, CA: 7,000 sq. ft., $1.5 million yearly sales, but restaurant formerly did $2.3 million sales three years ago; $7,000 NNN monthly rent versus 5% of sales, base term expires 12/31/06, and there are four 5-year options, and the rent is substantially below market until 2016. COE: 1/04; sales price: $240,000.

Restaurant 17, San Rafael, CA: 8,000 sq. ft., over $1.5 million spent on restaurant, $2.2 million sales; lease terms: 10-year term with rent at $11,000, NNN with yearly CPI increases, plus a 10-year option at market rent. COE: 10/2002; sales price: $450,000.

Restaurant 18, San Francisco, CA: 11,300 sq. ft., over $2 million was spent in building out building and brewpub, $2.2 million sales; lease terms: $6,460 month NNN, with yearly CPI increases then two 5-year options at market rent. COE: 7/2002; sales price: $250,000 through the Federal Bankruptcy Court Chapter 11 proceeding.

Restaurant 19, South San Francisco, CA: 6,300 sq. ft., $1.4 million yearly sales, but restaurant was closed a year before sale; lease terms: currently monthly rent $4,095 NNN with 5% yearly increases every 2 years until 1/31/08, plus two 5-year options at market. COE 5/13/02; sales price: $170,000 through the Federal Bankruptcy Court Chapter 11 proceeding.

Restaurant 20, San Francisco, CA; 8,000 sq. ft., $1.1 million yearly sales; lease terms: 6 years, monthly rent first year $4,200 fixed until 4/30/06, with 5-year option with CPI adjustment in the first year of the option period. COE: 8/28/01; sales price: $285,000.

Restaurant 21, San Mateo, CA; 5,400 sq. ft., $1.2 million yearly sales; lease terms: $10,000 per month NNN, with yearly CPI increases, and the lease expires in 11 years, and there is a 5-year option at market rent with yearly CPI increases thereafter. COE: 4/27/01; sales price: $150,000.

Restaurant 22, Los Gatos, CA: 6,200 sq. ft., $1.5 million sales; lease terms: $4,400 per month NNN, versus 4% of gross sales with yearly CPI increases, and expires 2016. COE: 4/27/01; sales price: $500,000.

Restaurant 23, San Francisco, CA: 4,000 sq. ft., $1.5 million yearly sales; lease terms: 10-year terms, monthly rent first year $11,000 NNN, with yearly CPI increases with minimum of 4% and maximum of 8%, 5-year option with the rent the first year of the option period, not to exceed 20% of the rent in the last year of the base term. COE: 3/3/00; sales price: $350,000.

Restaurant 24, Burlingame, CA: 11,000 sq. ft., $2 million sales; lease terms: initial term expires 3/2004, rent is $14,000 per month NNN fixed for several years; then $15,000 per month NNN fixed for several years; then $16,000 per month NNN fixed for several years. $2.8 million invested into the building and restaurant. COE10/1999 through the Federal Bankruptcy Court in a Chapter 11 proceeding; sales price: $700,000 through an aggressive bid process.

Restaurant 25, San Francisco, CA: 3,595 sq. ft., $1.3 million yearly sales; lease terms: 10-year term with monthly rent year 1, $8,500; year 2, $9,000; year 3, $10,000; then yearly CPI with a minimum increase of 3%, and a maximum increase of 5% plus two 5-year options at market. COE: 6/17/98; sales price: $280,000.

Restaurant #26, Livermore, CA: 4,985 sq. ft., $1.3 million sales; lease terms: 5-year base term lease: year 1, $4,566 per month NNN; year 2, $4,786 per month NNN; year 3, $4,985 per month NNN; year 4, $5,184 per month NNN; year 5, $5,384 per month NNN; plus two 5-year options at market. COE10/29/97; sales price $350,000 with $200,000 cash down and $150,000 seller carry back note.

Restaurant 27, Cupertino, CA: 7,800 sq. ft., $2.1 million yearly sales; lease terms: $15,00 per month NNN with yearly CPI adjustments until 9/20/02, then one 5-year option at market rent. COE 3/6/96; sale price: $160,000.

Restaurant 28, San Ramon, CA: 6,000 sq. ft., $2.1 million sales; lease terms: 15 year lease- years 1–5, $10,000 per month NNN; years 5–10, $11,000 per month NNN; years 11–15, $12,500 per month NNN; plus three 5-year options at market; $1.2 million spent on remodel. COE 11/6/96; sales price $445,000 with $200,000 cash down and $245,000 of assumed liabilities.

Restaurant 29, Corte Madera, CA: 6,500 sq. ft., $2.3 million yearly sales; lease terms: 15- year lease with rent as follows: $11,677 per month years 1–5, $12,841 per month; years 6–10, $14,129 per month; years 11–15, all minimum rents are versus 5.5% of yearly sales whichever is greater plus the rent is NNN. There are also three 5-year options with CPI adjustments. COE 9/27/96; sales price: $415,000.

Restaurant 30, San Francisco, CA: 3,000 sq. ft., $1 million yearly sales; lease terms: $5,300 month NNN with yearly increases based on the CPI, with minimum increases of 4% and maximum increases of 6%. COE 7/26/96; sales price: $139,000.

Restaurant 31, Redwood City, CA: 10,075 sq. ft., $2 million sales; lease terms: 10 years with two 10-year options, $7,700 month (76 cents per sq. ft.); years 1–5, $8,700 month (86 cents per sq. ft.); years 6–10, $9,700 month (96 cents per sq. ft.); years 11–15, $10,700 month ($1.06 per sq. ft.); years 16–20, $12,700 month ($1.26 per sq. ft.); years 21–25, $14,700 month ($1.46 per sq. ft.); and years 26–30. Expires 2027. COE 3/1996; sales price: $280,000.

Summary of Sales Price as a Percentage of Yearly Sales

Restaurant #	Business	Percentage
1	Mill Valley	10.5%
2	San Jose	11.1%
3	San Francisco	15.0%
4	San Mateo	38.6%
5	Menlo Park	20.8%
6	Menlo Park	21.2%
7	Walnut Creek	38.7%
8	Menlo Park	16.2%
9	San Francisco	26.5%
10	San Francisco	27.5%
11	Sonoma	23.3%
12	San Rafael	10.0%
13	San Jose	12.1%
14	San Francisco	6.7%
15	Calistoga	13.3%
16	San Mateo	16.0%
17	San Rafael	20.5%
18	San Francisco	11.4%
19	South San Francisco	12.1%
20	San Francisco	25.9%
21	San Mateo	12.5%
22	Los Gatos	33.3%

Restaurant #	Business	Percentage
23	San Francisco	23.3%
24	Burlingame	35.0%
25	San Francisco	21.5%
26	Livermore	26.9%
27	Cupertino	7.6%
28	San Ramon	21.2%
29	Corte Madera	18.0%
30	San Francisco	13.9%
31	Redwood City	14.0%

The average sales price, as a percent of yearly sales, for the above sold restaurants is 20.5%.

The average sales price, as a percent of yearly sales, of the above sold restaurants doing between $1 million and $1,999,999 in yearly sales is 21.1%.

The average sales price, as a percent of yearly sales, of the above sold restaurants doing $2 million and above in yearly sales is 17.7%.

Valuation Summary Using the Assets-in-Place Method

I will use the assets-in-place method to determine the value of the subject business, and will use the past 3 years, 2007, 2008 and 2009 for this analysis. Since the projected year-end sales for 2009 is approximately $1.7 million, I will use the 21.1% number above, which is the average sales price (as a percent of yearly sales) of the above restaurants doing between $1 million and $1,999,999 in yearly sales. Since the year-end sales for 2007 was $2,662,798, and the year-end sales for 2008 was $2,220,891, I will use the 17.7% number above, which is the average sales price (as a percent of yearly sales) of the above-mentioned restaurants doing between $2 million and $2.5 million yearly sales.

- If we take the projected 2009 sales of $1.7 million times 21.1% the value of the business is $358,700 ($1.7 million x 21.1% = $358,700).
- If we take the 2008 sales of $2,220,891 times 17.7% the value of the business is $393,097 ($2,220,891 x 17.7% = $393,097).
- If we take the 2007 sales of $2,662,798 times 17.7% the value of the business is $471,315 $2,662,798 x 17.7% =$471,315).

We next weight the past 3 years valuations. The most recent year's business performance (2009) is given more weight than the latter year's business performance (2007-2008) as the most recent year's business performance is more indicative of the businesses future performance.

Year	Pre-weighted Value	Weight Factor	Weighted Value
2009	$358,700	50%	$179,350
2008	$393,097	30%	$117,929
2007	$471,315	20%	$ 94,263
			$391,532

Total Value Based on the Weighted Value
Using the Assets-in-Place Method Valuation $391,542

Valuation Summary

The going-concern valuation method value is $379,795, and the assets-in-place valuation method value is $391,542. The average of the above two methods is $385,668—my recommended valuation for this business. This valuation is based on the business having a premises lease in place, with a minimum of a 10-year term with similar terms and conditions as the existing premises lease. The lease term can be a straight 10-year term, or a 5-year term with a 5-year option, with the rent defined for each year of the lease term.

Saleable inventory, if desired (food, alcohol, paper and cleaning supplies) would be paid for by the buyer, in addition to the price indicated, based on a physical inventory to be taken between buyer and seller at the close of escrow for both the valuation methods discussed above.

If you have any questions and would like to discuss the above further, please call me.

Thank you for the opportunity of working with you on this challenging project.

Sincerely,
Steven D. Zimmerman, CBB, CBI
President
RESTAURANT REALTY COMPANY
California's Largest Restaurant Business Brokerage

Chapter 25

HOW TO ARRIVE AT A VALUE FOR A BUSINESS YOU ARE PURCHASING

The basic ways of determining how to value a business is as follows:

1. The broker does a cash-flow analysis of the business from a buyer's perspective by reviewing the most-current yearly tax return as well as the year-to-date income-and-expense statement for the business.

2. Broker and buyer looks as sales comparables.

3. Recasting the seller's profit and loss statement. This is the most common method for determining the value of a business. Recasting the profit-and-loss statement accomplishes the following:

   a. normalizes income statements and balance sheets to show a more accurate picture of the cash available to a buyer as well as the real value of the assets

   b. minimizes their taxes, to show as little profit possible on their income statements.

   c. helps buyers compare apples to apples.

Earnings Definitions

1. Sellers discretionary earnings (SDE) is net income before taxes, depreciation and amortization, interest, owner (one owner) compensation, owner's perks (discretionary expenses) and non-recurring expenses.
2. EBITDA – earnings before interest, taxes, depreciation and amortization (SDE minus fair market salary and perks for a general manager).
3. EBIT – Above, less depreciation and amortization.

Adjustments to Income Statement

We look at adjustments to the recast income statement, or add backs to the seller's discretionary earnings, from a buyer's perspective.

Here are the items we recast:
1. Personal perk items – personal car lease payments, personal insurance (health, life and auto), personal meals, personal travel, country club memberships, major league sports season ticket, salaries to non-working spouse, etc.
2. Personal preference items – donation to charities, employee bonuses, etc. (be careful not to eliminate employee bonuses because it will demoralize the employees or make them quit).
3. Interest on debt that will not remain with the business.

Depreciation, Amortization and Other Non-cash Charges

- Be careful with adjustments.
- Auto – not all auto expense should be adjusted. If vehicles are not used in the business, you cannot add them into seller's discretionary earnings.
- Excess wages – buyers have a hard time accepting that the seller is paying someone more than they are worth unless it is a family member, plus it could cause morale problems, or cause an employee to quit if wages are changed. The same goes for paying someone under the table.
- Health insurance for employees – employees who have enjoyed health care benefits are not going to want to lose them. It could

cause morale problems, or cause an employee to quit if benefits are changed.

- Discontinuance of advertising that is not effective – how do you tell what worked and what didn't?

Recasting goes both ways. You need to subtract for:

1. Owner working 80 hours per week. A rule of thumb is a 45–50 hours week is appropriate to factor in for a working owner. If you need additional hours of labor above 50 hours for the owner to complete all his functions, increase the labor expense accordingly, which will reduce the seller's discretionary income.

2. Family member working without pay. If essential functions are being performed by family members who are not being paid, you'll need to add additional labor expense to cover them.

3. Lease costs. If seller owns the real estate and is not paying himself a fair market rent, or if the lease is going up, you'll need to make the adjustment.

Below is an actual tax return for a restaurant and bar business. Note the adjustments made to the tax return to calculate the Adjusted Cash Flow also known as Discretionary Earnings (DE), Sellers Discretionary Cash (SDC), Sellers Discretionary Cash Flow (SDCF) or Seller's Discretionary Earnings (SDE).

Explanation of Adjustments to XYZ Restaurant 2009 Tax Return

Adjustment Number	Explanation	Adjustment Amount
1	Food for home for managing partner, $500 month x 12 months = $6,000	$6,000
2A	Managing partner's yearly salary	75,000
2B	Managing partner's payroll taxes (10% of salary)	7,500
3	Interest expense	8,402
4	Depreciation expense	10,673
5	Auto and truck expense for managing partner's personal use	4,939
6	Life and health insurance expense for managing partner	4,500
7	Non-reoccurring/extraordinary legal expense for terminating employee	6,500
8	Cell phone expense for managing partner $100 month x 12 months – $1,200	1,200
9	Personal expense for managing partner	12,095

Total Adjustments $136,809

Ordinary Income on tax return line 22 $92,394

Adjusted Cash Flow, also known as Discretionary
Earnings (DE), Sellers Discretionary Cash (SDC),
Sellers Discretionary Cash Flow (SDCF) or Seller's
Discretionary Earnings (SDE) $229,203

Form **1065**		**U.S. Return of Partnership Income**		OMB No. 1545-0099	
Department of the Treasury Internal Revenue Service		For cal. year 2009, or tax year beg. _____ , 2009, and end. _____ , 20 ___ . ▶ See separate instructions.		**2009**	

A Principal business activity
RESTAURANT

B Principal product or service
FOOD & BEVERAG

C Business code number
722110

Use the IRS label. Otherwise, print or type.

Name, Number, street, room/suite no., City/Town, state, and ZIP code

XYZ Restaurant & Bar

D Employer identification no.

E Date business started

F Total assets (see the instr.)
$

G Check applicable boxes: (1) ☐ Initial return (2) ☐ Final return (3) ☐ Name change (4) ☐ Address change (5) ☐ Amended return
(6) ☐ Technical termination - also check (1) or (2)

H Check accounting method: (1) ☐ Cash (2) ☒ Accrual (3) ☐ Other (specify) ▶

I Number of Schedules K-1. Attach one for each person who was a partner at any time during the tax year ▶ **2**

J Check if Schedules C and M-3 are attached ....

Caution. Include only trade or business income and expenses on lines 1a through 22 below. See the instructions for more information.

				Adjustments
Income				
1a	Gross receipts or sales	1a	1,313,283.	
b	Less returns and allowances	1b	5,397.	1c 1,307,886.	1
2	Cost of goods sold (Schedule A, line 8)	2	538,305.	
3	Gross profit. Subtract line 2 from line 1c	3	769,581.	
4	Ordinary income (loss) from other partnerships, estates, and trusts (attach statement)	4		
5	Net farm profit (loss) (attach Schedule F (Form 1040))	5		
6	Net gain (loss) from Form 4797, Part II, line 17 (attach Form 4797)	6		
7	Other income (loss) (attach statement)	7		
8	Total income (loss). Combine lines 3 through 7	8	769,581.	
Deductions (see the instr. for limitations)				
9	Salaries and wages (other than to partners) (less employment credits)	9	324,680.	2A 2B
10	Guaranteed payments to partners	10		
11	Repairs and maintenance	11		
12	Bad debts	12		
13	Rent	13	138,589.	
14	Taxes and licenses	14	45,159.	
15	Interest	15	8,402.	3
16a	Depreciation (if required, attach Form 4562)	16a	10,673.	
b	Less depreciation reported on Schedule A and elsewhere on return	16b	16c 10,673.	4
17	Depletion (Do not deduct oil and gas depletion.)	17		
18	Retirement plans, etc.	18	1,927.	
19	Employee benefit programs	19	5,315.	
20	Other deductions (attach statement)	20	142,442.	See Detail Sheet
21	Total deductions. Add the amounts shown in the far right column for lines 9 through 20	21	677,187.	Next Page
22	Ordinary business income (loss). Subtract line 21 from line 8	22	92,394.	

Sign Here

Under penalties of perjury, I declare that I have examined this return, including accompanying schedules and statements, and to the best of my knowledge and belief, it is true, correct, and complete. Declaration of preparer (other than general partner or limited liability company member manager) is based on all information of which preparer has any knowledge.

Signature of general partner or limited liability co. member manager — Date

May the IRS discuss this return with the preparer shown below (see instructions)? ☒ Yes ☐ No

Paid Preparer's Use Only

Preparer's signature	Date 08/25/2010	Check if self-employed ▶ ☐	Preparer's SSN or PTIN
Firm's name (or yours if self-employed), address, and ZIP code		EIN ▶	
		Phone no.	

For Privacy Act and Paperwork Reduction Act Notice, see separate instructions.

Form **1065** (2009)

US 1065 — Other Deductions — 2009

Name: XYZ Restaurant & Bar

ID number:

Type:		Adjustments	
Accounting		6,336.	
Advertising		3,478.	
Amortization			
Answering service			
Auto and truck expenses		4,939.	5
Bank charges			
Commissions			
Computer expense		1,755.	
Delivery and freight			
Dues and subscriptions			
Entertainment and promotion			
Gifts			
Insurance		17,842.	6
Janitorial		22,784.	
Laundry and cleaning			
Legal and professional fees		25,180.	7
Licenses and permits			
Meals: 12,915. at 50%			
at 70% - DOT hours of service			
at 100% - See instructions		6,458.	
Miscellaneous			
Office expense		6,102.	
Outside service			
Parking fees and tolls			
Postage			
Printing			
Sales expense			
Security			
Supplies			
Telephone		5,458.	8
Temporary help			
Tools			
Trade show expense			
Training and seminars			
Travel		12,095.	9
Uniforms			
Utilities		30,015.	
Total		142,442.	

Chapter 26

UNDERSTANDING THE INCOME-AND-EXPENSE STATEMENT

The income-and-expense statement is the most important financial statement for a buyer to understand—in terms of measuring the performance of the business on a monthly and yearly basis. This statement is the owner's report card, so to speak, as it measures how well the business performed in terms of achieving its sales and profit goals, or how poorly it performed in not achieving its sales and profit goals. The income-and-expense statement is also the major financial tool used by the buyer to determine the value of the business they are considering purchasing in a going-concern transaction. The income-and-expense statement is recast by the broker, with the seller's assistance, to determine the value of a going-concern business, discussed further in this chapter. Recasting means the income and/or expense numbers on the financial statements of the business are adjusted to reflect the actual financial benefits of business ownership.

The major components of the income-and-expense statement are indicated below:

1. **Income** – This is the restaurant, bar, or club business sales, which is normally broken down as food sales and alcohol sales. Food sales typically includes non-alcoholic beverages, and alcohol sales include all alcohol sales. In some cases, food sales may be broken down in more detail, such as sales in the restaurant, take-out sales, banquet-room sales, and catering sales, etc. In California, sales tax is not applicable to some take-out sales. A properly prepared income-and-expense statement will take the sales tax out of the total sales, and only show the net sales on the statement.

2. **Cost of Goods Sold** – The cost of the food and non-alcoholic beverages used for a given period is called food cost. To properly control the food cost, the owner or manager should take a physical inventory monthly of all the food and non-alcoholic beverages on hand. The items are counted and then priced at the invoice price to determine the total value of food and non-alcoholic beverages at cost. To calculate the food cost, you take the opening monthly inventory and add all the purchases made for that given month to the opening inventory total. Take a physical inventory at the end of the month, and subtract the closing monthly inventory from the total opening monthly inventory plus monthly purchases, to calculate the monthly food cost as indicated below:

Cost of goods for food and non-alcoholic beverages

$10,575	Inventory of food and non-alcoholic beverages on March 1, 2012
7,800	Total food and non-alcoholic beverage purchases made in March 2012
$18,375	Opening inventory plus monthly purchases total
(9,500)	Inventory of food and non-alcoholic beverage on March 31, 2012
$8,875	Cost of goods for food and non-alcoholic beverages for March 2012

Cost of goods for alcoholic beverages

$5,500	Inventory of alcoholic beverages on March 1, 2012
3,250	Total alcoholic beverage purchases in March 2012
$8,750	Opening inventory plus monthly purchases total
(5,250)	Inventory of alcoholic beverages on March 31, 2012
$3,500	Cost of goods for alcoholic beverages for March 2012

3. **Gross Profit** – This is sales, less cost of goods sold. If we assume monthly sales are $40,000, with $30,000 being food sales, and $10,000 being alcohol sales, and cost of goods are $8,875 per above for food sales (also known as food cost), and $3,500 cost of goods for alcohol sales per above (also known as pouring cost), the monthly gross profit is indicated below:

Gross Profit Calculation for March 2012

Food sales	$40,000
Alcohol sales	10,000
Total sales	$50,000
Food Cost	(8,875)
Pouring Cost	(3,500)
Gross Profit	$37,625

4. **Operating Expenses** – These are all of the business's expenses other than the food and alcohol expenses. Operating expenses include such items as payroll, rent, repairs and maintenance, depreciation, insurance, interest, rent, supplies, utilities and rent, etc.

5. **Operating Income** – This is the gross profit less operating expenses. If we assume that total monthly operating expenses are $30,000, and the gross profit (per the example above) is $37,625, the operating income is indicated below. Operating income is also referred to as income from operations.

Operating Income for March 2012

Gross Profit	$37,625
Operating Expenses	(30,000)
Operating Income	$7,625

6. **Other Income and Expenses** – The other income category includes such income items as interest income from business monies invested earning interest, and gain on sale of assets if the business sells an asset. These income items are not related to daily income and expense transactions, and as such are categorized separately. Other expense items include Federal and State Income Tax penalties and fines, which are again not related to daily income and expense transactions.

7. **Taxable Income** – Operating income, less other income and expense, equals taxable income. See the next section which shows the ABC Restaurant & Bar Income and Expense Statement for the 12-month period ended 2012, which explains all of the major categories above.

ABC RESTAURANT & BAR INCOME AND EXPENSE STATEMENT FOR THE 12-MONTH PERIOD ENDED 2012

INCOME	EXPLANATION	
Food sales	$675,000	Total food & non-alcoholic beverages net of tax
Alcohol sales	200,000	Total alcohol sales net of tax
Total sales	$875,000	Total food, non-alcoholic and alcoholic beverages
COST OF GOODS SOLD		
Food cost	$202,500	
Pouring cost	50,000	
Total cost of goods sold	$252,500	Opening food/beverage inventory + food beverage purchases – closing food/beverage inventory
GROSS PROFIT	$622,500	Total sales less cost of goods sold

EXPENSES

Salaries & wages	$262,500
Payroll taxes	26,250
Advertising	10,000
Auto expense	14,000
Depreciation	10,000
Dues & subscriptions	3,000
Employee benefits	25,000
Insurance	32,000
Interest	5,000
Legal & accounting	12,000
Outside services	5,000
Rent	60,000
Repairs & maintenance	13,000
Supplies	30,000
Telephone	6,000
Travel & entertainment	19,000
Utilities	30,000
China, silver & glass replacement	4,000
Miscellaneous	<u>3,000</u>
Total operating expenses	$569,750
Operating income	$52,750

Gross profit less operating expenses.

Other income and (expenses)	
Interest income	$500
Gain on sale of assets	2,500
Federal Income Tax	(1,500)
State Income Tax	(1,350)
Penalties & fines	<u>(275)</u>
Net income (Loss)	$52,625

Chapter 27

UNDERSTANDING AND RECASTING FINANCIAL STATEMENTS

With the help of his broker, a buyer should be able to analyze the business's income-and-expense statement to determine the cash flow of the business he is considering purchasing. The main method for determining the value of a going-concern business is analyzing the Adjusted Cash Flow of the business. The Adjusted Cash Flow is also known by several other terms: Discretionary Earnings (also known an DE), Seller's Discretionary Cash (also known as SDC), Seller's Discretionary Cash Flow (also known as SDCF), and Seller's Discretionary Earnings (also known as SDE). The definition of all of the above items is adjusted earnings before taxes, interest income expense, non-operating and non-recurring income/ expense, deprecation and other non-cash charges and prior to deducting an owner's/officer's compensation—when adjustments are made before making adjustments for owner's compensation. All of these items are defined below.

Adjustments that can be made to the income-and-expense statement to determine the adjusted cash flow/discretionary income

- Sales adjustment. Sales tax monies are deducted from sales.

- Cost of goods adjustment. Any food or beverage that is taken home for the owner's use is deducted from the food and/or beverage categories. For example, if the owner takes home $1,000 of food at cost for his home use per month, this would be deducted from his food cost of goods sold, to determine the real food cost of the business. Also, if the owner takes home $500 of wine a month at cost for his home use, this would be deducted from the alcohol cost of the restaurant to determine the real pouring cost of the business.

- Operating expenses. The owner's compensation, including bonus, payroll taxes, pension, profit sharing, health and life insurance, auto, travel, and entertainment are always added back to the net income when determining adjusted cash flow/discretionary income.

- Depreciation/amortization. Depreciation is a non-cash expense for tangible fixed assets resulting from wear and tear. Assets are depreciated to recognize the loss of value of the assets over time. The definition of discretionary earnings says all depreciation is deducted from expense. So, when recasting, we add back all depreciation.

- Amortization, which is a pay down of equity on loan, is also added back when recasting as this expense is paying towards the equity of the business.

- Interest expense is added back to calculate adjusted cash flow/ discretionary earnings as if the business is being purchased for all cash, so there is no need for interest expense to finance the purchase of the business.

- Non-recurring items would include gain/loss on sale of assets, insurance proceeds from an insurance claim settlement, lawsuit settlements, bad debt, etc. Non-recurring items are add backs to adjusted cash flow/ discretionary earnings because they are not regular on-going expenses that occur yearly.

- Capital items are expensed.

Chapter 28

ASSUMPTIONS FOR RECASTING INCOME-AND-EXPENSE STATEMENTS

In the recast income-and-expense statement that follows, we will consider the points listed below regarding ABC's business for the year we are evaluating.

1. John is a working owner, and charges the business a base salary of $60,000 a year, and his payroll taxes are 10% of his base salary or $6,000.

2. John takes $5,000 (at the business's cost) of wine a year for his personal use at home, which is charged to the business, and takes home $12,000 (at the business's cost) of food for his personal uses, also charged to the business.

3. The business pays auto expenses for two of his vehicles, costing $14,000 year, and auto insurance of $3,000 per year—not expenses of the business.

4. Jane, John's wife, works full time in the business, but receives no salary. To replace her, it would cost $25,000 plus payroll taxes of

10%, or $2,500. Her job is an integral part of the business, and she'll need to be replaced.

5. The business pays health insurance premiums for John's family of $15,000 per year.

6. The business makes pension contributions for John in the amount of $12,500 per year.

7. Telephone expense includes three cell phones used by John's children at $150 per month.

8. John attends the National Restaurant Association show in Chicago every year at a total cost of $3,000.

9. This year the business spent $3,000 on new refrigeration that should have been capitalized rather than expensed.

10. John owns the building and charges the business $12,000 yearly— more than the current market rent—to reduce his taxable income, and if John sells the business, he will charge the buyer the normal market rent.

11. The travel and entertainment includes fees and expenses at a local country club, totaling $7,000 for the year. Not only is the business nature of this expense questionable, but membership in the club is very exclusive and nontransferable.

12. Legal expenses were $5,000 high due to a sexual harassment lawsuit settled by the company this past year.

In the income and expense example below, we will adjust all of the above items to recast the income-and-expense statement to determine the business's discretionary earnings. You would go through this same exercise when evaluating the discretionary earnings of any business you are considering purchasing.

In the recast income-and-expense statement below, although the taxable income is only $42,750, when you add back all the benefits the buyer gets out of the business, the discretionary earnings are $202,550 as indicated and explained below.

RECAST INCOME AND EXPENSE STATEMENT FOR ABC RESTAURANT & BAR FOR YEAR ENDING DECEMBER 31, 2012

	Owner's Income Statement	Adjustments	Adjusted Amount
INCOME			
Food sales	$675,000		$675,000
Alcohol sales	200,000		200,000
Total sales	$875,000		$875,000
COST OF GOODS SOLD (CGS)			
Food cost	$202,500	12,000 (a)	$190,500
Pouring cost	50,000	5,000 (b)	45,000
Total CGS	$252,500		$235,500
GROSS PROFIT	$622,500		$639,500
EXPENSES			
Salaries & wages	$262,500	60,000 (c) +(25,000) (d) = 35,000	$227,500
Payroll taxes	26,250	6,000 (e) + (2,500) (f) = 3,500	22,750
Advertising	10,000		10,000
Auto expense	14,000	14,000(g)	0
Depreciation	10,000	10,000(h)	0
Dues & subscriptions	3,000		3,000
Employee benefits	25,000	12,500(i)	12,500
Insurance	32,000	15,000(j) + 3,000 (k)=18,000	14,000
Interest	5,000	5,000 (l)	0
Legal & accounting	12,000	5,000(m)	7,000
Outside services	5,000		5,000
Rent	60,000	12,000(n)	48,000
Repairs & maintenance	13,000	3,000(o)	10,000
Supplies	30,000		30,000
Telephone	6,000	1,800(p)	4,200

Travel & entertainment	19,000	3,000(q) + 7,000(r) =10,000	9,000
Utilities	30,000		30,000
China, silverware & glassware replacement	4,000		4,000
Miscellaneous	3,000		3,000
Total operating expenses	$569,750		$439,950
Income before taxes	$52,750		
Discretionary Earnings / Adjusted Cash Flow			$199,550

EXPLANATION OF RECAST INCOME-AND-EXPENSE STATEMENT FOR ABC RESTAURANT & BAR FOR YEAR ENDING DECEMBER 31, 2012

Letter and Appropriate Explanation

a. The food cost was reduced by $12,000—the amount of food the owner took home for his personal use.

b. The pouring cost was reduced by $5,000—the amount of wine the owner took home for his personal use.

c. The salaries and wages expense was reduced by $60,000—the owner's salary.

d. This expense category was increased by $25,000—the owner's wife's salary as she was not paid, and a new owner will have to replace her as her position is an integral part of the business.

e. $6,000 was for the owner's payroll taxes—10% of his base salary.

f. The payroll taxes were increased by $2,500—the wife's payroll taxes.

g. The $14,000 cost of owner's two vehicles not used for the business.

h. Depreciation is a paper expense, and is added back to the buyer's discretionary earnings.

i. The business makes pension contributions for the owner in the amount of $12,500.

j. $15,000 is for the owner's health insurance.

k. $3,000 is for the owner's auto insurance.

l. $5,000 interest expense is added back as the business is always analyzed as an all-cash sale.

m. $5,000 is added back as an extraordinary legal expense incurred from a past sexual harassment lawsuit.

n. $12,000 is added back as this is extraordinary rent the owner charge in order to reduce taxable income.

o. $3,000 was for a new refrigeration purchase—should be capitalized rather than expensed.

p. $1,800 was added back for the owner's children's cell phones—not a business expense.

q. $3,000 was for the owner's expense in attending the National Restaurant Association show in Chicago

r. $7,000 is for the owner's country club expenses.

In determining the value of the subject business, we would use a multiple of the discretionary earnings, also referred to adjusted cash flow in this book. If the multiple was 2, the value of the ABC Restaurant & Bar would be $399,100, which is $199,550 discretionary earnings times 2 = $399,100.

Importance of Location

Chapter 29

THE MAJOR FACTORS IN SELECTING A STRONG LOCATION

Choosing the right restaurant location is one of the most important factors in contributing to one's success in the business. It is very challenging to be successful in the restaurant business, and having a strong location will enhance one's chances for success. The key factors in choosing the proper location are as follows: 1) rent affordability, 2) demographics match your concept requirements, 3) trade-area draw, and 4) major market generators in the neighborhood.

Rent Affordability

This means that you can afford the rent you will be paying. Frequently operators pay more rent than they should, and this can contribute to going out of business. Restaurant operators should not pay more that 6% to 8% of their sales in rent. This 6% to 8% factor also includes any additional costs you may be paying the landlord, which may include real estate taxes, fire insurance and common-area maintenance costs (CAM)—including security, landscaping, common-area utilities, and maintenance costs, etc. This means that if you are doing $600,000 in yearly sales, your annual rent should be no more that $48,000 ($600,000 sales x 8% = $48,000).

Demographics Match Your Concept Requirements

Demographics are the population statistics in the neighborhood of your proposed restaurant, within a given radius of your site. In researching your concept, you want to make sure that the neighborhood population can financially support your restaurant. Here concept means the name, menu, and format of the operation used in implementing their new operation.

The demographics include the following factors:

a. per capita income–the yearly earnings per person,

b. household income–the yearly earning per family household,

c. education level–broken down by persons holding a high school diploma, undergraduate degree, and graduate degree,

d. percent of income available for spending on food purchases away from home,

e. a breakdown of ethnic mix in the area, and

f. number of people living in the area.

Trade-Area Draw

This is the distance an average customer will travel to come to your restaurant. Most neighborhood restaurants draw customers from a one-mile radius of the site.

Outstanding planned dining restaurants such as the French Laundry in Yountville, or Michael Mina and Gary Danko's Restaurants in San Francisco, may draw customers from hundreds or thousand of miles away. Some restaurants gain a state-wide or even national reputation, and people will come from long distances.

Major Market Generator in the Neighborhood

Ideally you want to have a mix of the following in the immediate area of your restaurant:

a. a strong residential population,

b. a strong retail area with lots of both foot and vehicular traffic, and

c. strong traffic generators such as hospitals, theaters, colleges, shopping centers, and tourist attractions.

An example of a strong location in San Francisco would be the Irving Street Shopping Corridor, which includes Irving Street between 5th and 12th Avenue in the Inner Sunset District. This location has a large, well educated, residential population with a high household income. It is adjacent to the following: a) 9th Avenue, one of the major vehicular feeders into Golden Gate Park, a large tourist attraction which generates close to 75,000 cars daily and lots of foot traffic, b) UCSF or University of California at San Francisco Medical Center, which draws tens of thousands of people daily from staff, patients, visitors, etc. Also the University of San Francisco and St. Mary's Hospital is nearby, and c) strong retail area which generates additional foot traffic.

One cannot compromise in choosing the right location—this can be a make-or-break factor in your future success.

In our experience, we find that, overall, our most successful restaurants, year after year, are located in solid residential neighborhoods with a mix of retail and strong pedestrian traffic.

The strong residential base provides a regular customer base—the backbone of any solid business.

Chapter 30

HOW AN OPERATOR DETERMINES IF AN EXISTING SITE WILL WORK FOR HIS PROPOSED NEW OPERATION

For an assets-in-place transaction, where the operator is determining whether a proposed existing restaurant site will work for his new concept, he must do an extensive amount of research to determine if the site will meet his criteria.

The items of consideration include the following:

1. Complete comprehensive business plan,
2. Complete comprehensive feasibility study to evaluate the site,
3. Determination if the rent, terms and conditions the landlord is requiring are acceptable,
4. Determination if the price he is willing to pay for the business is economically acceptable, and
5. Evaluation of the business to determine if the concept does not work, what are the exit plans for the location.

Complete a comprehensive business plan

Before a buyer can move forward in any transaction regarding an assets-in-place transaction, he must first complete a business plan. The main components of the business plan include:

a. A definition of the concept—the menu, pricing, physical characteristics of the business which includes the number of seats, floor plans, square footage, equipment list, and design specifications.

b. A description of concept, type of service (i.e., full service, fast service, etc.) and hours of operation. Also included with the concept definition is an explanation as to who the customer profile is in regards to demographics as explained in Section 2 below.

c. A summary of management and staff, including resumes, financial statements, credit reports of key personnel including owner, manager, executive chef, etc.

d. Financial projections, including guest check averages, income and expense projections for at least 3 years, source, and use of funds statement. See Section II for more information on the essentials of preparing a business plan for future growth opportunity.

Complete a comprehensive feasibility study

Completing a site feasibility study includes the following items:

- A definition of the trade area of the business. The buyer needs to define the trade area of his business, which is the distance a customer will travel to patronize your business. In many cases, a restaurant's primary trade area is a one-mile radius of the proposed business site. In some situations, such as fast-food restaurants, coffee houses, and other impulse type fast-food service operations, the primary trade area may be just a few blocks from the subject site. The trade area needs enough potential customer activity to warrant your site selection.

Potential customer activity comes from the following factors:

1. Pedestrian traffic –How many customers walk by your proposed site daily.

2. Vehicular traffic – How many cars drive by your potential site daily.

3. Retail shops – These other businesses in the area create a synergy, attracting customers to the area. Ideally you want a number of complementary businesses that helps to minimize head-on competition to your business.

4. Major market generators – These are schools, churches, hospitals, shopping centers, movie theaters, museums, tourist attritions, office buildings, hotels, etc., which create a lot of potential customer activity. You want to have as many market generators as possible in the trade areas of your business to enhance your business's sales potential.

   a. A definition of the residential population in the trade area. Having a solid base of residential customers in your business's trade area is very important as residents contribute largely to your regular customer base. A regular customer patronizes your business frequently, on a daily, weekly and/or monthly basis, and can help give your projected sales a strong cushion. In the trade area of your proposed business, you want to have a dense population of single residential and multi-residential housing with residents who meet the demographic criteria for your concept so they have the economic ability to patronize your business on a regular basis.

   b. Completion of a demographic study of the proposed site – A demographic study is essential to determine if the demographics of the proposed site meet your customer demographic profile. A demographic study provides primarily the following information:
      - A breakdown of the household income per family in your trade area. Household income is the combined yearly income of the two primary wage earners living in a single family dwelling at the same address within the trade area of the proposed site. Income is broken down by in various income ranges as follows: Families making $200,000 per year or more; families making $150,000–$199,999 per year; families making $100,000–$149,999 per year; families making $75,000–$99,999 per year; families making $50,000–$74,999 per year; families making $25,000–$49,999 per year; and families making less than $25,000 per year.

- A breakdown of the per capita income in your trade area. The per capita income is the income per individual on a yearly basis living within a certain radius of the proposed site, broken down into various income ranges as follows: individuals making $200,000 per year or more; individuals making $150,000–$199,999 per year; individuals making $100,000–149,999 per year; individuals making $75,000–$99,999 per year; individuals making $50,000–$74,999 per year; individuals making $25,000–$49,999 per year; and families making less than $25,000 per year.
- A breakdown of the educational level of the population in your trade area. The educational level per individual living with a certain radius of the proposed site as follows: number and percentage of individuals with graduate degrees, number and percentage of individuals with undergraduate degrees, number and percentage of individuals with high school diplomas, and number and percentage of individuals with 8th grade education or less.
- The total population of residents living in your trade area.
- A breakdown of the ethnic mix of the population in your trade area. This is broken down as follows: number and percent of people living within a certain radius that are white, black, Asian, Pacific Islander, other/multiple races and Hispanic origin.
- A breakdown of the amount of money that is spent per person for food consumption away from home in a given year.

In your business plan, you will define what your customer profile is in terms of the demographic criteria listed above. In analyzing whether or not a proposed site is right for your concept, you will look very carefully when comparing the demographic criteria of your proposed customer profile with the actual demographics of the proposed trade area.

c. A definition of the major competition in the area. The buyer needs to physically walk the trade area of the proposed site and eat in the various restaurants to check out their operations and determine who is the competition in the area. If it appears that there are other businesses which are head-on competition to the proposed business, the buyer may want to reconsider his plans regarding opening his business in this trade area. Additionally the buyer should research the area to determine if any proposed new head-on competitive types of businesses plan to open in the proposed trade area. This research should consist of checking with the local building and planning departments to see if any new building permits are in the works. Also, if the buyer sees empty retail spaces with real estate signs, they should call the listing broker to learn what they may know about any new operators coming into the area, as well as asking what are the market rents for the space. Additionally if the buyer sees empty retail spaces without real estate signs, he can get the address of the building by calling a local title company. They can pull a property profile to determine who the landlord is, and the buyer should contact the landlord to inquire regarding the empty space.

d. Determining whether the location is vulnerable to a lot of new competition. If the proposed restaurant site is in an area that is already built-out, with no more space available for new building construction, then the next step would be to evaluate the existing building space to determine its status. This would include looking for any empty retail space which can be converted to restaurant space, or evaluating any existing restaurants in the area that look like they may be going out of business in the near future. If your proposed site is in an area where there is lots of surrounding space for new building construction, you need to carefully evaluate the area's zoning to determine how much new head-on competition could come in the area, impacting your business.

For example, in our area, several franchises have not done well. It wasn't because of their concept, but because they built too many like restaurants in a given area, cannibalizing sales in their other locations in the same area.

e. Determination whether any new restrictions are being proposed in the neighborhood that could negatively impact sales. The buyer needs to research the neighborhood to determine whether any new restrictions are being proposed that could have a detrimental impact on the sales of the proposed business. Such proposed restrictions could include the following:

- Minimizing vehicles into an area at certain times by implementing vehicle barriers. This has occurred in the North Beach district in San Francisco on weekends, having a dramatic negative impact on the sales in this area.
- Restricting the operating hours of businesses in the area as a result of the organized efforts of the local neighborhood associations. Often this is in response to a history of continued neighborhood complaints regarding noise, loitering, and vandalism in an area.
- Restricting any future businesses from the right to serve alcoholic beverages due to complaints from neighbors about an overabundance of businesses serving alcoholic beverages. This has resulted in many loud, rowdy, inebriated customers mingling in the area at various times throughout the day.

f. Determining whether there is enough parking in the area – If the buyer is going into a densely populated urban location where the customer flow is coming from primarily foot traffic, then having designated parking for your business is not a major concern. However, if your business is in a suburban area where customers' primary means of getting to your business is by car, adequate parking is imperative. Most municipalities have parking requirements based on the square footage or number of seats in the proposed business. Check with the local planning department that has jurisdiction for your proposed site to determine what the parking requirements are.

Determine if you can afford to pay the triple nets (NNN) rent, terms and conditions the landlord is requiring.

Total rent should not be more than 8% of total sales. Total rent includes the base rent plus any triple-net expenses, if applicable—additional expenses to the base rent charged by the landlord, which include property taxes, fire insurance, and common-area maintenance charges—(also referred to as all inclusive rent).

In the following case study, we are projecting that the optimum sales level will be $720,000 per year, which means that the yearly rent should be no more than $57,600 per year ($720,000 x .08% = $57,600 rent per year). To convert the yearly rent into monthly rent, take the yearly rent of $57,600 and divide by 12 months ($57,600 yearly rent / 12 months) which equals $4,800 monthly rent. The space is 2,000 sq. ft., which means that the monthly square foot rent is $2.40 or $4,800 per month which is calculated as follows: $4,800 per month rent / 2,000 sq. ft. = $2.40 square foot rent. $2.40 sq. ft. x 2,000 sq. ft. = $4,800 per month rent. $4,800 month rent x 12 months = $57,600 yearly rent.

This means that when the buyer is analyzing projected costs for a proposed business, the monthly rent should not be greater that $2.40 per square foot all inclusive. If the rent is going to be greater than $2.40 square foot all inclusive, then the buyer should look at a business that can do more than $720,000 yearly sales. For example, if the business, in an optimum sales projection, will do $1 million sales a year, the buyer can then afford to pay $80,000 a year in rent. $1 million x 8% = $80,000 yearly rent. The business's square footage is 2,000 sq. ft. which means the monthly square foot rent is as follows: $80,000 yearly rent / 12 months = $6,666.67 rent per month. If you take the monthly rent of $6,666.67 and divide by 2,000 sq. ft., the monthly per square foot rent is as follows: $6,666.67 monthly rent / 2,000 sq. ft. = $3.33 per square foot rent.

The higher the sales projection, the more the operator can afford to pay for rent. It is prudent to be conservative in projecting the financial statements for a business.

Rent per square foot varies greatly, depending on the location. For example, in 2008 San Francisco's monthly rents varied between $1.50 per square foot, all inclusive, to over $10 per square foot, all inclusive. Using the parameters of the case study of a 2,000 sq. ft. restaurant, this means that a $1.50 sq. ft. times 2,000 sq. ft. ($1.50 sq. ft. rent x 2,000 sq. ft.), the monthly rent will be $3,000. To determine the monthly sales level you must achieve to pay a $3,000 monthly rent, you calculate this number as follows (remembering that the rent should not exceed 8% of sales): $3,000 monthly rent / .08% = $37,500 monthly sales.

However, if you examine the high end of the rental market in San Francisco at $10 per square foot rent monthly, the calculation will be as follows: 2,000 sq. ft. times $10 per square foot equals $20,000 monthly rent (2,000 sq. ft. x $10 per sq. ft. = $20,000 monthly rent). To determine the monthly sales level, you must achieve to pay $20,000 monthly rent, you calculate this number as follows (remembering that rent should not exceed 8% of sales): $20,000 monthly rent / .08% =

$250,000 monthly sales. This translates into $3 million of sales annually –$250,000 monthly sales x 12 months.

In San Francisco, for $10 per square foot monthly rent, you must be located in one of the best locations in the city, such a Union Square. Union Square is located in the downtown area where there are thousands of hotel rooms, major shopping centers, including the major department stores in the city, thousands of residential units, many office buildings occupied by thousands of tenants, as well as a steady flow of tourists and locals walking by the proposed site daily.

Determine if the price you are paying for the business is economically feasible

The buyer should remember that the price he pays for an assets-in-place business is just a portion of the money he'll be investing in the business, due to all the additional expenses the buyer needs to budget for when purchasing the business. These other costs include costs for closing, remodeling, deposits, training, marketing, and reserves/working capital as discussed in more detail in other chapters.

Evaluation of the business to determine if the concept does not work, what are the exit plans for the location

To hedge against the risk that your business may not work out, a buyer needs to consider a couple of things explained below. Make sure you have flexibility in your lease-use clause so if the existing concept doesn't work, you have the right to change to another concept. For example, if you have an Italian restaurant that doesn't work, you want the flexibility to change the concept to either Chinese, Mexican, Greek, Mediterranean, or any other menu concept you choose. If it is clear that this location will not work out for you with the existing concept, or any other concept, you may have flexibility built in your lease so you have the right to assign the lease to another qualified buyer. Make sure you have the words "the landlord cannot arbitrarily without consent for assignment of the lease," included in the assignment section of the lease.

Also, in designing the restaurant, keep the décor somewhat neutral, other than some particular accessories, since you may need to give the operation some specific identity for the theme of the concept. Also design the cooking lineup so it can easily be changed to add or delete specific pieces of cooking equipment to accommodate different food concepts. By doing these things, the restaurant will be attractive to a buyer realizing that it is easy for him to make changes to accommodate his new operation.

Chapter 31

THE IMPORTANCE OF LOCATION

Types of Locations

Where you locate will vary, depending on the type and style of restaurant. Some types of restaurants require heavy pedestrian traffic and vehicular traffic, while others may depend on only one or the other.

Some restaurant chains require that a particular concept must be located in a certain type of regional shopping center, while some restaurants need to be situated next to a multi-screen movie theater. Below I've listed the various types of restaurant locations:

A. Impulse-Oriented Sites

These sites are for fast food, quick service, espresso cafes, and delis, etc. The criteria includes high visibility, easy access, heavy pedestrian traffic, and in many situations, a corner location. High visibility means that the restaurant's frontage is easily seen by its potential customers. Many customers who frequent these type of businesses do not plan to go but impulsively decide to visit this business based upon its close proximity and convenience. Easy access is a requirement, allowing customers to get in and out of this space. A heavy concentration of foot traffic is another requirement of an impulse-oriented site.

Often these sites include a corner location near other complimentary retail businesses that generate foot traffic, sites on the ground floor of large office buildings, and sites in downtown areas where a large concentration number of people come from office buildings, retail stores, residential building and hotels.

B. Planned-Dining Sites

Here customers have planned out their dining experience in advance, and as a rule, these sites are for more up-scale restaurants. The site criteria are generally not as stringent as the impulse-oriented site, however it requires good proximity to its customers, and adequate parking facilities. Many planned-dining sites are in destination-bound locations, such as several wine country locations in California, including the French Laundry in Yountville, where some of its customers come from all over the country. Reservations for this type of highly popular restaurants can sometimes require booking several months ahead.

- **Search for Sites in Built-out Areas Versus Sites in Large Open-Space Areas**

  For independent, non-franchised operators, it is more prudent to open a restaurant in a site that is fairly built out rather than open a restaurant in an area with lots of open space.

  If you're in a built-out area, there is a limit as to how much new competition can open, and the operator has a pretty good handle on his competition. In an area where there is lots of open space, an operator is vulnerable to having too much competition, and an operator's market share can be reduced, substantially limiting sales and profit potential.

- **Major Market Generators**

  It is prudent to choose a location near major customer generators such as colleges, shopping center sites, office buildings, hospitals, theaters and major tourist attractions, etc., as this gives the operator a base of regular customers. If the operator does a good job running the business, he will have a good chance of having the staff, employees, tenants, and residents become market generators—as well as having the customers and patients that are attracted to these businesses and institutions become regular customers.

- **Strong Neighborhood Base**

  It is important to have a strong neighborhood base of customers close to the operator's site as this will help provide a regular base of customers who become the backbone of the business. If the operator does a good job, he will have a good chance that locals will frequent his business on a daily, weekly, or monthly basis.

- **Site Restrictions**

  It is important that the operator research any possible restrictions about a site he may be considering. Check with the area's local building and planning departments regarding any special conditions or restrictions for the proposed site. Such restrictions may include no alcoholic beverages allowed, a limitation on the hours of operation, a limitation on customer capacity, special disabled requirements, or no entertainment activity allowed, such as live entertainment, live music, DJ music, with even some restrictions on recorded music. Generally, if an operator purchases a business in California with an alcoholic beverage license or entertainment license, these licenses are grandfathered in with the site when the business transfers to the buyer, assuming there are no major violations against the business. Such violations could include serving minors, having complaints filed by neighbors or businesses in the area regarding the unprofessional behavior of the business's customers such as loud noise, excessive drunks and litter in the area, etc. If these problems occur, it is possible to have the alcoholic and entertainment license revoked, or have stringent conditions put on these licenses; such as limitations on the days and hours of operation the business can use these licenses. This could greatly negatively impact a business and its ability to make a reasonable profit.

- **Moratoriums**

  In some locations, moratoriums are in place which prohibit new restaurants, bar, or nightclubs from opening in a given area. A moratorium is a temporary or permanent ordinance which prohibits a use, such as a restaurant, bar, or nightclub. These moratoriums usually exist for the following reasons: a) too many of these type of businesses in the area, b) too much foot traffic or car traffic in the area, c) a shortage of parking in the area, and d) complaints from neighbors regarding noise, intoxicated customers, drug problems, and damage to neighbors' property.

- **American Disabilities Act (ADA)**
  National, state, and local governments have passed laws regarding standards for a disabled person to have comparable access to a facility as a non-disabled person.

  These requirements vary depending on the operator's location. These requirements include primary access to entering and leaving a facility, seating areas, and restroom access. It is important that an operator analyzes the requirements so there are no surprises such as excessive costs to retrofit spaces to comply with laws to accommodate disabled individuals. In California, if an operator is remodeling a site, and the site does not meet the ADA requirements, the operator will be required to make the necessary changes to comply with the law.

- **Existing Competition**
  It is important that an operator checks out what competition might already be in the neighborhood of the proposed site. It is healthy to have some competition in the area, but the challenge of running a profitable business is difficult enough without having an excess amount of head-on competition. Complimentary competition is healthy as it brings customers to the area that perhaps would not come otherwise. The best competition would be other food concepts with price points that are different from the proposed operator's menu.

  For example, if the proposed concept was a popular-priced Italian bistro with guest check averages per person at lunch at $10 and at dinner $17 per person, complimentary competitors would be anyone such as coffee cafes, different ethnic restaurants, and operations with different menu items, and a varied assortment of price points.

  When these customers frequent these operations, they have exposure to the operator's business as well, and perhaps will try the operator's business the next time they are in the area.

- **Landlord Concerns**

  It is important that the operator has a good sense of what his landlord is like. When a operator enters into a long-term lease with a landlord, it is like a partnership, and having a good working relationship with a landlord is important. If the operator needs to make improvements to the business that affect the building, such as adding a new flue and hood system; changing the electrical or plumbing systems; modifying the heating, ventilating and air conditioning systems; installing signs and awnings; or painting the exterior of the building, these improvements require the landlord's consent. The operator needs to make sure, before he proceeds with the proposed project, that the landlord will approve the changes critical for the business's success

- **Adjoining Neighbors' Concerns**

  The operator needs to be familiar with any potential adjacent neighbors of the proposed site. This is especially important if you are on the ground floor of a multi-story building. If there are residential tenants above the proposed site, it is important to know if the operator's operation will create any conflicts with the neighbors upstairs as the operator may need to stay open late or have recorded or live music in the late evening hours. If the operator has a late-night operation, he needs to check the acoustical aspects of the building to make sure there is adequate sound insulation to minimize any sound transmission to the upstairs tenants.

Chapter 32

SPECIAL TYPES OF LOCATIONS

- **Tourist Attractions**

  If the operator chooses this type of location, he needs to make sure there is a strong enough base of regular customers in the trade area to assure he will be able to pay the business bills during the off season. Tourist locations are great during holidays, weekends, and during the tourist season, but when tourists aren't around, these types of locations can get a little scary. Tourist locations are frequently a turn-off to the normal regular customer base in the area, such as residents and employees in the area, as they won't want to hassle with large crowds and lack of parking And in many cases, the menu items are expensive, and the service and price value relationship are not good. Some tourist-oriented operators think they can get away with this because they'll never see these tourists again. This is obviously the wrong attitude for a business to have since the operator needs to be concerned about his restaurant's reputation to survive successfully long term.

- **Five-Day, Monday-thru-Friday, Breakfast-and-Lunch Operation**

  This type of location requires a heavy concentration of customers within a short time span. These locations are typically in financial district, downtown, business centers or industrial parks where customers are present Monday thru Friday 7 a.m. through 5 p.m., except holidays when they are closed. To be successful, the operator needs a physical plant capable of servicing a lot of customers quickly, since the highest percentage of business occurs during the lunch hours between 11 a.m. and 2 p.m.

  Most of these type of locations are set up to do a high percentage of take-out sales where customers eat their meals outside their office or take their food back to their office.

- **Twenty-Four-Hour Locations**

  High visibility and easy access are the main criteria for this type of location. In urban areas, these locations should be a corner location with a high concentration of both foot and vehicular traffic. It's important to be near live theaters, movie theaters, hospitals, bars, nightclubs, universities and colleges, sports areas, and public transportation stops. In suburban areas, freestanding buildings on major highways with heavy traffic, easy access, parking lots and high visibility are well-positioned. Another good location is a freestanding building on the periphery of a major regional shopping center, on a main thoroughfare.

- **Seven-Day-a-Week Breakfast, Lunch and Dinner Locations**

  Being anchored by a solid residential population with good demographics, coupled with an active retail area with stores and businesses in the immediate area, is helpful for this type of restaurant. The solid residential market provides a base for regular customers who will frequent the business on a daily weekly and monthly basis. It is also helpful to have some major employers in the area such as office buildings, hospitals and colleges and universities.

- **In-Plant Feeding Cafeterias**

  These locations are in buildings with a high concentration of employees who eat their meal in the building where they work, such as hospitals, factories, schools, and large office buildings. This type of operation can operate seven days a week serving breakfast, lunch and dinner, because most of the customers who frequent these operations work in these buildings, with visitors to these buildings comprising a small percentage of the customers.

- **Shopping Centers**

  The key for a successful location in this type of venue is high foot traffic all hours the center is open. Being near major entry and exit areas, a major anchor tenant, and a multi-screen theater, is helpful. Some shopping centers have food courts where many fast-food operators with different menu concepts are grouped together, with a shared central seating area. It is also helpful to have exterior exposure in the mall so the operator can attract both customers in the shopping center, as well as non-mall customers who see the site from the outside. Some operators prefer free-standing buildings on the periphery of the center where they don't attract the foot traffic in the center, but attract customers driving by the center, as well as those shopping. Exclusivity is essential, where the operator has the exclusive right for a particular food service concept, like the operator has the exclusive right to be the only Mexican operation in the center. It is important the center has a good mix of operations that complement each other and minimize head-on competition.

- **Restaurant Row and Nightclub Row Locations**

  Some restaurant and nightclub operations need to be located near a high concentration of either restaurants or nightclubs respectively. Why is this important? These other businesses create a synergistic customer base which brings a large volume of customers into the area. For this to work for a restaurant, it is best to have a diverse mix of restaurant concepts in the same area to minimize head-on competition, for example, one of each restaurant: Chinese, Japanese, Italian, Mexican, Mediterranean, Greek, French, Asian fusion, espresso café, American diner, and deli. Many nightclub operators are oriented to be in a concentrated nightclub area that don't require a diversified operating format. This is because many club goers like to jump from one club to another in a single night, as well as frequenting different clubs on various nights of the week, depending on what's happening at that club.

Chapter 33

HOW TO FIND
A GOOD RESTAURANT SITE

Individual restaurants have different site criteria. A fast-food restaurant, such as KFC, McDonald's or Burger King; a family coffee shop, such as Denny's, IHOP, or Baker's Square; and coffeehouses such as Starbuck's or Peet's, have similar site criteria. They are all looking for high visibility, easy access, high vehicular counts, and/or heavy foot traffic. Other types of restaurants, such as dinner houses or other upgraded operations, are looking for a strong, stable demographic base of customers. This might include a combination of a strong neighborhood population, a dense business district, a heavy concentration of office buildings, and/or a neighborhood or regional shopping center.

Many independent restaurant operators are competing against major chain operators for the best sites. Chain operators can routinely beat out independents in acquiring these sites, as they can afford to pay higher rents because they generate higher sales volumes. This is a result of their large advertising and marketing budgets, and their high physical presence in the marketplace.

Here are some of the ways independent operators can obtain good restaurant sites:

a. Look for a situation where an inexperienced operator has a good site, but is not doing well, and will most likely being going out of business in the near future.

b. Look at particular locations where local communities do not want chain operators, preferring only local independent operators.

c. Talk to restaurant vendors and suppliers who know which restaurant operators are late pays, and are having financial problems.

d. Check out restaurant sites where former operators are out of business, but it appears that the equipment is still intact.

e. Check the businesses for sale internet business websites for restaurants, bars, and clubs for sale as detailed in Chapter 48.

f. Call a restaurant broker specialist. More than likely a broker will be happy to follow up anonymously on your behalf in situations where it appears that the current operator is having trouble financially, or a business is closed, etc

Lease and Other Legal Aspects

Chapter 34

PREMISES LEASE

What is a premises lease?

A premises lease is a legal written contract normally between two parties. The two parties to the lease are the landlord, also known as the lessor, who owns the building of the prospective business, and the tenant, also known as the lessee, who leases the proposed space for monetary consideration. The tenant has the right of possession of a given space during the term of the lease, in exchange for paying the landlord monthly rent. The premises lease spells out the rights and responsibilities of both the landlord and tenant. If the premises lease is for a 5-year period, the tenant is responsible for paying $300,000 total accumulative rent over this period. If the tenant goes out of business after two years, the landlord can take legal action against the tenant for the balance of the $300,000 in the 5-year contract, and obtain a judgment against him for the loss of rent and also his legal costs. This can continue until such time the landlord releases the space for a comparable rent.

A premises lease is similar to a promissory note. This is used when one borrows money, and signs a written document that legally binds the borrower to the lender, stating that the borrower will pay back the loan over an agreed amount of time with an agreed interest. In a premises lease, the lessee personally guarantees that he will pay the landlord a pre-negotiated amount of money on a monthly basis for the duration of the lease. The rent is pre-negotiated before the lease is executed between the landlord and tenant. If the tenant does not pay his rent or fulfill the other terms and conditions of the lease, the tenant can be evicted, and be legally removed from the premises. Without possession of the premise, the tenant's business cannot operate at the site of the premises lease, and without a valid premises lease in place, the tenant has no business to sell, should he decide to sell his business.

What is a guarantor?
The tenant is financially responsible to perform the terms and conditions of the lease, and is the guarantor of the lease. The guarantor personally guarantees that he will pay rent on a timely basis, and will perform all the terms and conditions of the lease. In smaller transactions, and for entry-level buyers, the individual tenant is generallly required to personally guarantee the lease. This means that if the tenant does not meet the terms and conditions of the lease, he can be removed from the premises through a legal action. Then the landlord can go after the tenant for any lost rent and other costs he incurs as a result of this action. Before a tenant is accepted by a landlord, the tenant must be operationally and financially qualified (operational and financial qualification is discussed further in Chapter 3). In many cases, the landlord requires that the tenant owns a home, because if the tenants fails, and the landlord has to take legal action against the tenant, the landlord can get a judgment against the tenant. Subsequently the landlord can get a lien secured against the tenant's home to force the tenant to legally pay the landlord for all lost

damages, including loss of rent, attorney's fees, and commission costs for re-renting the space.

Tenants with a long, successful track record can usually negotiate having an entity such as a corporation, or limited liability company guarantee the lease. For a landlord to accept an entity other than an individual as a guarantor, the entity has to be adequately capitalized to assure the landlord that the entity can meet the financial requirements of the lease.

The Main Elements of the Lease

Term – Term is the length of the lease in number of years. It is recommended that the operator obtains minimally a 5-year term, which is called the base term, and a 5-year option discussed below, so the tenant has enough time to get a return of his investment and return on his investment. To ensure clarity, "return of his investment" means that whatever he invested in the business, he will get this amount back through the profits and/or his compensation from the performance of the business. "Return on his investment" means that if he spends $100,000 on his investment, and he has already received his investment back, he wants to make, let's say, a 10% a year return, or $10,000 per year. Some landlords do not grant options, in which case it is recommended that the operator obtain a 10-year-or-longer lease term. The advantage of having a shorter base term with options is that the tenant is only personally liable for the base term, and if the business is not successful, the tenant will not exercise the option, and will minimize his personal liability.

Generally, the more that is invested in the business by the tenant, the longer the lease term the tenant requires in order to be able to recoup his investment, and obtain a reasonable profit on the money the tenant has invested in the business.

Rent – Rent is the monthly payment the tenant is required to pay the landlord for the tenant's right to occupy the space. Most rent amounts are determined by the amount of square footage the tenant occupies, times the market rent per square foot for the space. For example, if the operator occupies a 2,000 sq. ft. space, and the market rent is $2 per sq. ft. , the monthly rent will be $4,000–2,000 sq. ft. x $2 sq. ft.

Determining the Market Rent – If the operator is negotiating a new lease, or renewing an existing lease, the best way to determine the market rent is to talk to several reputable commercial real estate brokers who specialize in retail restaurant, bar, or nightclub leases in the area of the proposed business. Rents in large metropolitan areas vary dramatically, depending on where the business is located. For example, in San Francisco, monthly market rents will vary between $1.50 to $10.00 a square foot. Another method for determining market rent is to drive around the area of the proposed location looking at "for lease" signs, and call the brokers and ask them what is the asking rent for these spaces. The operator can then take an average of the rents he has surveyed, and use this information as a basis for negotiating the base rent with the landlord.

Additionally the operator can call existing restaurant, bar, and nightclub owners in the area of the proposed site, and ask them how much rent they are paying. However, in most cases, the owners will feel this is proprietary information, and in many cases, the owners may have older leases with substantially rents below current market. If the operator is negotiating a new lease, and has a good prior track record, he can sometimes negotiate a below-market rent as the landlord feels his risk factor has been reduced, based on the operator's past success. If the operator is renewing a lease, he should capitalize on his past success as a tenant—in terms of paying rent on time, keeping the premises well maintained, and being an asset to the building—as a tool in negotiating a favorable lease.

The Landlord's Perspective on Rent – Although the landlord wants his tenant to be successful, he is very concerned with obtaining the maximum market rent for the space leased as this determines the value of their building. For example, if a tenant is paying $60,000 a year rent, and the formula for determining the value of the landlord's building is using a capitalization method and a 6 cap rate, the value of the landlord's building is $1,000,000 ($60,000 annual rent / .06 cap rate = $1,000,000). If, however, the market rent for this space is $75,000 per year, and using the same valuation formula above, the building is worth $1,250,000 ($75,000 annual rent / .06 cap rate = $1,250,000)

Yearly Rent Increases – Yearly rent increases should be tied to either pre-negotiated fixed yearly rent increases on the Consumer Price Index

(CPI). A consumer price index (CPI) is an index number measuring the average price of consumer goods and services purchased by households. It is one of several price indices calculated by national statistical agencies. The percent change in the CPI is a measure of inflation. The CPI can be used to index (i.e., adjust for the effects of inflation) wages, salaries, pensions, or regulated or contracted prices. The CPI is, along with the population census and the National Income and Product Accounts, one of the most closely watched national economic statistics. The average CPI in the San Francisco-Oakland-San Jose area in the past several years has been approximately 3.5% a year.

When the CPI is used, it is common to have a minimum yearly increase, also called a floor, and a maximum yearly increase, also called a ceiling. When floors and ceilings are used with CPI rents, floors usually are in the range of 2 to 4% a year and CPI ceilings are in the range of 5 to 7% a year.

a. Flat Rent – Although rents are usually adjusted yearly on the anniversary date of the commencement of the lease, in some cases, if the operator has a strong track record, or the rental market is weak and it is a lessee's market, the operator can negotiate a flat rent—rent is fixed at a certain level for a given number of years. For example, there is a 10-year lease, and the rent for the first 5 years is $2,000 per month, and the rent for second 5-year period is $2,500 per month. If there are additional rent expenses required with a flat rent, such as property taxes, fire insurance, and common-area maintenance expenses (discussed later in this chapter), usually the landlord will pass the yearly increases for these expenses through to the tenant as he does not want to be out of pocket for these costs.

b. Fixed Rent – This means the rent is fixed either at a stated dollar amount, or at a yearly fixed percentage. An example of a stated fixed-amount dollar rent is as follows: in a 5-year base term lease, the monthly rent is stated as follows: year 1–$2,000, year 2–$2,100, year 3–$2,200, year 4–$2,300, and year 5–$2,400. An example of a stated fixed-percentage rent is as follows: there will be a yearly 3% increase of the base rent as follows: year 1–$2,000, year 2–$2,060, year 3–$2,121.80, year 4–$2,185.45, and year 5– $2,251.02

c. Percentage Rent – If the landlord insists on a percentage rent, the operator should cap the percentage at 5 to 6% of yearly sales. In exchange for a percentage rent, the operator should negotiate a below-market minimum rent, and have the landlord make a monetary contribution to any remodeling the operator plans to do, without having the landlord's contribution amortized as additional rent. The rational for percentage rent is that since the landlord is making a monetary contribution to the tenant, the landlord is in effect becoming a minority partner, so to speak, with the tenant, and is entitled to a percentage of sales based upon his investment. Percentage rent usually kicks in at a determined natural break point, which is as follows: if the base rent is $60,000 per year, and the percentage rent is 6% of gross sales, and the natural break point is $1 million per year of sales, the operator does not pay percentage rent until he does at least $1 million in sales a year. This is determined as follows: Divide the annual minimum rent of $60,000 by the percentage rent, which is as follows: $60,000 minimum rent / .06% percentage rent = $1million natural break point of yearly sales. If the operator does $1.5 million sales in a given year, his rent will be as follow: $1.5 million in sales times .06% percentage rent = $90,000 rent.

Calculation of Percentage Rent Natural Versus Artificial Breakpoints

Breakpoints in general: Percentage rent is typically not payable until the tenant's gross sales exceed the "breakpoint" in the applicable lease year.

Example: Tenant pays percentage rent in an amount equal to three percent (3%) of the amount of gross sales in excess of $500,000 made during any lease year—$500,000 is the "breakpoint."

Natural breakpoint: A "natural breakpoint" is calculated by dividing the rent by the applicable percentage. In other words, percentage rent is paid to the extent the gross sales at the premises exceeds the base rent.

Example: If base rent was $5,000 per month ($60,000 per annum), and percentage rent was 7%, then, percentage rent would be paid on monthly gross sales in excess of $71,429 (5,000/0.07 = 71,429). Percentage rent would be paid on annual gross sales in excess of $857,143 (60,000/0.07 = 857,143)

Sliding Scale Percentage Rent – In some cases, if the landlord is making a large contribution toward the tenant's remodeling, a sliding-scale percentage rent formula may be negotiated. With this method, the landlord's rent is calculated using different percentages at different sales levels. An example of a sliding-scale percentage rent formula is as follows – on the first $1 million in sales the operator does in a given year, the landlord will get 6% of yearly sales, and on any sales the operator does in the same given year between $1 million–$1.5 million, the landlord will get 7% of yearly sales, and on any sales the operator does in the same given year above $1.5 million in sales, the landlord will get 8% of yearly sales. In the above-mentioned example, if the tenant does $2 million in sales, the tenant's rent formula would be as follows – the percentage rent formula on the first $1 million of sales is $1,000,000 x .06% = $60,000, plus the percentage rent formula on sales between $1,000,001 and $1,500,000 of sales is $500,000 x .07% = $35,000, plus the percentage formula on sales between $1,500,001 and $2,000,000 of sales is $500,000 x .08% = $40,000. The total rent owed to the landlord would then be $60,000 + $35,000 + $40,000 = $135,000 for that given year.

Additional Occupancy Expenses – In addition to base rent, the tenant may be charged what is called triple net expenses (NNN). In addition to the base rent, the tenant will be charged monthly for real estate taxes, fire insurance on the building, and common-area maintenance costs (CAM costs). CAM expenses can include these expenses – landscaping, security, common area utility, and building maintenance. The lease spells out expenses as determined by a predetermined formula. The formula is usually tied to a pro-rata share of the total building NNN costs, based on the percentage the given rentable space has relative to the total rentable space for the building. For example, if the given rentable space is one third of the entire rentable space of the building, the NNN expenses would be equal to one-third of the yearly real estate taxes, building fire insurance expense, and CAM charges of the building. Specifically, if the building's yearly real estate taxes were $24,000, the yearly fire insurance expense was $12,000, and the yearly CAM charge was $6,000, the total building's yearly NNN expenses would be $42,000.

The tenant for the given rentable space would then be responsible for paying one third of the $42,000 NNN expenses on a monthly basis as follows – $42,000 x .333% = $14,000 or $1,166.67 per month ($14,000 per year / 12 months = $1,166.67 monthly NNN expense). This NNN rent is paid monthly in addition to the base rent, and the tenant is usually billed monthly by the landlord, with the invoice breaking down the various components of the NNN expense. In the above example, if the tenant is occupying 100% of the building, the tenant would then be responsible for paying 100% of the $42,000 NNN expense or $3,500 per month NNN expense ($42,000 yearly NNN expense / 12 months = $3,5000 monthly NNN expense).

In some cases the tenant's additional occupancy expenses may be limited to a single net lease (N) where the tenant pays only real estate taxes, or to a double net lease (NN) where the tenant pays only real estate taxes and the fire insurance on the building.

Recapture of Percentage Rent – In a large number of percentage leases, the tenant is paying additional occupancy expenses in the form of either a single net lease (N), double net lease (NN) or triple net lease (NNN) as described above, in addition to the base and percentage rent. If the operator has any of the above additional occupancy expense leases, he should try to negotiate a recapture provision in the lease. A recapture provision means that the operator can deduct any of the NNN components against percentage rent. For example, if the tenant's total rent is $80,000 per year, of which $60,000 is base rent, and $20,000 is additional percentage rent, and his NNN expenses are $15,000 per year, the operator would be able to deduct the $15,000 of NNN expenses from his percentage rent. So instead of paying $95,000 ($60,000 base rent + $20,000 percentage rent + $15,000 NNN expenses =$95,000 total occupancy expense) a year in total occupancy expenses, the operator would deduct $15,000 of NNN expenses against the $20,000 of percentage rent he would have paid, so his total rent would be $80,000 ($95,000 total yearly occupancy costs before recapturing $15,000 NNN expenses or $95,000–$15,000 = $80,000 total occupancy costs). This results in the operator's total occupancy costs being reduced from $95,000 to $80,000 a year, for a savings of 16.7% a year of occupancy expense to the tenant.

Use Clause – This is a very important section as it states the allowable use a tenant is allowed to have in a given rentable space. The best-use clause a tenant can get is the one with the broadest language, such as "a restaurant serving alcoholic beverages." This clause gives the tenant the right to have any type of restaurant, and serve a full alcohol menu. In most leases that are in a shopping center or in office building where there are multiple restaurant tenants, the language in the use clause will be very specific, such as "a café serving breakfast and lunch items, excluding submarine sandwiches, deli sandwiches and specialty coffee drinks." The exclusion of submarine sandwiches, deli sandwiches and specialty coffee drinks is because probably a sub/deli sandwich business and specialty coffee business are already in the complex.

Most landlords of retail spaces that have multiple food service tenants, do not want to have head-on competitors. They'll routinely allow only one of each type of food service operation such as Chinese, Thai, Vietnamese, Korean, Mexican, Italian, hamburger franchise, coffee specialty operation, hot dog operation, etc. in the given complex. This provides exclusivity to the existing tenants, allowing them to have a reasonable market share of the food service customers in the complex. Having diverse food service tenants also attracts more customers to the complex, and provides a synergistic effect helpful to all of the tenants. If a tenant is having a problem making his operation financially successful, and needs to change the menu and concept, he'll be limited to concept and menus not already in the complex. Having a broad-use clause in the tenant's lease also makes it easier to sell the business.

Assignment and Subletting – Having the right to assign the tenant's lease or to be able to sublet a tenant's space is very important as there is a high probability that the tenant will not be successful, and will want to minimize his financial exposure to continued lease liability. The key language to look for in the lease that is advantageous for the tenant is "the landlord cannot arbitrarily withhold consent to an assignment." This language means that if the proposed new tenant is operationally and financially qualified, the landlord cannot arbitrarily deny the proposed new tenant the right to have the lease assigned to him. When an assignment occurs, the two parties in the assignment are the assignor, who is the existing tenant, and the assignee, who is the proposed new tenant. In an assignment agreement, it is stated that the assignee assumes all of the rights and obligations of the lease being assigned, and this agreement is executed in writing by the assignor, assignee and the landlord.

In most assignments, the assignor has secondary liability for the remaining term of the base lease. This means that if the assignee's business fails, and the tenant can't continue to pay rent or meet the other conditions of the lease, and the landlord is unable to recoup their financial losses from the assignee, the landlord can go after the assignor to be made whole financially. If you are an assignor, try to negotiate a release of continued lease liability, which becomes effective at the close of escrow. This is hard to do unless the assignee is significantly stronger financially and operationally than the assignor. Even in these circumstances, the landlord will want the assignor to have continued lease liability for at least one or two years of the remaining base term of the lease being assigned. There can be situations in an assignment whereby the assignees want to change/modify some of the terms and conditions of the lease, and require a modification section in the lease assignment.

It is generally understood in a lease assignment that the assignor has secondary liability; the assignee has primary liability. Secondary liability means that the landlord must exhaust the financial resources of the assignee, who has primary liability, before he comes after the assignor's financial resources. If the assignee breaches the lease, the landlord has to take legal action to be made whole against the assignee, before the landlord takes legal action against the assignor to be made whole. Being "made whole" means the landlord gets all of his rent money paid current from the tenant, in addition to any other expenses the landlord may incur, such as legal expenses, late payments, and interest fees on late rent, etc., which have occurred as a result of the tenant's late rent history. It is also generally understood that if there are options in the lease, other than the remaining base term that is being assigned, the assignor has secondary liability only for the base term and not the options, as the assignor has no control in exercising the options.

Subletting – In this situation, the existing tenant is called the sublessor, and the new proposed tenant is called the sublessee, and the document that is executed between these two parties is called the sublease. In most cases, a sublease situation requires the written permission of the landlord as does the lease assignment. Unlike an assignment, the sublessor who is the existing tenant, still has primary liability to the landlord, and the sublessee has secondary liability. This means that if the sublessee fails to pay the rent or meet the other conditions of the lease, the sublessor is responsible to the landlord. In many sublease situations, the rent is paid directly by the sublessee to the sublessor, and the sublessor pays the rent directly to the landlord. Frequently, wording in the sublease agreement states that if the sublessee breaches the sublease, the sublessor has an expedited method of taking over physical possession of the premises. In some situations, if there is a base term of the lease, and an option in the future, wording in the sublease states that if the sublessee is in good standing in the base term of the lease, he will have the right to exercise the option. In this case, the sublease will be converted into an assignment of the lease, and the sublessee now becomes the assignee, and the sublessor becomes the assignor, and the primary liability shifts to the new assignee, who was formerly the sublessee.

In both the assignment and sublease, it is important that the existing tenant has a comfort level with the new proposed tenant's financial and operational history to assure himself that the new proposed tenant will be successful, and he will not have to bail out the new proposed tenant at his own expense.

Maintenance, Repairs and Alterations – It is spelled out in the lease what the tenant's and landlord's respective responsibilities are regarding maintenance, repairs, and alterations. In most cases, the lessee is responsible for the repairs of all items within its premises—electrical, wiring, plumbing, plate glass, heating, ventilating and air conditioning systems. In most cases, the landlord is responsible for the roof, sidewalls, and foundation. However, in some cases where there are NNN leases, and freestanding buildings, the lessee could be responsible for the maintenance of the roof and parking lot.

There have been cases where the tenant was on the ground floor of a multi-story building, and water leaks coming from the upper floors caused damage to the ground-floor tenant. In this case, the landlord was responsible for these damages. Other situations where the ground-floor tenant had a basement with sub pumps for pumping out any excess water that accumulates after heavy rainfall, and flooding caused damage to the ground-floor tenant, the landlord was responsible for the damage.

Alterations –When a tenant wants to do major remodeling to the building, the landlord usually requires written consent given in a timely manner, and he often reviews the plans and specifications before giving his written approval. In these circumstances, the landlord will require that all work is done up to code, with the proper permits pulled, and the work completed by licensed contractors. Additionally, the landlord will require the tenant to make sure the contractor posts a notice of non-responsibility which states – 1) the landlord is not responsible for anything that goes wrong during the remodeling, 2) the contractors are insured, and 3) the lien releases will be prepared after the work is completed so no mechanics liens can be attached to the building. If any mechanics liens are attached to the building, it will be the tenant's responsibility working with their contractors to get them removed.

Utilities – It is the tenant's responsibility to pay all their utilities, which include electric, gas, water, and most tenants have their own separate meters that read their respective utility usage. It is also the tenant's responsibility to pay his garbage expense. In some circumstances, where there are no separate gas, water, and electric meters, or a separate garbage area for the tenant, a formula is spelled out in the lease stating what the tenant's financial responsibility will be for these items. In some cases, these utility costs are included as part of the rent.

Indemnification of Lessor – This section states that the lessee will be legally responsible for any damage or injury to any person or property on the lessee's premises, and will indemnify and hold the lessor harmless for any legal action resulting from any injury to any person or property damage. Additionally, if the lessor has to legally defend himself regarding the above, the lessee will be responsible for any expenses the lessor incurs in defending himself.

Lessee's Insurance – The lessee will have in place the necessary insurance to cover plate glass, public liability, and property damage to the business. Usually the minimum limits of liability insurance to be carried by the lessee are mentioned in the lease. The lessee is responsible to provide an insurance certificate which states that the landlord, as well as the lessee, is named as an insured on this policy, and should be provided to the landlord yearly.

Lessor's Insurance – The lessor is required to carry hazard insurance to cover 100% of the actual cash value of the improvements throughout the leases. However, the lessor is not responsible for insuring the lessee's personal property, leasehold improvements, or trade fixtures.

Abandonment of Premises – If the lessee abandons the premises and leaves its trade fixtures behind, the landlord, after taking the appropriate legal action, is entitled to retain these trade fixtures.

Condemnation – The process of taking private property, without the consent of the owner, by a governmental agency, for public use through the power of eminent domain.

Eminent Domain – A power of the state, municipalities, and private persons, or corporations authorized to exercise functions of public character to acquire private property for public use by condemnation, in return for just compensation.

Traditional Fixtures – In the restaurant, bar, and nightclub business, there are different interpretations, normally spelled out in the lease, for which fixtures a tenant can remove at the expiration of their lease, and which they must leave behind for the landlord. As a rule, any fixture attached to the building such as a hood-and-duct system, sinks, some forms of built-in shelving, walk-in refrigerators that are not prefabricated. etc., belong to the landlord. However, in most cases, if you are building a freestanding bar top with refrigeration included in the structure, the tenant can remove this item as long as they properly cap off all plumbing lines and refrigeration lines. In order to minimize confusion, it is best to spell out in the lease which fixtures belong to the tenant and which belong to the landlord.

Destruction of Premises – A damage or destruction clause in a landlord-tenant lease agreement defines the rights and obligations of the parties to the lease in the event that the leased premises are damaged or destroyed during the term of the lease. The damage or destruction clause serves the following purposes –

1. Notice and Repair Timeframes. A damage or destruction clause will state the tenant's obligation to notify the landlord of a casualty, and identify the landlord's timeframe for repairing the damaged premises.

2. When to Repair the Premises, When to Terminate the Lease. A damage or destruction clause will identify when a landlord is obligated to repair the premises, and when one (or both) parties may choose to terminate the lease.

3. Abatement of Rent During Repairs. A damage or destruction clause will also entitle the tenant to an abatement of rent for the period in which the landlord makes repairs to the premises.

4. Consequences of Tenant's Casualty. A damage or destruction clause will also state the consequences of a casualty caused by a tenant or the tenant's agents. Above definition taken from Contract Standards Destructions of Premises – www.contractstandards.com.

Hazardous waste – This is waste that is dangerous or potentially harmful to our health or the environment. Hazardous wastes can be liquids, solids, gases, or sludges. They can be discarded commercial products, such as cleaning fluids or pesticides, or the byproducts of manufacturing processes.

Default – The general failure to perform a legal or contractual duty or to discharge an obligation when due. Some specific examples are – 1) Failure to make a payment of rent when due, and 2) The breach or failure to perform any of the terms of a lease agreement.

Deposit Refunds – This clause states that if the tenant, at the end of the term of his lease, has left the premises in the same condition as he received it at the beginning of his lease—with normal wear and tear, and he has met all the terms and conditions of his lease, then he will get the security deposit back at the end of the lease. Conversely, if the tenant has not met all the terms and conditions of the lease, and/or have left the premises in unsatisfactory physical condition, then the landlord can keep the tenant's deposit, and in some cases, go after the tenant if extensive damage was done to the premises.

Attorney Fees – In a lease, it is spelled out that if there is legal action taken by either the tenant or landlord, the legal fees must be paid by each respective party. Many leases state that if there is a legal action, the losing party must pay for the winning party's legal fees.

Hold Over Tenant/Holding Over – A tenant retaining possession of the leased premises after the expiration of a lease.

Heirs, Assigns, Successors – A Successors and Assigns clause determines whether the parties' successors and assigns are subject to the benefits and obligations of the agreement. The clause may seek to a) bind the non-assigning party to perform obligations in the favor of the assignee, and b) bind the assignee to perform in favor of the non-assigning party. It is also sometimes used to determine whether rights and obligations can be assigned, or delegated, and may overlap with clauses titled "assignment" or "parties in interest." This agreement shall be binding upon, and shall inure to, the benefit of the parties and their [permitted] successors and assigns and benefits and binds the parties and their [permitted] successors and assigns. Above definition taken from Contract Standards–Successors and Assigns at www.contractstandards.com.

American Disabilities Act (ADA)– Americans With Disabilities Act passed by Congress in 1994, with intent to provide persons with disabilities accommodations and access equal to, or similar to, that of the general public.

Lessors Liability – This means the potential liability that a landlord may have as a result of some person or someone's property getting hurt as a result of damage to the premises. It is usually spelled out in a lease how damages are handled by the landlord, tenant and/or other persons affected by such damage.

Estoppel Certificate – A signed statement certifying that certain statements of fact are correct as of the date of the statement, and can be relied upon by a third party, including a prospective lender or purchaser.

In the context of a lease, a statement by a tenant identifies that the lease is in effect, and certifies that no rent has been prepaid, and that there are no known outstanding defaults by the landlord (except those specified).

Subordination – A subordination agreement is a written contract in which a lender, who has secured a loan by a mortgage or deed of trust, agrees with the property owner to subordinate the first loan to a new loan. Therefore, in the case of foreclosure, the new loan has priority to be paid ahead of the old loan. The agreement must be notarized and recorded in the county recorder's office. Almost without exception, shopping center leases contain subordination provisions stating that the rights of the tenants, under the leases, will be subject to the rights of any lender whose mortgage affects the shopping center. Generally, if the lease is recorded, or if the tenant takes possession of the premises prior to the recordation of a mortgage on the property, of which the leased premises is a part, the lien of the lease has "priority" over the lien of the mortgage.

A subordination provision changes the priority. The tenant agrees that the lien of its lease will be subordinate to the lien of a mortgage. A landlord generally includes subordination language in its lease in anticipation of the requirement of its lenders. Above definition taken from us.legal.com – landlord/tenant subordination.

Triple Net (NNN) Rent – A lease in which the tenant pays, in addition to rent, certain costs associated with a leased property, which may include property taxes, insurance premiums, repairs, utilities, and maintenances. There are also "Net Leases" and "NN" (double net) leases, depending upon the degree to which the tenant is responsible for operating costs.
Option – An option is a legal tenant's right to extend his occupancy of the premises for a given period of time. For an option to be enforceable, it needs to be in writing, and included as part of the lease. In some cases, the option is personal to the tenant, and the option right cannot be assigned to a proposed new tenant. To make certain that the option is assignable to the new tenant, it is best to state in the assignment agreement that the assignee will have the right to exercise the option, if he is in good standing with the lease. The option language will usually spell out the number of years of the option period, as well as any changes regarding the terms and conditions of the lease that will occur in the option period.

Option periods can vary from as little as 1 to 3 years, to as long as 10 years or more; average is 5 years. Most options keep the same terms and conditions of the lease other than the rent, and the formula for the yearly increase in the rent. If there is not specific language in the option as to what the rent will be, one of two formulas, which are traditionally used, should be stated in the option, and both are tied to the fair market rent for the premises.

One formula that is frequently used is tied to binding arbitration. Binding arbitration is a legal procedure whereby, if the landlord and tenant cannot agree on the fair market rent, they agree to have the fair-market rent determined by the arbitrator whose decision is final, and cannot be appealed. An arbitrator is usually a retired judge (or an attorney) who understands the law. The landlord and tenant are also represented by counsel, each presenting their research as to what they feel the fair-market rent should be; then they present their respective findings to the arbitrator in a formal arbitration. After the arbitrator hears both sides' presentations, he makes a ruling as to what the fair-market rent will be. If the tenant is dissatisfied with the arbitrator's final decision, he has no further obligation to occupy the premises after his lease term expires. He then gives the landlord notice he wishes to vacate, and can remove his trade fixtures. Arbitration is expensive, and can range between $10,000 to $20,000. The arbitrator's cost is split 50/50 between the landlord and tenant, with each party paying his own attorney fees.

The other primary, and generally preferred, method used to determine the fair-market rents is the commercial real estate broker method. The tenant and landlord each choose an experienced commercial real estate broker who has recently completed comparable retail leases in the area of the proposed tenant's site. Each broker comes up with a recommended fair-market value rent, and if the brokers cannot agree on the fair-market rent, the two brokers agree upon a third qualified commercial real estate broker who then determines the fair-market rent. With this method, as in the arbitration method, if the tenant does not agree to the new fair-market rent, he can then give notice to the landlord, vacate the premise at the expiration of this lease, and remove his trade fixtures.

There is specific language in the option section of the lease which spells out what is the minimum and maximum amount of time, prior to the expiration date of the lease, when the tenant is allowed to give written notice to the landlord. He must do it by certified return receipt mail, detailing his interest in exercising the option. For example, it can be no earlier than 360 days before, and no later than 180 days before the expiration of the lease. The 180-day maximum notification time frame regarding the option period is because the landlord wants enough time to find another tenant to rent the space, should the existing tenant decide to vacate. There is usually language in the lease that gives the landlord the right to put up a "for lease" sign, and start showing the space to prospective new tenants a certain amount of time before the lease's expiration date. In some situations, the tenant has the right to have more than one option in the lease. If this is the case, the tenant has to be in good standing prior to exercising each subsequent options, and the terms and conditions for each subsequent option can be different, although they are usually the same. If the tenant has more than one option, and does not exercise the previous option in a timely manner, he loses the right to exercise subsequent options to the lease. Many landlords do not like options because they work primarily to the benefit of the tenant, in terms of trying up the premises. The landlord will not be receptive to a having an option in the lease if he is considering selling his property in the near future and wants to:

- maximize his right to get the highest price for his building,
- have the flexibility to sell the building to an owner/operator, and
- have the ability to deliver the building without a tenant.

Chapter 35

HOW A TENANT CAN NEGOTIATE A GOOD LEASE, AND RENEW IT ON FAVORABLE TERMS

Here are the things a tenant needs to know when negotiating a good tenant's lease:

1. A knowledge of the market rents for comparable restaurant space, obtainable from a real estate broker.
2. A viable concept that will motivate the landlord to lease to the tenant.
3. A business plan that includes the following:
    a. operators tenants resume,
    b. business financial information, including financial projections for the new operation. (The landlord wants to make sure that the tenant has enough working capital to get him through his start-up period with several months of reserve capital to weather any possible unanticipated negative events).
    c. copy of the proposed menu,

    d.   proposed remodeling plans, and

    e.   proposed hours of operation.

4.   A financial package which should include:

    a.   a current personal financial statement,

    b.   two years' most current tax returns,

    c.   a current credit report, and

    d.   a list of at least three business and three personal references.

5.   A history of successful restaurant experience to include:

    a.   past menus,

    b.   financial statements,

    c.   customer testimonials, like complimentary letters andcomment cards, and

    d.   the names, addresses and phone numbers of past landlords.

Here are the things a tenant needs to negotiate a renewal of an existing lease on favorable terms with a landlord:

1.   History with the landlord of being a good tenant, including meeting all of the terms and conditions of the lease, and paying the rent and other occupancy expenses on time.

2.   A knowledge of the market rents for comparable restaurant space.

3.   In negotiating an existing lease, the tenant should do that as far in advance as possible, prior to the lease's expiration date. The closer the tenant gets to the lease's expiration date, the more difficult it could be for the tenant to negotiate favorable terms, since when time passes, usually rents increase. Also the landlord knows that if the tenant wants to continue his business at the same location, the landlord has an advantage in the negotiating process. If the tenant waits till the end of the lease to negotiate extensions, and he can't come to an agreement with the landlord, the tenant could be forced to relocate his business, which could be economically prohibitive. However, if the tenant is in good standing with the landlord, he will have some leverage in renewing his lease. Most landlords would rather work with a known quantity than be at risk with a new tenant, and possibly lose rental income during the period when the old tenant leaves and the new tenant comes in.

Chapter 36

HELPFUL TECHNIQUES IN NEGOTIATING YOUR LEASE

As a former restaurant owner, and now as a restaurant broker who has negotiated over 1,000 leases, I have diverse experience. I thought it would be helpful to discuss some of the most important aspects of negotiating a lease.

1. Yearly Rent Increases – Yearly rent increases should be tied to either pre-negotiated fixed yearly rent increases or the Consumer Price Index (CPI) —with a maximum or ceiling, and preferably no minimum or floor. Typical yearly fixed increases range from 2 to 4%, and yearly CPI adjustments have a ceiling of 5 to 6%. If you have to agree to a floor or minimum, they range in the 2 to 3% range. Needless to say, it is helpful if you can lock your rent in for several years at a time, and have adjustments every 2 to 5 years.

2. Percentage Leases – If the landlord insists on a percentage lease, you should cap the percentage to 5 to 6% of yearly sales. In exchange for a percentage rent, you should negotiate a below-market minimum rent, and have the landlord make a monetary contribution to any remodeling you plan to do. If you have a NNN lease, where you are paying the real estate taxes, building insurance, and common-area expenses (CAM), which includes landscaping, security and other maintenance costs, you should negotiate a recapture provision whereby you can deduct from your percentage rent (dollar for dollar) any of these NNN expenses. For example, if your total rent is $80,000 per year, of which $60,000 is base rent and $20,000 is additional percentage rent, and your NNN expenses are $15,000, you should be able to deduct those $15,000 of NNN expenses from your percentage rent. So instead of paying $95,000 ($60,000 base rent + $20,000 percentage rent +$15,000 NNN expenses = $95,000) a year of base rent plus NNN expenses, you are only paying a total of $80,000 ($95,000–$15,000 of NNN expenses against your percentage rent =$80,000) rent, which is a savings of 16%.

3. Determining Market Rent – If you are negotiating a new lease or renewing a lease, the best way to determine the market rent is to talk to several reputable commercial brokers who do retail restaurant leases in the area of your restaurant. Also, drive around your area and look at "For lease" signs. Call the brokers and ask what the rent is. Then talk to several restaurant owners in your area, asking the amount of their rent. Take an average of the rents you've surveyed, and use this number as a basis for negotiating with the landlord. If you are negotiating a new lease, and have had a good prior track record as an operator, use your background to get the landlord to give you a favorable rent. If you are renewing a lease, capitalize on your past success as a tenant, in terms of paying your rent on time, keeping the premises maintained etc., as a tool to negotiate a favorable rent.

4. Assignment and Sublease Rights – Having the proper language in this section of the lease is extremely important in helping you sell your business. It should include the words, "the landlord will not unreasonably withhold consent" in consenting to an assignment. Additionally, you want to have the right to sublease, and keep any of the excess monies from a prospective sublease (this is called a spread—the difference between the rent you are paying the landlord, and the rent you are receiving from the sublessee, or at the minimum, being able to share this spread 50/50 with the landlord).

5. Options – These are helpful in giving you the added years necessary to operate your business, as well as making it easier to sell your business. Try to get the first year's rent of each term of the option nailed down, so you aren't the victim of runaway rent increases that make it economically unfeasible to operate. If possible, avoid the market rent formula, and try to have the rent tied to a rollover of the Cost of Living (CPI) in the proceeding year. For example, if you have a 5-year base term with a 5-year option, and the rent in the fifth year of the base term is $4000, set up the rent in the first year of the option period so it is tied to CPI (assuming CPI is 3% for the proceeding year, the rent for the first year of the option would be $4,120 or $4000 x 103% = $4,120). Make sure that the options are also assignable.

6. Right of First Refusal – This very helpful tool gives you the right to purchase the building, should the landlord put the building on the market during your tenancy. The means that if the landlord gets an acceptable offer from a third-party buyer, he has to give you the opportunity to match or exceed that offer, usually between 15 to 30 days from the date this offer is received.

7. Landlord Contributions – Having the landlord contribute capital improvement money to you, based on so many dollars a square foot (e.g., $25 per square foot), is helpful in reducing your initial investment. If the landlord is willing to do this, have it structured so you are not obligated to pay back this contribution through increased rent.

Chapter 37

WHY LANDLORDS WANT TO MAXIMIZE THEIR RENT

It is important for tenants to know what their rent will be as far in the future as possible, in order to determine whether they can afford to stay in the same location, as well as to determine their rent expense for the ensuing years.

Most landlords in the San Francisco Bay area don't want to tie up their properties long term as yearly rent increases have traditionally grown faster than general inflation in the area, and the rent the building generates determines the building's value.

I always recommend to tenants that they have at least a 5-year lease with a 5-year option, and it is best to lock in a realistic formula for determining the rent in the option years.

Frequently the rent in the option period is tied to market rent, meaning the tenant's rent could go up so high that he could no longer afford to stay in the premises.

An example of how rent increases the building's value is illustrated as follows: the current yearly rent for the building is $48,000 per year after expenses before debt. If buildings sell for a 6 cap, the value of the building will be $800,000 ($48,000/.06 cap rate = $800,000). If the income after expenses but before debt service, (if any), for the same building now goes up to $72,000 per year, the value of the building will be $1,200,000 ($72,000 / .06 cap rate = $1,200,000) or a 50% increase in value. This is why landlords want to keep their building rents at market rents.

Put simply, the cap rate is a measure of the return a property's net operating income (income less expenses) will generate as a percentage of its cost. A property that generates $100,000 worth of income from rents after paying for all expenses to own and manage the property (but before paying debt service) would sell at a $1,000,000 price if the cap rate was 10%. ($100,000/10% = $1,000,000).

Steps to the Sale

Chapter 38

THE SELLING PROCESS FROM THE OFFER STAGE THROUGH THE CLOSE-OF-ESCROW STAGE

The items below are important because some of you who buy a business will eventually be selling it, so it is crucial to understand the selling process from both the seller's and buyer's perspective.

1. Receiving the Offer – Once a business has been listed and marketed, and a buyer is interested in acquiring the business, we write up an Asset Purchase Agreement contract that is signed by the buyer, with an initial deposit check attached. The Asset Purchase Agreement contract spells out the terms and conditions of the sale, and contains an expiration date.

2. Responding to the Offer – Upon receipt of the offer, the seller has three options: 1) accept the offer by signing the contract, 2) write a counter offer, changing the terms, or 3) reject the offer by not responding. Once the seller receives the offer, he will have a designated time, spelled out in the contract, to respond. If he doesn't respond in the designated time, the offer will terminate, and any subsequent response will be considered a counter offer.

3. Acceptance of the Offer – Once the offer has been accepted by the seller, the broker puts the initial deposit check into escrow, and the buyer customarily has ten days, or more, to remove the contingencies described below.

4. Removal of Contingencies – Conditions need to be satisfied by the buyer before he increases his deposit to (normally) 10 percent of the sales price, and the actual escrow process begins. The standard contingencies include the following: 1) review of the business's books and records, 2) physical inspection of the premises, and 3) the landlord's approval of assignment of the existing lease, modifying the existing lease or negotiating a new lease with the buyer. In some cases, the transfer of special licenses such as Department of Alcoholic Beverage Control (ABC) license, entertainment license, or approval of the franchisor (if a franchise) are required as additional contingencies. There may be a financing contingency where the buyer has a certain time to acquire necessary third-party financing.

5. Now we will cover the remaining steps necessary to close escrow: 1) the escrow process, 2) obtaining licenses and setting up tax accounts, etc., 3) transferring licenses, 4) taking inventory, and 5) closing escrow.

The Escrow Process

An escrow is a process whereby a third party becomes involved in assisting in the completion of a transaction. The first and second parties to the escrow are buyer and seller and the third party is the escrow company. This is a neutral entity hired by buyer and seller to hold and disburse all monies in the transaction, as well as to perform title procedures to assure that the seller's outstanding creditors will be paid, and that the buyer will receive title free and clear of all liens and encumbrances. The escrow fees are usually paid 50/50 between buyer and seller, and average between $1,200 to $1,500, depending on the size of the transaction. As provided by the Uniform Commercial Code of California, all monies (including consideration for stock inventory) must pass through escrow, and no monies can be released prior to close of escrow.

The escrow process consists of the items listed below:

1. Escrow Instructions – Once an offer is accepted, a copy of the signed offer and the buyer's deposit are submitted to the escrow company. Upon receipt, the escrow company sets up an escrow, issues an escrow number, issues a receipt for the deposit, and generates escrow instructions. Escrow instructions must be signed by all parties and delivered into escrow, together with initial deposits, before the Notice of Bulk Transfer is published or recorded. This document is part of the escrow instructions authorizing the escrow company to publish an announcement in the newspaper regarding the pending sale, giving notice to the seller's creditors to file any outstanding claims they have against the seller into escrow Once the notice is published, creditors have twelve business days to file their claims against the seller into escrow. Any subsequent claims are filed against the seller, after this period.

2. Tax and Lien Clearances   The escrow obtains clearance certificates from the Employment Development Department, State Board of Equalization, Franchise Tax Board and from the county where the business is located. Any secured liens against the business such as equipment leases, seller carry-back notes, etc., must be paid off by the seller at the close of escrow

3. Escrow Closing Papers – The items listed below are included with Escrow Closing Papers:

   A. The Bill of Sale – This document includes a list of all the fixtures and equipment included with the sale.
   B. The Covenant Not to Compete – This document, if applicable in the transaction, prohibits the seller from competing within a certain radius of the subject business for a given period of time. There is

a written agreement, which is signed by the buyer and seller prior to the close of escrow, outlining the terms of the covenant not to compete. Included in the agreement is a statement by the seller that he will not compete in a similar business within a certain radius from the location for so many years.

C. Closing Statement – One is prepared for both the seller and the buyer, and each statement breaks down the total accounting of the transaction, showing the total debits and credits paid by each party. On the closing statement, the following items are prorated: unsecured personal property taxes (taxes paid on the personal property), and rent and real estate taxes, if applicable. The sales tax on the fixtures and equipment is paid by the buyer, who usually allocates the purchase price, subject to approval by the seller. The only portion of the sales price which is subject to sales tax are the fixtures and equipment.

D. Promissory Note – If part of the sales price is being carried back by the seller in the form of a note, escrow draws up a promissory note that is secured by a security agreement (called UCC1), and recorded with the Secretary of State's office. It stays as a lien on the buyer's business until the loan is paid off.

E. Inventory – Saleable inventory includes food, beverages (alcohol and non-alcoholic), paper and cleaning supplies. These are paid for by the buyer, usually at the seller's cost, and an inventory is taken at the close of escrow to determine how much the buyer pays for these items.

F. Liquor License Transfer – If there is a liquor license transfer, the escrow company must confirm that all the money is in escrow before they notify the Department of Alcoholic Beverage Control to complete processing the license transfer. The escrow must be notified that the liquor license has transferred before the escrow is closed.

Licenses, Inventory, and Closing Escrow

The final steps in the selling process are as follows: 1) obtaining licenses and setting up tax accounts, getting insurance in place, etc., 2) transferring licenses, 3) taking inventory, and 4) closing escrow.

1. Obtaining Licenses, Setting Up Tax Accounts, Getting Insurance in Place, etc.– The buyer needs to apply for the following: a) resale permit from the State Board of Equalization, b) an affidavit of Fictitious Business Name with the county clerk, c) Business License with the local governmental office, and d) an Employer's Tax Identification Number with the State of California Employment Development Department. Also the buyer must get his liability insurance in place, and arrange to have the utilities changed to his name at the close of escrow.

2. Transferring Licenses – The Department of Alcoholic Beverage Control License (ABC) is transferred during the escrow process. The broker or ABC expeditor handles this process, which typically takes about 6 to 8 weeks. They work closely with the buyer and ABC investigator through the entire process to assure that the license will be transferred in an expeditious manner. If this is a club sale, entertainment licenses and dance licenses need to be transferred. If this is a brewpub sale, special alcohol manufacturing licenses need to be transferred, which would also be handled by the broker or ABC expeditor. Also if this is a franchise sale, they need to get the franchisor's approval of the proposed franchisee.

3. Taking Inventory – If saleable inventory (food, beverage, cleaning and paper supplies) is being transferred, a physical inventory is taken by the buyer and seller immediately before the close of escrow. Saleable inventory is paid to the seller at seller's cost, in addition to the purchase price. An inventory of the fixtures and equipment is also taken by buyer and seller immediately before the close of escrow. This is to assure that all the inventory indicated on the inventory list given to the buyer when the purchase contract was executed is still there. Also the buyer checks all the equipment immediately before the close of escrow to assure that it is in good operating condition.

4. Closing Escrow – Once all of the above items are complete, the buyer calls his broker, and tells us he is ready to close escrow. The broker calls the title company and tells them to close escrow. We instruct the seller to give the buyer the keys, and tell the buyer to immediately change the locks.

Chapter 39

DEALING WITH THE MOST COMMON PROBLEMS RELATED TO THE SALE, AND HOW TO ENSURE A CLOSED ESCROW

Many problems can occur during the sales process, and having closed over 800 escrows, Restaurant Realty has experienced many of these problems. This chapter is to prepare the seller to take a proactive approach in dealing with some of the most common problems. It is also to help them obtain the maximum price for their business, as well as to assure a closed escrow. The most common challenges that occur during the sales process are as follows:

1. problems with the lease and the landlord,
2. incomplete business financial statements,
3. deferred maintenance, and
4. health department violations.

1. Problems With the Lease and the Landlord

This is the most common problem that contributes to a failed escrow. The best way to handle this problem is to deal with it up front. It is best to speak with your landlord early in the game, either before or immediately after you list the business for sale. This way the landlord feels he is part of the sales process from the get-go, and you can assure the landlord that you are going to present only buyer/tenants to him that are operationally and financially qualified. Additionally, you can find out from the landlord what the terms of the new lease are going to be, and you can negotiate with him up front what you perceive to be competitive lease terms for the buyer. There are situations where the landlord will not negotiate reasonable terms and conditions, making it prohibitive to sell the business. If you are the seller, it is best to know up front what the landlord will accept so you do not waste time on a sale that can't occur. If your landlord won't negotiate a reasonable lease with your buyer, you can then implement creative ways to make the best use of your remaining lease term.

2. Incomplete Business Financial Statements

If you are selling a business that is making money, and the buyer is buying the business largely due to the cash flow, you have to provide complete and timely financial statements. You also need to provide the immediate past three years' tax returns, year-end income-and-expense statements, the current year's sales tax returns, and year-to-date income-and-expense statements. Don't put your business up for sale until you have gathered all these items as you may have only one chance to capture a buyer's attention. Even if you are selling a business with unreported sales, or a business that is not profitable, or marginally profitable, it is still important to have accurate income and expense information for the buyer.

3. Deferred Maintenances

First impressions are lasting impressions. It is important that your business shows well when you put it on the market. Make sure all pieces of equipment are in good working order, and if you have equipment in need of repair, either fix it, or remove it from the premises. Make sure all your plumbing, electrical and heating, air conditioning and ventilation systems are in good working order. Cleanliness is a key element in a buyer's impression of what he is purchasing, so make sure your entire facility is clean, including the dining room, back of the house, and restroom areas.

4. Health Department Violations

It is the seller's responsibility to pass a change-of-ownership health department inspection prior to the close of escrow. This inspection has a higher standard than a routine health department inspection, and a seller should have this inspection completed by the time the business goes on the market. This allows time to take action to satisfy any heath department corrective issues. If the seller is unable financially or chooses not to bring his business up to standards regarding maintenance and health department issues, the seller should be prepared to adjust the business price accordingly.

Chapter 40

OVERCOMING THE MOST COMMON OBSTACLES IN DEALING WITH THE LANDLORD

From my current experience in negotiating over 1,000 restaurant, bar, and/or club leases, my former experience as a restaurant owner negotiating many leases for myself, and currently as a restaurant landlord, I am very sensitive to the needs of the landlord in qualifying a prospective new tenant.

The major reason deals fail to close escrow is due to the landlord not approving a new tenant, or not coming to an agreement on the terms and conditions of the lease. Landlords are very sensitive to the high failure rate of the restaurant, bar, and club industry, and consequently they want to deal only with prospective tenants who are financially and operationally qualified. Specifically, they want to deal with tenants who have had extensive experience (usually a minimum of 3 to 5 years) in the management and/or ownership of a restaurant, bar, and/or club. Additionally they want a tenant that is financially qualified, which includes a good FICA credit score, usually 680 or above; a strong financial statement, showing a minimum $500,000 net worth, including the tenant owning a home and having adequate cash reserves available, above and beyond the cash required to purchase the business.

In some circumstances, the prospective tenant has a strong operation's background, but may not have the financial qualifications. In order to overcome this problem, the prospective tenant could find a guarantor. A guarantor secures the performance of the lease so that if the tenant gets into trouble, then the landlord can go after the assets of the guarantor to satisfy the economic requirements of the lease.

If the prospective tenant can't find a guarantor, in some cases the tenant can satisfy the landlord by offering a large security deposit. The normal security deposit is one to two times the monthly rent. In the case of a tenant with weaker financials, the tenant will sometimes be asked to come up with as much as 6 months to a year's rent as a security deposit. This means that if the tenant fails, the landlord has enough money in the security deposit to remove the current tenant, to re-lease the space, cover the costs of loss of rent, attorney fees and leasing commissions, and to obtain a replacement tenant. If the tenant doesn't fail, the landlord will usually give back a portion of the security deposit to the tenant after 2 to 3 years of successful performance, and will hold between 2 to 3 months rent as a security deposit for the remaining term of the lease.

Another way to financially satisfy the landlord is to have the current tenant stay on the lease for a certain number of years until the landlord is comfortable that the new tenant has a proven himself successful in meeting the terms of the lease.

Another method landlords use to deal with a prospective tenant with weaker financials is for the tenant to give the landlord a UCC1 security agreement on the fixtures and equipment of the premises. This means that a security agreement (similar to a recorded trust deed on a piece of real estate) is recorded with the Secretary of State. This puts a blanket lien on the fixtures and equipment, ensuring the tenant cannot transfer the assets of the business until this lien is removed by the landlord.

Conversely, if the tenant is strong financially, and weak operationally, the way to overcome this deficit is for the prospective tenant to team up with a strong operational person, giving him/her a piece of the equity tied to the operating results of the business. For a landlord to get comfortable with a prospective operational partner, he will want to see the proposed partner's existing business operation, review the partner's references, the business plan, and the operation's income and expense projections for the first three years of business. He will also review the resumes of all key management personnel for the new business. and review the menu, etc.

Chapter 41

THE MAIN THREE PARTIES IN THE TRANSACTION: THE BUYER, THE SELLER, AND THE LANDLORD

The Buyer

The buyer is the party purchasing the business. He needs to be operationally and financially qualified to purchase the business. The standard operational qualifications for the buyer are at least three to five years of experience working in a restaurant, bar, or nightclub as either an owner or manager.

Experience includes overall management experience, either as a bar manager, dining room manager, kitchen manager, assistant manager or general manager. The buyer also must have completed a comprehensive business plan spelling out his concept, including any physical changes planned to the premises, financial projections, a copy of his resume, and resumes of the management team. The financial qualifications for a buyer include: a FICA score of a minimum of 680, and a net worth, including the value of the buyer's residence of approximately $300,000 or more, depending on the price of the restaurant. Some net-worth requirements may be in excess of $1 million, depending on the size of the deal. The buyer also must have adequate cash (in addition to the sales price and closing costs), to include monies available for reserves, training costs, marketing costs, fees and permits, and remodeling costs, etc.

The strong financial and operational qualifications are for the benefit of all parties in the transaction – the seller, the buyer, and the landlord. Due to the high failure rate in the industry, the seller's landlord wants to assure himself that the buyer will be successful. If the buyer fails, the seller will possibly have to take back the business if there is an assignment of the lease. The seller, as the assignor, has continued lease liability until the initial term of the lease expires. Also, the landlord is concerned that he'll get his rent on a timely basis, and the buyer will be an asset, increasing the value of his building.

If the buyer fails, and a new lease is executed with this buyer, and the seller has no future lease liability, the landlord's recourse will be to evict the buyer, thus costing him legal fees, loss of rent, some potential remodeling costs to prepare the space for re-lease, and a leasing commission to obtain a new tenant.

The Seller

The seller is the owner of the business, and wants to make sure the buyer is financially and operationally qualified before he commits himself to tying up the business with the buyer. This is where careful screening by a restaurant broker is vital. If the buyer is not qualified, and gets into a contract, this could possibly tie up the business for an extended period of time. Additionally, if this is a confidential sale, as most are, and it becomes known to the employees, vendors, competitors, and customers that the business is for sale, this could create problems for the seller. The employees may quit due to lack of job security, and customers may stop frequenting the place due to the uncertainty of the business's future.

Usually the only recourse the seller has against the buyer who doesn't perform, is to threaten him with legal action unless the buyer releases the deposit to the seller. Most often, the deposit represents 10% of the sales price, and it usually does not compensate the seller for the damages he has sustained, in terms of the potential loss of employees and customers, and the potential reduced value of the business.

The Landlord

The landlord owns the building, and has the authority to accept or reject the buyer as a prospective tenant. He must be satisfied that the buyer is operationally and financially qualified, assuring himself that the buyer will perform his responsibilities as the tenant, like paying his rent on time, keeping the leased space in good condition, and meeting all the terms and conditions of the premises lease.

Chapter 42

HOW THE SALES PROCESS WORKS

The sales process is a delicate balance between the needs and requests of the buyer and seller. Added to that is the collaboration and cooperation related to financing and escrow; and the guidance, work, and expertise of the restaurant broker. Here are the steps in detail:

1. Buyer makes offer, and sends us their initial deposit of $1,000 made payable to the escrow company. The uncashed check is held in our office until escrow is opened. If escrow is not opened, the check is returned to the buyer.

2. Once the offer is agreed upon between the buyer and seller, the buyer is sent our "Landlord Package" with information they must prepare to present to the landlord.

3. The buyer usually has 10 days from signing to request any additional information from the seller, and to examine equipment, etc.

4. The restaurant broker contacts the landlord with the buyer's information—financial statement, credit report, resume, etc.— requesting the landlord's approval of them to either do an assignment

of the lease, or get a new lease. This process can take some time. It depends upon the availability of the landlord, and what additional things they request, etc.

5. Once the landlord's response looks promising (and if there is an ABC license to be transferred), we send the necessary forms to the seller for his signatures and have him prepare the necessary diagram. We also send the ABC forms to the buyer, and assist him in completing them.

6. Once the landlord contingency and all other contingencies, such as financing, have been removed, escrow is opened. We mail the escrow company the initial deposit check, and the buyer sends the escrow company his increased deposit.

7. The escrow officer prepares the escrow documents, and mails/emails them to the buyer and seller, along with a demand for the escrow fees.

8. If there is an ABC license to be transferred, we will have the buyer make his appointment with his ABC district office, which usually takes a few days. The restaurant broker will arrange with the seller to get his original forms to the buyer–either directly or by using overnight mailing, rather than Fed Ex-ing them to our office.

9. Once the escrow documents and escrow fees are received by the escrow company, the bulk sale notification is published in the local newspaper.

10. When the buyer goes to his ABC appointment, he is given an official notice that must be posted at the business for 30 days. The seller should prepare his employees for the change in ownership. It is usually a good idea to have a meeting with the buyer and the employees at this time.

11. Unless it is otherwise stipulated, the contract requires that "the seller shall continue to operate the business in the usual way, protect and preserve its assets and goodwill…maintain good relations with suppliers, customers and employees."

12. During this time the buyer will order a "Change of Ownership" Health Department inspection, which is paid for by the buyer. The seller is responsible (unless otherwise stipulated) for whatever repairs are required to satisfy the Health Department.

13. Twenty-one days after the ABC notice is posted, the escrow company will draw up closing documents, and send them to the buyer and seller for their signatures.

14. The buyer must now put the balance of his money, including any prorated expenses (rent, etc.) and security deposit, in escrow.

15. The escrow company will send form 226 to ABC, informing them that all monies are in escrow.

16. The ABC investigator will finish up his file, and turn it over his supervisor who will review it, and if all is okay, send it to Sacramento headquarters. This usually takes about 10 days after the 30 day posting is up. There is no definite date.

17. The buyer and seller need to arrange a meeting (usually the day/night before the ABC license transfers) to do an inventory count—if it so stipulates in the contract. They also need to do a walk-through with the fixtures and equipment list to verify that all listed items are there, and in good working order.

18. The buyer and seller must sign and date a copy of the salable inventory (if applicable), and the fixtures and equipment list, which is then faxed or emailed to the restaurant broker's office before we can authorize the closing.

Chapter 43

EXPLANATION OF THE ASSET PURCHASE AGREEMENT

To better understand what has to be done, and who does it, I will explain some terms.

- **Signing** means the contract has been agreed to, and signed between seller and buyer.
- **SBW** means signed both ways between seller and buyer.
- **COP** means changes of possession. This is when physical control of the premises changes from seller to the buyer. This is usually done at the close of escrow. In some circumstances, the buyer and seller agree to an early possession, whereby, the buyer takes physical possession of the business before the close of escrow.
- **Early Possession** means that in this situation, the buyer and seller agree to the items indicated below, which is memorialized in an addendum to the asset purchase agreement.
  a. The buyer agrees not to make claims to seller regarding defects in the premises, and/or equipment from the time he takes possession.

b. The buyer is responsible for payment of rent and all lease requirements to the landlord as of the date he takes early possession. Payments will be made to the seller, who will, in turn, make the payments to the landlord until the close of escrow, at which time the buyer will make the rent payments directly to the landlord.

c. The buyer will obtain any permits or licenses required to operate the restaurant, including a temporary ABC license.

d. The buyer has deposited all monies in escrow needed to close escrow, including closing costs, escrow fees and security deposit, etc., before taking early possession.

e. The buyer will have liability insurance in place, naming the seller and landlord as the insured, and will submit said endorsement to seller before early possession.

f. The buyer will submit a complete executed lease assignment with buyer's and landlord's signature to the broker.

g. The buyer shall be responsible for all costs and expenses of operating the restaurant from, and after, the date buyer takes possession of the premises.

h. The buyer and seller will execute an Interim Operating Agreement that includes the items indicated below as an integral part of the transaction, and becomes an addendum to the purchase agreement.

    1. The business name, premises address, buyer name, seller name, purchase agreement date, possession date, and closing date.

    2. Possession: Transfer of legal ownership of business to buyer shall occur only upon closing, and not upon any prior possession. During the period between possession and closing, the party in possession shall do all of the following:

        • protect and preserve the business and its assets;

        • conduct the business in the normal manner with due diligence and skill, and make no material changes in the manner of operation;

- retain all business assets at their normal location and use them in the normal manner, except that inventory may be sold in the ordinary course of business with prompt replacement;
- permit the other party to inspect the business and its assets at all reasonable times;
- immediately inform the other party of any developments that may jeopardize the business or any of its assets;
- retain all receipts, and pay all costs applicable to the operation of the business during this period: and
- verify to the other party that liability and business asset protection insurance (with mutually satisfactory amounts) and coverage is in force.

3. Rescission: If the sale is rescinded after possession, and prior to closing, for any reason whatsoever, the buyer shall promptly return possession of the business to seller. The parties shall immediately account to each other for any changes that have occurred during buyer's possession in asset, liabilities, or other conditions of the business. The seller shall be entitled to receive full payment for all costs incurred from the buyer.

We do not usually recommend early possession as it puts the seller in a compromising position. Why? Because the buyer gets possession of the premises; the seller's asset—and the seller does not get the money until the close of escrow. If something goes wrong in the business during the early possession stage, even if the buyer agrees in writing not to come after the seller, inevitably something will come up in the early possession period which will undoubtedly cost the seller money. Another concern is that if the buyer dies or gets severely injured and can't close the escrow, it becomes messy trying to unwind the deal and have the seller take back possession of the premises.

- Closing – This is also known as the "close of escrow," when 1) all the paperwork has been completed, 2) the tax clearances have been received from all taxing agencies, indicating all of seller's taxes have been paid, and 3) all monies are ready to be disbursed to the parties, including vendors, brokers and the seller. In California, per state law, when there is an alcoholic beverage license transferring as a condition of the escrow, the license must transfer from the seller to the buyer before the escrow can close. Before the close of escrow, the premises lease documents are signed, all equipment lease or rental agreements have been transferred to the buyer, the buyer has his liability insurance in place, and all his tax accounts have been set up.

- Inventory – When we discuss inventory in the contract, we are talking about saleable inventory—food, beverage, cleaning and paper supplies, which are paid for in addition to the purchase price. On the close of escrow, a physical inventory is taken between both buyer and seller, and the buyer pays for the inventory at the seller's cost.

- A not-to-exceed amount is written into the contract at the time the contract is signed, and if the saleable inventory turns out to be more than this not-to-exceed amount, the buyer can reject it and have the seller take the excess inventory, or the buyer can buy it at the seller's cost.

- Assets – Assets of the business include, but are not limited to, any equipment, trade fixtures, property lease, leasehold improvements, contract rights, business records (with seller retaining a reasonable right of inspection), software and software licenses, other licenses, franchises, goodwill, covenant not to compete, trade secrets, patents, intellectual property, trade name, telephone and fax numbers, websites, email addresses and inventory. Assets being sold shall not include bank accounts, deposits, cash, financial records (but the buyer shall have a right to make copies prior to closing).

The Purchase Price Section

Initial Deposit – Usually a nominal amount between $1,000 to $5,000, this initial deposit is traditionally held by the broker until the contingencies are removed. In order to have a binding contract, it is necessary to have consideration, and the initial deposit serves as that consideration.

Increased Deposit – This amount with the initial deposit usually equals 10% of the sales price, and as soon as the contingencies are removed (other than the alcoholic beverage license transfer contingency), the initial deposit and increased deposit are put into escrow. Once the deposits are put into escrow, the escrow papers are signed, and the escrow process begins. When the escrow process has begun, if the buyer tries to back out of the deal, he becomes liable for damages unless he has acceptable grounds. No money can be removed from escrow, prior to the close of escrow, unless both buyer and seller agree in writing.

a. The remaining cash required in the deal – When there is an alcoholic beverage license transfer involved as part of the transaction, we ask that the buyer put his remaining money into escrow in the form of a cashier's check made payable to the escrow company. He needs to do this no later than 21 days after the alcoholic beverage license has been posted. This allows adequate time for the alcoholic beverage control to transfer the license in a timely manner.

b. If there is no alcoholic beverage license involved, the buyer's money in the form of a cashier's check made payable to the escrow company, is usually due in escrow no later than two days before the close of escrow.

c. Additional money from third-party financing – If the buyer is going to get third-party financing, both the time frame for getting his letter of commitment, and for getting the loan funded, is spelled out in the contract. The normal time frames are 15 days from acceptance to get a letter of commitment, and somewhere between 30 to 45 days to get the loan funded.

d. Assumption of a note balance – If the buyer is going to assume an existing loan, such as an equipment lease, the balance of the loan being assumed, and the interest rate, are spelled out in the contract. If the balance of the loan is less than anticipated at the close of escrow, the difference is usually made up of cash put into the deal by the buyer.

Seller carry-back note – If the seller is going to carry-back part of the financing, the amount of the loan, the interest rate, the term of the loan, and monthly payments are spelled out in the contract. This loan is usually secured by the assets of the business, and in California this is done with a UCC1 security agreement recorded with the Secretary of the State. This loan can usually be prepaid without penalty, and is personally guaranteed by the buyer. The loan documents are usually prepared by the escrow company.

Saleable Inventory Count – During the early stages of the transaction, the operator reviews the quality and quantity of the saleable inventory— food , beverage, papers and cleaning supplies—to determine if he is interested in purchasing any of this inventory at the close of escrow. If so, there is a not-to-exceed amount indicated on the purchase contract so the operator does not get stuck with excess inventory he does not need. Saleable inventory is sold to the operator at the seller's cost when he purchased the inventory, and the buyer and seller take a physical inventory at the close of escrow, and the seller produces his purchase invoices to support the actual cost of the saleable inventory. At times, if the parties agree, they hire a outside inventory specialist to count the inventory.

Accounts Receivable – Generally most restaurant, bar, and nightclub businesses do not have accounts receivable, but if they do, the amount of the collectable accounts receivable would be determined and transferred to the buyer, and would be part of the price consideration. If the total of the collectable accounts receivables varies from the purchase price, the down payment would be adjusted accordingly. If the collectable accounts receivable were higher at the close of escrow than originally anticipated, the cash down at the close would be adjusted lower. If the collectable accounts receivable at the close of escrow were less than originally anticipated, then the cash at the close of escrow would be adjusted upward.

Gift Certificates – At times, in a restaurant transaction, gift certificates have been issued, and the buyer customarily wants to accept them so he maintains goodwill with customers, and doesn't alienate a future customer. Because gift certificates are prepaid, the seller already has received the monies from them, and the normal redemption rate is approximately 50%.

So if $5,000 in outstanding gift certificates were issued by the seller at the close of escrow, the buyer would get a credit of $2,500 (50% redemption rate). This would be a credit to the buyer on his closing statement at the close of escrow.

Purchase Price Allocation – During the escrow period, the buyer determines how he wishes to allocate the purchase price for tax purposes. The rules of thumb for price allocation are as follows: fixtures and equipment can be written off over seven years; goodwill and covenant not to compete can be written off over fifteen years; and lease-hold improvements can be written off over 39 years. In California, the only component of the sales price subject to sales tax for the buyer, is fixtures and equipment, which are taxed at the sales tax rate based on rate of the city where the asset is being purchased. This tax is a one-time charge paid at the close of escrow. For example, if the buyer allocates $100,000 of the purchase price towards fixtures and equipment, and the local sales tax rate is 8.5%, the sales tax will be $8,500 ($100,000 fixtures and equipment allocation amount times 8.5% = $8,500 sales tax).

Also, the amount allocated toward fixtures and equipment is part of the basis the county uses to calculate the buyer's annual unsecured personal property tax—which is approximately 1% of the sales price allocated to fixtures and equipment. So in the above example, the yearly unsecured personal property tax the buyer would have to pay would be $1,000 ($100,000 x 1% = $1.000 yearly unsecured personal property tax). Once the buyer determines the price allocation, it is reviewed with the seller. There could be circumstances where the seller's tax situation is not compatible with the buyer's price allocation, and they may need to adjust the buyer's allocation to accommodate the seller's needs. The seller does not want the buyer to allocate very much of the sales price towards the covenant not to compete, as this category is taxable at ordinary income tax rates, unlike the other components of the sales price, which are taxed at capital gain tax rates.

Conditions Section

This section deals with the conditions that need to be satisfied by the buyer before the buyer moves forward in the transaction, and begins the escrow process. The time frame for the buyer to remove these conditions is usually 10 to 15 days from acceptance. It is spelled out in the contract whether these conditions need to be signed off in writing. If not, they are considered approved by the buyer, unless he gives contrary written notice to the seller within so many days. It has to be stated in the contract that the buyer does not approve.

The normal conditions in this section are as follows:

a. Physical inspection of the premises – The buyer has the right to bring though the premises various building-related parties such as plumbing, electrical or general contractors, food facility engineers (who design and layout kitchen equipment), architects, or others needed to check out the physical premises.

b. Review of books and records – The buyer usually wants to review three years of the business's tax returns, including the year-end income-and-expense statements, the current year's sales tax returns, including a year-to-date income-and-expense statement. Additionally, the buyer will want the right to have his bookkeeper or accountant go through the seller's books and record to review invoices, sales forms, and other material related to the income and expense history of the business. This includes all contracts, the premises lease, equipment lease or rental agreements if applicable, franchise agreement if applicable, and the seller's disclosure statement.

c. In addition to the above, the landlord's approval of the buyer, and the buyer's satisfaction with the lease terms and conditions, set the requirements for the buyer.

d. Additionally, if there is a loan contingency from a third party, this is also a condition for the buyer.

e. Transfer of alcohol license

f. Transfer of other licenses

g. Approval by franchisor, if applicable

Escrow – This section states who the escrow company will be, that all parties will cooperate with the escrow, and the broker will be a party to the escrow and to the payment of any broker's fee.

Sellers and Buyer's Disclosure Statement – This section states that the buyer will review and sign the seller's disclosure statement, and the seller will review and sign the buyer's disclosure statement, no later than three days after acceptance of the contract.

Representations and Warranties – This section acknowledges that the seller makes the following representations to be true at the time of the close of escrow. If there is any change in these warranties, prompt notice will be given to the buyer, and the seller's disclosure statements shall be amended to reflect these changes, and then signed by both buyer and seller. Seller further agrees to indemnify and hold the buyer and broker harmless for any misrepresentations made regarding these warranties.

The seller is running the business per all the laws and regulations that operators are required to abide by, and the business will pass all applicable inspections upon change of possession.

Getting the Proper Clearances from Governmental Agencies – Before closing escrow, it is essential that the buyer gets clearance from all the governmental agencies that regulate the business—the health department, fire department, and building and planning departments. Specifically, when a restaurant, bar, or nightclub is in the process of being sold, the health department uses this opportunity to require that the business's physical premises are brought up to current code requirements. It is usually the seller's responsibility to bring the existing premises up to code (per the health department's change of ownership inspection completed during the escrow process). Any physical changes made to the premises by the buyer, after the close of escrow, are the buyer's responsibility to meet the health departments requirements associated with this remodeling.

It is important for the buyer to have a sign-off by the fire department before the close of escrow. This inspection includes: having the proper egress and ingress area; compliance with maintaining the required customer-capacity requirements; having the proper fire protection equipment, including current fire extinguishers; a fire-suppression system over all the cooking equipment; and fire sprinklers, if applicable. The buyer needs to check with the building department to make sure all the building's mechanical, electrical and plumbing systems meet code requirements, and that the business meets disabled requirements. The American Disabilities Act (ADA) mandates that the requirements for disabled customers include egress and ingress requirements, and access requirements to restrooms and all other public areas in the facility. In most cases, the existing premises need to get clearances from these agencies before the close of escrow to protect the buyer, unless an "as-is" clause is negotiated in the purchase contract. That clause spells out specifically that the buyer is buying the business in its "as-is" condition, and the buyer is responsible for meeting all governmental clearances.

a. No claims and investigations are pending which will effect the business assets being sold. This means the business will close escrow free and clear of all liens and encumbrances, and there are no pending lawsuits which could effect the title of the business being sold.

b. All of the lease and contract requirements related to the ownership and operation of the business are complete, and have been disclosed to the buyer, and there are no undisclosed amendments.

c. Similarly to above, all of the financial record and information are complete and accurate as of the date these statements were prepared. In some transactions, there is unreported income that should be disclosed to the buyer. If the buyer is counting on the undisclosed income to be a material part of the financial performance of the business, the buyer needs to complete his own due diligence with the seller to receive supporting documentation, such as food servers' guest checks and cash register tapes, to support any unreported income.

d. All accounts receivable are from the business, none of them have been pledged, and they are fully collectable

e. All assets used by the business are free from liens and encumbrances, and are in good working condition. This means that at the close of escrow, no liens are against the equipment, and the buyer will test all the equipment immediately, before close of escrow, to make sure it is in good working condition. If it is in not good working condition, the seller will either repair the equipment, or give the buyer a credit for repairing the equipment before close of escrow. The only exception to this clause will be if the purchase contract states that the business is being sold in its "as-is" condition, and it specifically states in the contract which pieces of equipment are not in good working order.

f. Seller does not guarantee that all employees will remain employed after transfer of ownership, but the seller has no knowledge that employees (other than owner or owner's relatives) will leave after the business has been sold. In many situations, the employees need their jobs and don't want to relocate to another business, if they are happy working there. If the new buyer is postured properly with the employees before the close of escrow, he has a strong chance they will stay on and give him a chance. If the employees are told that the new buyer is going to make improvements to the business, thus increasing business, this will create excitement for the employees who will want to stay on with new owner.

Continuity – This section states that the seller will continue to run the business operation in the same way it was run at the time the parties got into contract. Additionally, the seller will maintain its goodwill and assets, as well as maintain good relations with vendors, employees, and customers. He will also allow the buyer to make reasonable inspections throughout the escrow period. In some situations with business escrows the seller cannot maintain the continuity of the business due to the following potential situations: a.   the seller is in poor health, b. the seller has lost key employees, c. the business is generating unsustainable operating losses and d. the seller has other personal problems. Under these circumstances, the seller is responsible for notifying the buyer regarding this, before the business is closed, and these conditions should be memorialized in writing as an amendment to the purchase contract, and signed by both parties.

Also, in these circumstances where the lease specifically states that the business is required to operate for minimum operating hours, especially in shopping centers, it is important for the seller to notify the landlord before he closes the business. This ensures that a closure won't be a breach of the premises lease, whereby the seller could lose his lease, and not be able to sell the business.

Taxes and Expenses

On the escrow closing statement, many of the operating expenses—such as utilities, personal property taxes, other taxes, insurances and other operating expenses—will be prorated at the change of possession. Also, the buyer is responsible for reimbursing the seller for any deposits the seller has made such as: security deposit to the landlord, utility company, or a deposit on an equipment lease. The seller is then credited on the escrow closing statement for these items, and the buyer is debited for these items on his escrow closing statement.

If, after the close of escrow, the buyer receives refunds for overpayments on any bills, including workers compensation, taxes, or vendor bills that were for the period prior to the close of escrow, it is the buyer's responsibility to remit these refunds to the seller.

Each party is responsible for his operating expenses while they were in possession of the business. In other words, any bills that were generated by the seller, prior to the buyer taking possession of the business, are the responsibility of the seller, and any bills that were generated after the buyer took possession of the premises, are the buyer's responsibility.

License fees such as alcohol licenses, business licenses, or franchise fees shall not be prorated, and the buyer shall pay any transfer or issue fees for permits and licenses required.

- The buyer and seller split the escrow fees and costs, and other transfer costs 50/50, unless agreed to otherwise. Each party pays his own attorney, accountants, and other consultants.
- The buyer is responsible for paying the sales tax on the fixtures and equipment.

Part of the escrow process is for escrow to get tax clearances for the buyer from the California Employment Development Department, the California Franchise Tax Board. The California State Board of Equalization and from the county where the business is located. This is for all business activities generated by the seller during the seller's possession of the business, through the close of escrow. The seller further holds the buyer harmless for any liability from these agencies during the period of time it operated the business, through the close of escrow. The escrow will hold back reserves from the seller for projected taxes owed to these agency, until such time as the escrow receives written releases from these agencies that the seller has paid them in full.

Miscellaneous Leases, Etc. – This section states that if any leases are going to be assumed by the buyer at the close of escrow, such as equipment leases, advertising contracts, vending machine contracts, etc., the specific leases that will be assumed are detailed. It is best to present copies of all these lease agreements to the buyer during the conditions period so the buyer can be privy to all the details of these leases. If the buyer finds a problem with any of these leases, he should not remove the contingencies until he is satisfied. If not, the purchase price will be adjusted accordingly.

Closing Date – This sections spells out the approximate closing date, and states that the seller and buyer will make their best efforts to close on that date, or earlier. This section also states that the change of possession will be at closing. In earlier discussion, the only exception to this is early possession, as discussed in Chapter 43. Also, if there is an ABC license transfer involved as part of the transaction, it is very difficult to project the exact closing date as it could take weeks or months, to transfer the license. This depends on the competency of the investigator, the degree of follow up with the buyer to make sure all the required items are submitted on time to the ABC office, and includes the buyer putting his money in escrow on a timely basis. As discussed earlier, per California law, the escrow cannot close until the ABC license has transferred. If no ABC license is involved, there can be a "date certain"—a specific date targeted as the escrow close date—near the close of escrow date. Once the bulk sales has begun, and the notice of publication regarding the sale has been published in the newspaper, the creditors have 12 business days to put their claims into escrow. Once this 12 business day period is over, the escrow can close.

Broker – This is a section which holds the broker harmless; the buyer and seller indemnify the broker. Furthermore, both buyer and seller must look to one another for any legal claim for misrepresentations made by either party. Examples would be the seller's misrepresenting the financial statements, business records, contracts, or any other pertinent facts regarding the business to the buyer, and the buyer misrepresenting his financial and operating qualifications to the seller.

Also stated in this section is that the broker may receive a referral fee from an institutional lender, if the broker is responsible for putting a lender together with a buyer, which leads to funding a loan for the specific transaction that results in the sale of the business.

Training – The purchase contract spells out the amount of training the seller will provide the buyer. Most training is done by the seller immediately after the close of escrow, as it is confusing to the employees to have the seller and buyer working together before the close of escrow. This can create split loyalties, in terms of the employees responding to the buyer and ignoring the seller, or the employees playing the buyer against the seller, creating a chaotic business environment. Most training includes an orientation of the operational, financial, administrative, and marketing functions of the business, specifically: a detailed review of all the personnel, hiring and firing procedures, scheduling procedures, ordering procedures, preventative maintenance, repairs and maintenance procedures, accounting, bookkeeping and banking procedures. Training for all the standard operating procedures regarding the back of the house, includes all cooking and preparation procedures and plate set ups, and front-of-the-house procedures regarding guest check accountability, customer recognition procedures, all drink and salad set-up procedures, etc.

Covenant Not to Compete – An agreement needs to be included in the purchase agreement that states that the seller cannot directly or indirectly compete in a similar business for a given period of term within a given radius from the business being sold. Common time periods and radiuses for this section are 5 years and 5 miles respectively, but these periods and radiuses can vary dramatically depending on the individual location. For example, in San Francisco the distance spelled out could only be a few blocks, but in remote areas, the radius clause could be 25 to 50 miles, or even a non-compete in certain counties. Part of the sales price allocation includes a portion of the sale price assigned to the value of the covenant not to compete. The covenant not to compete is very important to assure that the buyer is protected regarding the business's customer base, menu and concept the operator is purchasing.

Mediation of Disputes – This states that if there is a disagreement in the transaction between buyer and seller that cannot be settled between them, the parties will mediate their differences before pursuing an arbitration or court action. The mediation will be confidential. If the parties cannot agree on a mediator within 30 days of the first party seeking mediation, the Superior Court judge of the county, in the appropriate venue for filing the complaint, will pick a mediator.

Brokers Fees – This section states who (the buyer or seller) the broker is representing in the transaction, and what is his compensation. The section also explains that if either the buyer or seller breaches this contract, they are liable to the broker for his sales commission.

Summarizing this section: The entire agreement of the parties, relating to the sale of the business, is set forth in the Asset Purchase Agreement, and can only be modified in writing, and signed by the parties. There are no other representations, agreements, arrangements, or understandings, either oral or written, between or among the parties relating to the subject matter of this Agreement that are not fully expressed. This Agreement shall bind and benefit the parties and their legal successors, and shall supersede any prior written or oral agreements. This Agreement may be signed in counterparts (faxed and electronic signatures may be considered as originals). Captions in this Agreement are for convenience only, and shall not be considered in construing its meaning. In any action, proceeding, or arbitration between buyer and seller arising out of this Agreement, the prevailing party shall be entitled to reasonable attorney's fees and costs.

Acknowledgment and Personal Guarantee: Here the buyer and seller each acknowledge that they have carefully read, and fully understand, the Asset Purchase Agreement and have received a copy of it. The parties warrant that their signatures are legally sufficient to bind the buyer and seller. If the buyer and/or seller is a corporation or other entity, the parties signing the agreement personally guarantee the performance of this Agreement, and any other agreements necessary to complete the purchase.

Acceptance: This section states that the offer shall expire, by a certain time and date, unless it is accepted in writing by seller, and that acceptance is communicated by fax or personal delivery to buyer or buyer's agent. Any later acceptance shall constitute a counteroffer. Also, this section states that an offer can be withdrawn or revoked before acceptance is properly communicated to buyer or buyer's agent.

Asset Purchase Agreement

INTRODUCTION: This is an offer and an agreement to buy and sell business assets, dated _____

A.   DEFINITIONS: The following definitions and designations shall apply regardless of number or gender:

BUSINESS _____

Address _____ City, State Zip _____

BUYER _____ SELLER _____

Contact Person _____ Contact Person _____

Phone Fax _____ Phone Fax _____

Email _____ Email _____

Address _____ Address _____

City/State Zip _____ City/State Zip _____

BUYER'S BROKER _____ SELLER'S BROKER _____

Phone _____ Fax _____ Phone _____ Fax _____

Email_____ Email _____

AGENT _____ AGENT _____

SIGNING: Signing of this Agreement by both Buyer and Seller.

COP: Change of possession of business assets from Seller to Buyer

CLOSING: Transfer of ownership of business assets from Seller to Buyer

INVENTORY: Current raw materials, work in progress, saleable finished goods and consumable supplies valued at lower of cost or market

ASSETS: Assets of the Business include, but are not limited to, any equipment, trade fixtures, leasehold, leasehold improvements, accounts receivable, contract rights, business records (with Seller retaining a reasonable right of inspection), software and software licenses, other licenses, franchises, goodwill, covenant not to compete, trade secrets, patents, intellectual property, trade name, customer lists, telephone and fax numbers, web sites, email addresses, inventory and backlog. Assets being sold shall not include bank accounts, deposits, cash, 1inancial records (but Buyer shall have a right to make copies prior to Closing), or _____ .

SALES ORDER BACKLOG: The sum of all unfulfilled sales orders at net invoice amount.

GROSS PROFIT MARGIN: Gross profit divided by revenue expressed as a percentage based on the most recent Federal Tax Return

B.   SALE OF BUSINESS ASSETS: Seller agrees to sell to Buyer and Buyer agrees to buy from Seller the Assets for the price and on the terms and conditions set forth below.

C.   CONSIDERATION: The total consideration shall be paid or credited as follows:

1. $ _____   as a deposit by Buyer upon signing this Agreement andI included as part of the down payment" Broker is authorized to:

2. $ _____   additional deposit upon opening of escrow, also included inthe down payment"

3. $ _____   additional down payment to be deposited in escrow in cash or cash equivalent days before Closing"

4. $ _____   additional down payment provided from third party financing as described in paragraph 6rd"

5. $ _____   O Total Down Payment

6. $ _____   assumption of a note payable to with monthly payments of (Estimated Closing costs will also be deposited) remaining as of Closing. If the actual balance differs at Closing, ____the note to the Seller, or ____the down payment, shall be adjusted

7. $ _____   approximate balance of a non-negotiable Seller note payable in equal monthly installments, including per month), with payments to begin one month from. Note shall be secured by a security agreement on the Assets with right of offset, contain a right to prepay without penalty and be assumable with Seller's consent, which shall not unreasonably be withheld" Seller note shall be subordinated to any third-party 1inancing described in 6.d"

8. $ _____   Total Consideration

Business _____ Buyer _____ Date _____

INVENTORY, ACCOUNTS RECEIVABLE and BACKLOG:
　　The consideration shall include Inventory of $ _____ at cost and collectable accounts receivable of $ _____ . If the actual amount of Inventor) and accounts receivable at COP is less than the total of these figures, the consideration and down payment shall be decreased accordingly, and if the actual amount is more than these figures, then the consideration and note due Seller shall be increased accordingly., If the amount has increased and there is not a note due to Seller, Buyer shall execute a non-negotiable promissory note to Seller with night of offset and right to prepay without penalty, payable in equal monthly installments, including % per annum interest computed from COP, so as to fully amortize over _____ months, with payments to begin one month from COPA. Note shall otherwise contain the same provisions as the note described in 3.g above, or
　　The Inventory at cost shall be paid for at Closing in addition to the total consideration above.,
Notwithstanding the above, the inventory shall not (and the Buyer can reject any part of the Inventory over that amount) or be less than .i The Inventory count shall be made on COP　　by Buyer and Seller, or　　by an independent inventory service, with the fees to be divided equally between Buyer and Seller., Work in progress and finished goods shall be valued at the actual cost of material and direct labor incurred by Seller.
　　If the Sales Order Backlog (if applicable) at Closing is less than the Sales Order Backlog at Signing, then the purchase price and down payment shall be reduced by the difference multiplied by the Gross Proñt Margin"

SELLERS AND BUYER'S DISCLOSURE STATEMENTS:
a.　Buyer has received and read the completed Sellers Disclosure Statement, or
　　Seller shall provide to Buyer the completed Sel|er's Disclosure Statement within three days after Signing"
b.　Seller has received and read the completed Buyer's Disclosure Statement, or
　　Buyer shall Seller the completed Buyers Disclosure Statement within three days after Signing.
The parties warrant the accuracy and completeness of their respective Disclosure Statements. The parties warrant that these representations are true, shall be true as of Closing and shall survive Closing.

CONDITIONS: This Agreement is subject to the following conditions:
a. Buyer's due diligence:
　　i: Within _____ days of signing Bwer shall request in writing any and all information and an appointment(s) for access to inspect the premises as may reasonably be required evaluate the Business`
　　ii.Within_____ days of Buyer's request Seller shall provide all requested information and accessi.
　　iii. Within_____ days of Buyer's receipt Buyer shall have reviewed and approved in writing information requested and provided"
b. Seller's due diligence:
　　i. Within_____ days of signing Seller shall request in writing any and all information as may reasonably be required to evaluate Buyer's qualifcations to purchase and operate the Business"
　　ii. Within _____ days of Seller's request Buyer shall provide all requested information
　　iii. Within _____ days of Seller's receipt Seller shall have reviewed and approved in writing information requested and provided.,
Should either party not approve in writing, as provided in 6 al. iii or 6 br iii, as applicable, within the time specitied, the other party may terminate this agreement with written notice and the other party's failure to cure within 48 hours of such notice"
c. Lease contingency:
　　The written consent of the landlord to assignment of the existing premises lease, or
　　The making of a new lease between the landlord and the Buyer which is acceptable to the Buyer within COP if sooner
d. Financing contingency:
　　i. Buyer receiving a commitment letter for third party financing in the amount of $ _____ within _____ days after signing
　　ii. Buyer receiving funding in the amount indicated in 6d. within _____ days after Signing.
Buyer shall use its best efforts to obtain said financing and Seller shall fully and promptly comply with lender requests for information and to inspect the Business.
If Buyer is unable to satisfy the conditions in or within the specified time limits, either party may terminate this Agreement by giving written notice to the other party's Broker,
e. Other contingencies: (Liquor license, franchise agreement, etc.) _____
_____ .

ESCROW: The purchase and closing adjustments shall be paid through an escrow to be established with _____
_____
the escrow holder. Separate escrow instructions shall be signed to define the duties of the parties and the
escrow holder" All parties shall cooperate with the escrow holder in completing any documents and performing any acts necessary to complete the transfer of the Business Assets. The Broker is a party to the escrow as to the payment of any broker's fees and an irrevocable assignee of the sale proceeds to the extent of such fees.

PURCHASE PRICE ALLOCATION: Before Closing, Buyer and Seller shall endeavor to allocate the purchase price among the Assets purchased and submit the allocation to escrow"

REPRESENTATIONS AND WARRANTIES: Except as noted in paragraph 91, Seller and its owners acknowledge and represent as follows:
a. Seller is operating the Business in compliance with all applicable laws, environmental regulations and contracts. This compliance will not be violated by this sale and the Business will pass all applicable inspections upon COP. If a Change of Possession Health Inspection is required to consummate this Agreement, Seller shall make whatever repairs are required to satisfy said inspection, and if repairs are not complete and paid for by Closing, then sufficient monies shall be held in Escrow to fundA and or pay for the completion of such repairs
b. There are no claims or investigations pending which would affect the Business or Assets being sold.
c. All leases and contracts relevant to the ownership and operation of the Business and furnished to Buyer are complete and in effect, and there are no undisclosed amendments.

Page 2 of 4

Business _____ Buyer _____ Date _____

d. All the financial information and statements furnished or to be furnished to Buyer are complete, accurate, prepared in a manner consistent with prior statements and fairly present the financial condition of the Business as of the dates stated on them. Since the date of the last financial statements furnished, there have been no material adverse changes in the aggregate in the assets, liabilities, revenues, expenses or any other items shown on such statements.

e. All accounts receivable of the Business arose from the normal course of business, none have been previously assigned and they are fully collectabler

f. All resale Inventory of the Business is marketable and in good condition"

g. All Assets currently used in the Business are owned by Seller free from liens and encumbrances, and they are in good working condition, except as otherwise noted in 9. i.

h. Seller does not guarantee that all current employees will remain employed in the Business after Closing, but Seller has no knowledge indicating that any employee who is not an owner would leave in the event of a sale"

i. Exceptions: _____
_____

Seller warrants that these representations are true, shall be true as of Closing and shall survive Closing l Prompt notice will be given to Buyer of any event which materially alters the accuracy of the above Seller Representations and Warranties or Seller`s Disclosure Statement" Seller shall indemnify and hold Buyer and Broker harmless from any damage resulting from their falsityi.

CONTINUITY: Pending Closing, the Seller shall continue to operate the Business in the usual way, protect and preserve its Assets and goodwill, maintain good relations with suppliers, customers and employees and allow the Buyer to make reasonable inspections

TAXES and EXPENSES: .

a. Utilities, personal property taxes, other taxes, insurance, rent, vacation pay and other expenses of the Business not othen/vise provided for in this Agreement shall be prorated to COP. Buyer shall reimburse Seller at Closing for facility lease deposits and other miscellaneous deposits transferred to Buyer and shall receive a credit from Seller at Closing for any customer deposits and assumed warranty obligations.

b. Buyer shall remit to Seller upon receipt any refund of overpayments of worker's compensation premiums, taxes, trade payables or the like which relate to the period prior to COP.

c. Except as otherwise noted in this Agreement, each party shall pay when due all operating costs incurred while that party is in possession and hold the other party harmless therefrom.

d. Any liquor or other license or franchise fees shall not be prorated and Buyer shall pay any transfer or issue fees for permits and licenses required

e. The Buyer and Seller shall pay equally all escrow fees and costsl and other transfer costs except _____
_____

f. The Buyer shall pay at Closing any sales taxes assessed on the sale of the Business Assets.

g. Seller shall hold Buyer harmless from any liability to the California Employment Development Department, the California Franchise Tax Board or the California State Board of Equalization arising from the operation of the Business until Prior to the receipt by the escrow holder of releases of transferee liability from these agencies, the Buyer shall be protected from the possible imposition of transferee liability reserve set by the taxing agencies or approved by the Buyer and retained in escrow until such releases are obtained.

MISCELLANEOUS LEASES, ETC; The Seller shall transfer to Buyer the following contracts used in the operation of the Business, and the Buyer shall assume obligation for them:

- ☐ Alarm system lease or maintenance agreement
- ☐ Telephone system lease or purchase contract
- ☐ Vehicle leases or purchase contracts
- ☐ Vending machine contracts
- ☐ Cell Phone numbers/contracts
- ☐ Other equipment lease(s) or purchase contract(S)
- ☐ Equipment or software maintainence agreements
- ☐ Music Service contract
- ☐ Advertising contract(s), including yellow pages
- ☐ Other: _____

CLOSING DATE: The estimated date for Closing is _____ , 20_____ , Buyer and Seller shall make their best efforts to complete Closing on or before that date. COP shall occur at Closing.

BROKER: Buyer acknowledges that Broker has furnished to Buyer financial and other information obtained from Seller and other sources, the accuracy and completeness of which have not been verified by Broker, and that Buyer is relying solely on his own inspection of the Business, its Assets, financial statements, business records, contracts, any assumed liabilities, operational history, future protitability and the representations by the Seller, and not on any representations of the Broker Seller acknowledges that he is relying solely on his own investigation of the Buyer's creditworthiness and ability to complete this transaction and to successfully operate the Business, and not on any representations of the Broker, Should any such representations of Seller or Buyer be untrue, Buyer and Seller agree to look solely to each other for relief and shall release, hold harmless, indemnify and defend the Broker from any such claims, Buyer and Seller acknowledge and agree that Broker may receive a referral fee from an institutional lender.

TRAINING: Seller and _____, individually, shall train Buyer in the operation of the Business for a period of _____ consecutive weeks from COP, for_____ hours per week, without additional cost to Buyer.

COVENANT NOT TO COMPETE: Seller and _____ , individually, shall not directly or indirectly carry on a similar business ☐ within a radius of miles of the present location ofthe Business, or ☐ within the counties of_____. attempt to hire any existing employees of the Business, solicit any customers of the Business or assist anyone else except the Buyer to do so within these limits, or have any interest, directly or indirectly, in such business, except as an employee of the Buyer, for a period of consecutive years from COP, This covenant shall become an asset ofthe Business and may be transferred as part of any future sale of the Business.

Page 3 of 4

Business _____ Buyer _____ Date _____

MEDIATION OF DISPUTES: Buyer and Seller shall mediate any dispute or claim between them arising out of this Agreement or any resulting relationship or transaction between them, The mediation shall be held prior to any court action or arbitration The mediation shall be confidential and in accordance with applicable sections of the California Evidence Coder In the event the parties are not able to agree on a mediator within thirty (30) days of the tirst party seeking mediation, the presiding judge of the Superior Court of the county in which venue would lie for the tiling of a complaint for relief in such dispute shall have jurisdiction to appoint a mediator" In the event the mediator determines that a second mediation is necessary, it shall be conducted in accordance with this paragraph Should either party attempt an arbitration or a court action before attempting to mediate, that party shall not be entitled to attorney fees that might be othen/vise available to it in a court action or arbitration and the party who is determined by the arbitrator orjudge to have resisted mediation may be sanctioned by the arbitrator orjudge Mediation fees, if any, shall be divided equally between Buyer and Sellerl

BROKER'S FEES: The Broker(s) identified in paragraph 1 has/have acted as the only Broker(s) for this sale and earned a brokers fee., Seller agrees to pay a fee to Broker(s) for services as follows:

☐ _____ percent of total purchase price to _____, Broker and
☐ _____ percent of total purchase price to _____, Broker,or
☐ _____ as per representation agreement between Seller and Sellers Broker.

Broke's fees shall be payable (a) at Closing, or (b) if completion of sale is prevented by default of Seller, upon Seller's default.. If Closing is prevented by default of Buyer, the Buyer shall be responsible for and agrees to pay the total Broker's fee immediately upon default.. Any amount that the Buyer has deposited with the escrow holder may be applied against Buyer's obligation under this paragraph, In any action, proceeding or arbitration relating to the payment of such afee, the prevailing party shall be entitled to reasonable attomey's fees and costs

SUMMARY: The entire agreement of the parties relating to the sale of the Business is set forth in this Agreement and can only be modified in writing signed by the parties: There are no other representations, agreements, arrangements or understandings, either oral or written, between or among the parties hereto relating to the subject matter of this Agreement that are not fully expressed herein, This Agreement shall bind and benefit the parties and their legal successors and shall supersede any prior written or oral agreements" This Agreement may be signed in counterparts and faxed and electronic signatures may be considered as originals.. Captions in this Agreement are for convenience only and shall not be considered in construing its meaning In any action, proceeding or arbitration between Buyer and Seller arising out of this Agreement, the prevailing party shall be entitled to reasonable attorney's fees and costs, except as provided in paragraph 17"

ACKNOWLEDGMENT AND PERSONAL GUARANTEE: By signing below, the Buyer and Seller each acknowledge that they have carefully read and fully understand this Agreement and have received a copy of it" The undersigned warrant that their signatures are legally sufficient to bind the

ACCEPTANCE: This offer shall expire unless it is accepted in writing by Seller and that acceptance is communicated by fax or personal delivery to Buyer or Buyer's agent by _____ ☐a.m. or ☐p.m. on _____, 20_____. Please note, any offer can be withdrawn or revoked before acceptance is properly communicated to Buyer or Buyer's agentiy The undersigned Seller accepts and agrees to sell the Business on the terms on the above terms and conditions.

THE CALIFORNIA ASSOCIATION OF BUSINESS BROKERS MAKES NO REPRESENTATION AS TO THE LEGAL VALIDITY OR ADEQUACY OF ANY PROVISION OF THIS FORM IN ANY SPECIFIC TRANSACTION. THE BROKER IS NOT QUALIFIED TO GIVE LEGAL OR TAX ADVICE" FOR SUCH ADVICE, THE PARTIES SHOULD CONSULT THEIR ATTORNEYS OR ACCOUNTANTS,

Subject to attached addendum

Buyer _____ Date _____   Seller _____ Date _____

Buyer _____ Date _____   Seller _____ Date _____

Corporation (or other entity)   Corporation (or other entity)

by: _____ ____   by: _____ ____
Name and Title   Date   Name and Title   Date

Brokers Agent _____ Date ____   Broker's Agent _____ Date ____

LIST OF ATTACHMENTS

A. Equipment List
B. Sellefs Disclosure Statement
C. Buyer's Disclosure Statement
D. _____
E. _____
F. _____
G. _____

Page 4 of 4

Buyer's Disclosure Statement

Business _____ Broker _____
Buyer _____ Agent _____

This series of quetions and answers is is to inform the seller about potential buyers of the business. It is supplied to
help the seller determine their qualifications to buy and operate the business, but does not take the place of the
seller's investigation of te buyer's qualifications to buy and operate the business. This should be determined by the
seller. The broker has not verified the accuracy or completeness of any information supplied here by the buyer.
PLEASE EXPLAIN ALL "YES" ANSWERS ON THE ADDENDUM

		YES	NO
1.	Have you been the subject of any bankruptcy filing, assignment for benefit of creditors or insolvency proceeding of any kind during the last five years, or consulted with an attorney or advisor regarding such proceedings?	☐	☐
2.	Have you been late or defaulted on a business premises or equipment lease?	☐	☐
3.	Is there anything about your personal or business operating or credit history that, if disclosed to the seller, might adversely affect the seller's decision to sell the business to you?	☐	☐
4.	Are there any representations you have made to the seller regarding your financial statement, expereience and education that are not true?	☐	☐
5.	Is there any reason you would not be able to investigate the suitability and performance of this business yourself? If yes, please name the independent adisor(s) you intend to use in assisting you with this investigation.	☐	☐
6.	Is there any reason that you will not have sufficient operating capital for this business after paying the downpayment and closing costs?	☐	☐
7.	Is there any reason why you might be denied any of the necessary licenses or permits to operate this business?	☐	☐
8.	Have you ever been convicted of a felony?	☐	☐
9.	Is there any person or entity other than yourself who will have an equity interest in the business?	☐	☐
10.	Will you have to borrow or obtain from other sources the funds you will need for the downpayment, closing costs and operating capital?	☐	☐
11.	Are there any other facts or conditions not disclosed above that might adversely affect your ability to operate this business or prevent you from fulfilling the terms of your purchase agreement?	☐	☐

**IF YOU ANSWERED "YES" TO ANY OF THE ABOVE QUESTIONS,
PLEASE GIVE A COMPLETE EXPLANATION ON THE ADDENDUM**

BUYER(S)

_____ _____ _____ _____
Buyer Signature   Date   Buyer's Agent Signature   Date

_____ _____
Buyer Signature   Date

Buyer(s) certifies that the above information is true and correct and acknowledges receipt of a copy of
this disclosure statement

Seller(s) acknowledges having reviewed the information relating to the buyer contained in this
disclosure statement and having received a copy.

_____ _____ _____ _____
Seller Signature   Date   Seller Signature   Date

Addendum to Disclosure Statement

☐ Seller's ☑ Buyer's

Business _____

Question#   Explanation of "YES" Answer

_____   _____
_____   _____
_____   _____
_____   _____
_____   _____
_____   _____
_____   _____
_____   _____
_____   _____
_____   _____
_____   _____
_____   _____
_____   _____

(Attach additional sheets if needed)

The undersigned certifies that the above information is true and correct and acknowledges receipt of a copy of this disclosure statement.

_____   _____
Seller(s) - Print Name(s)   Buyer(s) - Print Name(s)

_____ _____   _____ _____
Seller Signature   Date   Buyer Signature   Date

_____ _____   _____ _____
Seller Signature   Date   Buyer Signature   Date

Seller's Disclosure Statement

Business _____	Seller _____
Address _____	Broker _____
City _____ Zip _____	Broker's Agent _____

This series of questions and answers is to inform prospective buyers about this Business. It is supplied by the Seller to provide relevant information and to answer frequently asked questions, but it does not take the place of the Buyer's inspection of the Business and its financial and other records. Those must be carefully examined and approved by the Buyer. The Broker has not verified the accuracy or completeness of any of the information supplied here by the Seller.

PLEASE EXPLAIN ALL "YES" ANSWERS ON THE ADDENDUM

A. **Business Conditions**   YES   NO

1. Are you aware of any circumstances in the industry or market area that may adversely affect future profitability of the Business? ☐ ☐

2. Are there any revenues, expenses, assets or liabilities of the Business that are not clearly and accurately reflected in its financial statements or tax returns? ☐ ☐

3. Is the Business in default of any of its financial or contractual obligations? ☐ ☐

4. Has the Business or any of its owners been the subject of any bankruptcy filing, assignment for the benefit of creditors or insolvency proceeding of any kind during the last five years or consulted with any attorney or advisor regarding such proceedings? ☐ ☐

5. Are there any individual customers who account for more than 10% of annual gross sales? If yes, list each by name and indicate the approximate percentage of annual gross sales and any relationship to the Business or its owners. ☐ ☐

6. Are there any commitments to employees or independent contractors regarding future compensation increases, promotions or ownership interests? ☐ ☐

7. Are there suppliers or customers who have a personal or special relationship with the Business or its owners? If yes, list each such person or entity, the nature of the relationship, the approximate total of annual purchases and any special discounts, pricing or other favorable terms that may not be available to a buyer. ☐ ☐

8. Are any of the employees or independent contractors related to any of the owners of the Business or to one another? If yes, list them by name and describe the relationship. ☐ ☐

9. Have you had or do you anticipate any disputes with the landlord or problems with the premises the Business occupies? ☐ ☐

10. Does the premises have any deferred maintenance for which the tenant is responsible? ☐ ☐

11. Are you aware of any work done to the premises without the proper permits? ☐ ☐

Page 1 of 3

Business _____

	YES	NO
12. Have there been any deaths, violent crimes or other criminal activity on the premises within the last three years?	☐	☐
13. Are you aware of any substances, materials or products on or near the premises which may be an environmental hazard such as, but no t limited to, asbestos, formaldehyde, radon gas, paint, solvents, fuel, medical waste, surface o r underground storage tanks or contaminated soil or water?	☐	☐
14. Is there any equipment used in the Business that is not in good and operable condition, or for which maintenance has been deferred or that is not suitable for current usage?	☐	☐
15. Are there any items used in the Business that the Seller does not own, such as leased or loaned equipment, consigned resale inventory or employees' tools?	☐	☐
16. Does the Business have a franchise, distributorship or licensing agreement? If yes, please provide a copy of each such agreement.	☐	☐
17. Are there any errors or omissions on the pro forma or adjusted income statement prepared by the Broker from information provided by you?	☐	☐
18. Have you received notice of pending increases in workers' compensation insurance premiums, revised billings for previous periods or any indication that your insurance carrier may terminate coverage?	☐	☐
19. Have there been any workers' compensation insurance claims or injuries in the past 12 months that might lead to such claims?	☐	☐

B. Regulations

	YES	NO
1. Is the Business or its operators required to have any licenses or permits other than a local business license?	☐	☐
2. Are you aware of any pending zoning changes, redevelopment or nearby construction that might affect the Business?	☐	☐
3. Are there any alleged violations filed or under investigation by the following authorities?	☐	☐

	YES	NO		YES	NO
1. Police Department	☐	☐	9. Bureau of Alcohol, Tobacco & Firearms	☐	☐
2. Health Department	☐	☐	10. EDD	☐	☐
3. Fire Department	☐	☐	11. Alcoholic Beverage Control	☐	☐
4. Building Inspector	☐	☐	12. IRS	☐	☐
5. Zoning Commission	☐	☐	13. Board of Equalization	☐	☐
6. Water Pollution Control Agency	☐	☐	14. Franchise Tax Board	☐	☐
7. Environmental Protection Agency	☐	☐	15. Immigration and Naturalization Service	☐	☐
8. OSHA	☐	☐	16. Other	☐	☐

C. Other Considerations

Does the Business have any of the following?	YES	NO
1. Union or other employment agreements	☐	☐
2. Any employee hired after 11-6-86 without a completed INS Form I-9 on file	☐	☐
3. Employee stock ownership plan (ESOP)	☐	☐
4. Underfunded pension liabilities	☐	☐

Page 2 of 3

Business _____

	YES	NO
5. Profit sharing plan	☐	☐
6. Accrued back wages, vacation pay or sick leave or claims for same	☐	☐
7. Unpaid medical or other insurance premiums	☐	☐
8. Lease agreements (other than the premises)	☐	☐
9. Advertising contracts (including Yellow Pages)	☐	☐
10. Equipment maintenance agreements or any other contracts or agreements	☐	☐
11. Pending or threatened litigation	☐	☐
12. Unresolved insurance claims	☐	☐
13. Product liability exposure	☐	☐
14. Customer warranty obligations	☐	☐
15. Pending tax or Workers' Compensation refunds	☐	☐
16. Anticipated supplier rebates	☐	☐
17. Any outstanding gift certificates, coupons or store credits	☐	☐
18. Unpaid federal, state, local or other taxes	☐	☐
19. Customer deposits for security, prepaid goods or services	☐	☐

D. General

Are you aware of any other facts or conditions not disclosed above that may adversely ☐ ☐
affect the operation of the Business, a buyer's decision to purchase it or the price a
buyer might pay for it?

IF YOU HAVE ANSWERED "YES" TO ANY OF THE ABOVE QUESTIONS,
PLEASE GIVE A COMPLETE EXPLANATION ON THE ADDENDUM

**SELLER CERTIFIES THAT THE ABOVE INFORMATION IS TRUE AND CORRECT, AGREES TO
NOTIFY BROKER IMMEDIATELY OF ANY MATERIAL CHANGES AND ACKNOWLEDGES
RECEIPT OF A COPY OF THIS DISCLOSURE STATEMENT.**

_____	_____	_____
Name	Signature	date
_____	_____	_____
Name	Signature	date
	By:	
_____	_____	_____
Corporation	Signature and Title	date

**BUYER ACKNOWLEDGES HAVING REVIEWED THE INFORMATION CONTAINED IN THIS
DISCLOSURE STATEMENT AND HAVING RECEIVED A COPY.**

_____	_____	_____
Name	Signature	date
_____	_____	_____
Name	Signature	date
	By:	
_____	_____	_____
Corporation	Signature and Title	date

Page 3 of 3

Addendum to Disclosure Statement

☑ Seller's   ☐ Buyer's

Business _____

Question#   Explanation of "YES" Answer

_____   _____

_____   _____

_____   _____

_____   _____

_____   _____

_____   _____

_____   _____

_____   _____

_____   _____

_____   _____

_____   _____

_____   _____

_____   _____

_____   _____

(Attach additional sheets if needed)

**The undersigned certifies that the above information is true and correct
and acknowledges receipt of a copy of this disclosure statement.**

_____   _____
Seller(s) - Print Name(s)   Buyer(s) - Print Name(s)

_____   _____
Sign   Date   Sign   Date

_____   _____
Sign   Date   Sign   Date

California's Largest Restaurant Business Brokerage
*Specializing in Sales, Acquisitions and
Leasing of Restaurants, Bars and Clubs*

EQUIPMENT LIST

THIS IS A SAMPLE EQUIPMENT LIST - USE NEXT PAGE
YOU CAN TYPE IN & PRINT OR PRINT & HAND WRITE

#	DESCRIPTION/SIZE/BRAND	#	DESCRIPTION/SIZE/BRAND	#	DESCRIPTION/SIZE/BRAND
	KITCHENS		MISC. EQUIPMENT		DOWNSTAIRS BAR
1	Walk-in 6x12x7 Refrigerator	4	ATT Partner Phones	1	Blender
1	Walk-in 6x9x7 Freezer	1	ATT Cordless Phone	2	19" TVs
1	Stainless Steel table with sink	1	Aloha POS Systems	1	6 Door Under Counter Refri
1	Stainless steel shelf above door	6	Terminal and Keyboards	2	Stainless Steel Wells
14	Metro storage shelving units	9	Printers	2	Stainless Steel Sinks
2	Range Guard Fire Systems	1	Power backup		
1	Bakers Rack	1	Matrix printer		UPSTAIRS BAR
1	Vegetable Rack	7	Custom Padded Booths	1	Freezer
1	Amana radarrage	4	Custom Planter Boxes	2	Stainless Steel Wells
1	R-4 Food Processor	25	Cocktail Trays	1	Stainless Steel Sink
1	Sunkist Juice Extracotr	15	Waiter Trays	2	Two Door Refrigerator
1	Globe Meat Slicer	9	Stainless Steel platters/tray	2	19" TVs
1	Ounce Scale	10	Plastic storage containers	1	Satellite Dish
1	Manilowdoc Ice Maker	10	Silverware racks		
1	Gas 3x3 Grill	20	Bus tubs		
1	Well steam table	50	plastic ramakins		
2	Monague Convection Ovents	50	Hotel Pans		
2	Custom spice shelfs 12x18	100	9.75" round plates		
1	Gas 3x3 Grill	100	100 6" salad plates		
1	Randell #9200-32 cooler base	25	Oval platters		
1	New 100 gallon water heater	25	Creamers		
12	Burners, 2 cold drawers	25	Sugar caddies		
1	3ft High Soup Warmer	200	White wine glasses		
2	Wood shelving liquor storage	200	Red wine glasses		
1	Montague with 6 burners	20	Rocks glasses		
2	Montague standing w/2 burners	50	Pint Glasses		
		10	Martini Glasses		
	LIST EVERYTHING!!!	30	Champagne Flutes		
		60	Coffee cups		
		17	Bar Stools		
		252	Chairs		
		7	Banquet Tables		
		55	Dining Room Tables		
		9	Bar Tables		
		10	Round Tables		
		1	Ice Machine in Storeroom		
		1	TV Under Staircase		

Business Name, Location: SAMPLE BUSINESS, SAMPLE LOCATION

X_____   _____   X_____   _____
Seller Signature   **Date**   **Buyer Signature**   **Date**

California's Largest Restaurant Business Brokerage
Specializing in Sales, Acquisitions and
Leasing of Restaurants, Bars and Clubs

EQUIPMENT LIST

Enter Quantity in 1st column & description/size/brand in 2nd column.
FILL IN YOUR NAME, SIGN AND DATE AT THE BOTTOM

# DESCRIPTION/SIZE/BRAND	# DESCRIPTION/SIZE/BRAND	# DESCRIPTION/SIZE/BRAND

Business Name, Location: _____

Seller - print name(s) above & sign below   **Buyer** – print name(s) above & sign below

X_____   _____   X_____   _____
Seller Signature   **Date**   **Buyer Signature**   **Date**

X_____   _____   X_____   _____
Seller Signature   **Date**   **Buyer Signature**   **Date**

Chapter 44

THE BUYER'S
DUE-DILIGENCE PROCESS

Typically, the buyer has somewhere between 10 and 20 calendar days from the time the asset purchase contract is accepted to complete his due diligence. The due diligence includes the items indicated below:

Inspections

Physical Inspections – The buyer should hire a general contractor or building inspector who is capable of evaluating all the mechanical systems—plumbing, refrigeration, electrical and heating, ventilating and air conditioning—to make sure they are working correctly, and have a reasonable life remaining. Additionally, all the equipment and fixtures should be inspected to make sure they are in good working condition. The recommended procedure is that, upon the initial inspection of the equipment and fixtures, the buyer and seller walk through the business and check off all the equipment to make sure it is there. This list is prepared by the seller immediately after listing the business for sale, and the equipment list is signed by both buyer and seller at the time the purchase contract is executed. The equipment list is also signed again by both buyer and seller after the final walk thru is completed by the parties, immediately before the close of escrow.

Health Department Inspection – In most counties in California, before a business license is issued to a new owner, a change-of-ownership health department inspection must be signed off by the county health inspector. This means that before the sale is completed, the health department does an inspection for a change of ownership, and this has higher standards than a routine health department inspection that was done periodically while he was operating the business. On a change-of-ownership health department inspection, the inspector will call out all items that are now required as a result of code-upgrade changes and are typically required for a change of ownership—such as three compartment sinks, mop sinks, hand sinks, special floor drains; all surfaces including walls, floors and ceilings must be smooth and washable, etc. It is usually the buyer's responsibility to pay for the inspection report, which is a couple hundred dollars, and it is the seller's responsibility to clear all these items before the close of escrow. If the seller does not want to clear these items, usually the price is adjusted downward accordingly for an "as-is" sale, making the buyer responsible for these changes. If the buyer plans to undertake a major remodeling of the business after the close of escrow, then the health department inspection is not that meaningful. The buyer's remodeling plans will have to be approved by the health department.

Fire Department Inspection – If you have a type 1 hood (a hood system for a full kitchen with open flame cooking), you need to have a fire suppression system built into the hood system. If a fire occurs over the cooking area, the fire suppression system will activate, and hopefully extinguish the fire.

All of the fire extinguishers need to be checked and filled regularly.

You must have proper egress and ingress areas for customers and employees.

The duct system which connects between the hood and roof needs to be cleaned out quarterly by a professional hood-cleaning company.

Your electrical system must be up to code, and have the proper electrical work completed throughout, including updated circuit breaker systems.

American Disabilities Act (ADA) – This is the Federal law set up to assure that you have the proper facilities for disabled customers. Such areas as entry ways, front doors, restrooms, parking spaces, table heights, and seating areas must be properly adjusted to accommodate disabled customers. If you are buying an existing restaurant which does not accommodate disabled customers, you need to check with the local building and planning department to see what the requirements are to comply with ADA. In some cases, you may be grandfathered in, which means that as long as you don't make any major changes to the restaurant, the existing conditions will be acceptable. However, it is best to update your business to accommodate disabled customers, as society is becoming more conscious about incorporating the disabled, and you want to minimize any exposure to possible litigation for non-compliance.

Other Areas to Inspect – If you have a NNN lease, it means you are usually responsible for taking care of the entire building, rather than just the foundation and side walls. It is likely that you are then possibly responsible for maintenance of the roof, parking lot, and other parts of the building.

Therefore, make sure you have the roof inspected by a roofing company, the parking lot inspected by a paving company, etc., so you know the condition of these areas, and won't have any surprises after you close escrow. If work is needed, make sure the work is done before the close of escrow, or that you receive the proper credits from the seller towards the purchase price to cover this corrective work.

Review of Books and Records

a. **Federal Tax Returns and Sales Tax Returns** – The actual sale of a business is determined by a review of the Federal tax returns for prior years' sales history, and a review of the sales tax returns for the current year's sales history.

b. **Unreported Sales** – Frequently, in the restaurant, bar, or nightclub business, single-unit owner operators do not report all of their sales—which is a violation of the law. Typically the sellers do not receive credit for any sales not reported for tax purposes, as they have already been compensated by receiving increased profits (the result of not paying taxes on unreported sales). However, to truly determine the actual sales of the business, a good restaurant broker will recast the actual sales by tying in the cash register, or point-of-sales system sales tapes, with the guest checks and the invoices, to determine the true sales.

c. **Income-and-Expense Statements and Balance Sheets** – Specifically, a buyer needs to review the income-and-expense statements and balance sheets for the prior three years, and for the current year's year-to-date income-and-expense statement and balance sheet.

d. **Bank Statements** – Additionally, the buyer will want to review bank statements for the prior twelve months, evaluating the cash sales and charge sales to help further support the actual reported sales.

e. **Invoices** – The buyer will also want to review invoices for various items including: 1) a detail of the premises rent. This is especially true if there are NNN expenses which will detail the monthly common-area maintenance costs such as taxes, insurance and maintenance costs, or 2) any tax bills the buyer may be responsible for, such as property taxes or unsecured personal property taxes.

f. **Buyer's Discretionary Cash Flow Statement** – The broker will also prepare a buyer's discretionary cash flow statement, which is the actual income-and-expense statement recast. This means adjusting the income and expense categories to truly reflect the actual cash benefits the owner is receiving.

Review of Special Licenses

If the business being purchased has a license allowing the owner to serve alcoholic beverages, you want to examine those licenses to see if there are any special conditions attached, such as restrictions on certain days and hours when you can't serve alcoholic beverages. If you are buying a nightclub with an entertainment license, you need to review the conditions to see what days and hours you are allowed to provide entertainment, and what type of entertainment you can provide, such as dancing, live music, DJ, and karaoke. Specifically some licenses will allow live music, but only certain types, such as live music, but with no amplified instruments.

Review of the Premises Lease

Make sure if you are assuming an existing premises lease that all of the terms and conditions, and length of the lease are adequate. Make sure the lease is transferable, subject to the approval of the landlord, and that the existing rent and future rent schedules will work for your operation.

Other Agreements to Review

- **Franchise Agreement** – If you are purchasing a franchise business, make sure to review the terms of the franchise agreement in detail. Make certain that the length of the franchise agreement is long enough to satisfy your business requirements.

- **Equipment Lease** – If you are assuming an equipment lease, make sure you understand the terms of the equipment lease, and determine if the equipment will belong to you at the end of the lease, or if it reverts back to the equipment lessor. Most equipment leases at the end-of-the-lease period belong to the owner of the business for a nominal payment (like $1) at the end of the lease.

- **Phone Book Yellow Page Contract** – In some cases, you will be assuming the "Yellow Page" phone book annual contract, so review this contract.

- **Equipment Rental Agreements** – Some equipment is rented on a month-to-month basis. If you do not want to continue this agreement, you can usually give a 30-day notice to terminate this agreement.

- **Seller's Disclosure Statement** – This agreement discloses all of the seller's possible business problems, and is completed by the seller, and submitted to the buyer before he enters into the purchase contract. Review it carefully to make sure there are no pending lawsuits, no major future developments in the area which may hurt your business, or any other factors which will negatively impact your business.

- **Attorneys Review of Documents** – The buyer must have his attorney review the various legal documents used in the business. If the operator is not familiar with some legal points, there could be legal restrictions that are unacceptable to him, but need to be re-negotiated before the operator purchases the business. It is prudent to have the lease reviewed by the operator's attorney to assure that the current and future terms and conditions are acceptable, Section VII has additional information regarding the lease. The operator's attorney should also review any other legal documents, if applicable, including the franchise agreement, the equipment lease, and all use permits—food permit, alcohol license, conditional-use permit and entertainment permit, etc. All of the above-mentioned documents have terms and conditions which legally bind the operator. Non-compliance with the terms and conditions could result in the operator losing his right to continue running the business, or force him to run the business in a compromising way, which could have a negative impact on the his sales and profits.

- **Accountant Review of Financial Statements** – It is important to have the operator's accountant review all the business financial books and records. This assures that the seller had properly recorded all of the businesses income and expenses activities, and that the financial statements accurately reflect the true financial picture of the business.

Chapter 45

THINGS THAT CAN GO WRONG DURING A SALES TRANSACTION THAT A SELLER NEEDS TO KNOW —AND A BUYER SHOULD, TOO

Why should a seller use a specialized restaurant broker to help sell his restaurant, bar, or nightclub? It helps to get the seller the highest price possible, in the quickest time, on a confidential basis. Other reasons relate to the many things that can go wrong during the sales transaction process, which a good restaurant broker has the ability to resolve—and get the deal closed.

What can go wrong during the sales transaction is broken down by the major parties involved in the transaction: buyer, seller, landlord, broker, governmental agencies, and the escrow/title company. For a transaction to close properly, all parties must be in agreement: the buyer, the seller, landlord, funding, legal, government, and your professional advisor—the restaurant broker. But things do go wrong, so it's better to beware than have your head in the proverbial sand.

The Buyer:

a. can't raise the money,

b. gets cold feet,

c. gets struck with family problems,

d. becomes ill,

e. can't qualify for the ABC license or entertainment license, etc.

The Seller:

a. has remorse about putting his business up for sale,

b. goes bankrupt during the transaction,

c. gets evicted during the transaction,

d. can't support the financial statements,

e. finds the health department correctional work so overwhelming financially that most of his proceeds will get wiped out,

f. is hit with a lawsuit during the transaction,

g. discovers that the tax liens are so large they will wipe out his equity.

The Landlord:

a. is very uncooperative towards most new transactions,

b. becomes greedy,

c. has unrealistic rent expectations,

d. has very tough criteria for buyer qualifications.

The Broker:

a. has a high level of incompetence,

b. doesn't follow up,

c. lacks timeliness,

d. has little experience doing business transactions.

Governmental Agencies:

a. make the transaction prohibitive,

b. have inefficient staff at government agencies

c.   enforce health department guidelines that crush the deal,

d.   delay deal closing because of tax audits conducted during the escrow.

Escrow/Title Company:

a.   Doesn't perform in a timely manner to get out escrow papers, monitor receipt of deposits, start the bulk sales, complete the tax lien searches, get out closing papers, send out the 226, and follow up with various part of the paperwork.

How the buyer's actions can break the deal

- **Not being able to raise the money.**

  One of the roles of a good restaurant broker is to screen the prospective buyer up front to make sure he has the proper amount of money to purchase the business. This is done by examining the buyer's financial statement, including reviewing current bank statements to see his source of cash, securities account statements, and/or equity in the buyer's properties. If the buyer tries to get his cash from getting an equity line on her property, the broker looks carefully at the appraised value of the buyer's property and the respective loan-to-value ratio, to make sure the buyer has enough equity to obtain the cash for the transaction from the loan. If the cash is coming from a third-party investor rather than the buyer, we review the same items (indicated above) from the investor.

- **The buyer gets cold feet.**

  After the buyer signs the purchase contract and his offer is accepted, he may have second thoughts about moving forward on the transaction. After completing his due diligence—reviewing the books and records, completing physical inspections, and getting approval for assignment of the existing lease or negotiating a new lease with the landlord—the buyer may develop reservations. If the business is a going-concern business, and the buyer plans to continue the existing operation, the buyer, after further consideration, may conclude that he is not capable of maintaining the same business activity level as the current owner. If the business is an asset sales, and the buyer has to change the menu and concept, and also complete some remodeling, he may think that his original income and expense projections are not achievable.

- **Family problems.**

  The restaurant, bar and nightclub business requires long hours, and in some cases, family pressures regarding the owner's lifestyle priorities, may get in the way of the buyer's ability to close the transaction. The family may not be supportive of the time demands once they discover the difficulty of finding a balance between time spent in the business, and time spent with the family. Various family problems may develop with the buyer, his spouse, or with members of his family, after the purchase contract is executed. These may include a pending divorce, health problems with the buyer or members of the buyer's family, or the necessity to relocate due to personal family needs. Although many of these issues cannot be anticipated, to minimize the problem areas indicated above, we carefully review the buyer's background before he gets into contract to determine his stability, and that of his family.

- **Can't qualify for necessary business licenses**.

  There are various requirements for obtaining certain licenses such as the ABC license (alcohol license), whereby the applicant can't have any past felonies or DUIs (driving under the influence citations). As part of our initial screening process, we question the prospective buyer regarding any of the above-mentioned problems to eliminate any problems in this process.

Restaurant Realty Company, having completed over 800 transactions, has experienced most of the situations above. This has given us the ability, in many cases, to eliminate or minimize these problems—and get the deals closed.

How Seller's Actions Can Void the Deal

The seller may want to back out of the deal for several reasons, which might include "seller's remorse," which occurs when the seller has second thoughts about selling his business.

Other reasons may be that the seller:

- Thinks he is not getting enough money for his business.
- Feels it is the wrong time to sell the business, and if he waits to sell it during better economic times, he may get more money.
- Is concerned that he may not know what to do with himself if he no longer has a business to run.
- Has younger children, and starts thinking that one of his children may want to come into the business someday.
- Feels that with the new development going on in the area, the business may get significantly better, and may become substantially more profitable.
- Examines the tax consequences of the proposed transaction, and realizes that his after-tax proceeds are not sufficient to live on. A broker will have extensive conversations with the seller, before the business is listed for sale, to determine the reasons he wants to sell. If the seller is not fully committed to selling the business at this time, the broker should discourage the seller from listing it.
- Goes bankrupt during the transaction. In some situations, a seller is forced to file bankruptcy during the transaction, which means the business is no longer saleable, and physical possession of the premises is taken back by the landlord. Without a premises lease, the business is not saleable.
- Gets evicted during the transaction. In several situations, the seller was evicted during the transaction for non-payment of back rent. After the seller is delinquent for back rent, the landlord can file a 3-day notice which legally states that if the tenant can't pay the back rent within 3 days, a legal process will begin, whereby the tenant will be evicted from the premises, and the landlord takes back possession of the premises.
- Can't support the financial statements. In some situations, certain representations are made by the seller regarding the financial condition of the business, however, these representations cannot be supported by the appropriate financial documentation. Thus, the buyer decides to withdraw from the transaction. If you use a broker, he will review the tax returns, and profit and loss statements for the

past three years, as well as the year-to-date sales tax returns, and year-to-date profit and loss statements for the current year, before he takes the listing.

- Realizes that the premises corrective maintenance and repairs work is too extensive. Sometimes during the buyer's due-diligence period, the inspection of the physical premises, reveals that the corrective work necessary is so extensive that the buyer might walk from the deal. In many cases, this can be solved by the seller giving the buyer a credit for completing this corrective work after the close of escrow, or the seller completes the work, to the satisfaction of the buyer, before the close of escrow. A broker will advise the seller to make sure everything is in good working order. He will also have completed a change-of-ownership health inspection report so he knows exactly what corrective work the health department is going to require, before putting the business on the market.

- Gets hit with a lawsuit during the transaction – Sometimes a lawsuit is filed against the seller during the escrow period that will, in most cases, prohibit the deal from closing until the escrow closes. There is not much a broker can do in this case other than advise the parties not to proceed further in the transaction until this issue is resolved.

- Incurred tax liens so large that they wipe out seller's equity. In numerous situations, the seller has incurred tax liens larger that his equity, which can result in the deal not closing. A broker needs to review the possibility of these items occurring before he lists the business for sale.

The Landlord Can Typically Be One of the Major Obstacles in Getting the Deal Done

Why is this? Many landlords might not want to tie up the building in a long-term lease because they might want to sell the building in the near future, and may feel the building is more marketable to a buyer/user. Landlords also have a tendency to be very greedy and want an exorbitant rent, making it economically unfeasible for the prospective restaurant, bar, or nightclub tenant to rent the space.

Restaurant Realty, in most cases, will talk to the landlord in the early stages to determine if the landlord will offer reasonable lease terms and conditions. If we determine that the lease terms and conditions will not be reasonable for a prospective buyer, we tell the seller that the business is not sellable, and decline listing the business for sale.

The Broker – If a party uses an inexperienced broker, his incompetency may cause the deal to be voided as a result of his not obtaining all the pertinent facts necessary to the transaction: the physical and financial conditions of the business, the details of the premises lease, and an understanding of any of the potential operating restrictions of the business. Also an inexperienced broker may not follow up in a timely manner, which could result in a voided transaction.

Restaurant Realty's professional experience in selling over 800 restaurants, bars, and nightclubs gives us the ability to effectively and efficiently get the deal closed in a timely manner.

Governmental Agencies – The various governmental agencies one has to interact with during a transaction include the Alcoholic Beverage Control Agency, the health department, the fire department, and the planning and building departments. They also include various taxing agencies, such as the Internal Revenue Service, the Franchise Tax Board, the California State Board of Equalization, the Employment Development Department, and other local taxing authorities, etc.

Unless you keep on top of every step through the Alcohol Beverage Control license transfer process, the transfer of the license can be delayed weeks or months. This could cause a prospective deal to fall apart if the seller is having serious economic problems and can't keep the business going.

The health department can also impose onerous health correction recommendations. These could break a transaction because it may become economically unfeasible for the parties to deal with these correction costs.

If tax agencies are not paid in full by the seller, these agencies can put liens in the escrow, preventing the escrow from closing until the liens are paid off. If not enough monies are in the escrow to pay these tax liens, and the seller does not have additional monies to pay off these liens, or do an installment payment with the taxing agency, the deal could fall apart.

Restaurant Realty's experience in dealing with all of these governmental agencies gives us the ability to handle the multitude of problems that regularly occur.

Escrow Company – If the escrow company does not perform its functions in a timely manner— which include: getting all escrow papers out to the parties, monitoring all deposits and other cash requirements of the parties, starting the bulk sales, completing the tax lien search, getting out closing papers, and interacting with the ABC on a timely basis, etc.—the transaction could be delayed. This delay could ultimately result in the deal falling apart.

Restaurant Realty works only with professional escrow companies with whom we have an extensive pre-existing relationship, which ensures that the escrow function will be performed correctly and in a timely manner. Our extensive experience in dealing with all of the various influences will minimize the potential problems, and get the deal closed.

Chapter 46

ADVANTAGES AND DISADVANTAGES OF AN ASSET SALE VERSUS A STOCK SALE

Asset Sale–Advantages

- No legal liability for the corporation prior to the purchase. In California, when an escrow is utilized, a bulk-sales process assures that the buyer will get title to the assets free and clear of all liens and encumbrances.

- No liabilities for employees –The seller's employees are terminated at the close of escrow, even if the buyer is going to rehire all of them. This cuts off any liability the former owner had with the employees, such as back wages, payroll taxes, and vacation pay.

- Costs paid for the assets are depreciable. A new, depreciable base is set up by the buyer, subject to the allocation of the purchase price he made at the close of escrow, so he can establish a new basis for depreciating assets. Assets can be depreciated as follows: furniture and fixtures–7 years; goodwill and covenant not to compete–15 years, and leasehold improvements–39 years.

- Clean credit, reputation, workers compensation rating, etc. The new owner has a fresh start. If the prior owner had a high workers compensation risk rating, had a poor reputation for food quality and service, and/or had poor credit, the new owner will not be penalized for these items, and will start out with a clean record.

Asset Sale–Disadvantages

- No established credit. When you're starting a new business, unless you have had a prior business with a good credit history, initially it will be harder to get credit.
- Rehire the employees. The employees don't automatically roll over to the new owner unless he rehires them, although for a new owner, this feature has more advantages than disadvantages.
- Negotiate transfer of leases and contracts. Leases and contracts have to be formally assigned by the landlord and lessor, and the new owners must be qualified both financially and operationally by the landlord and lessor before they can formally assume these leases. In some cases, a new premises lease must be negotiated per the requirements of either the landlord and/or tenant.
- New licenses—all licenses need to be either newly applied for, or transferred.
- Must comply with California Uniform Commercial Code–Bulk Sales, which can cause additional time to close, and requires mandatory public notification of sale.
- Must pay sales tax on furniture, fixtures, and equipment.

Stock Sale–Advantages

- Established credit. The buyer of the stock sale continues to do business with the same vendors, and enjoys the benefit of the credit history previously established by the seller.
- Many times, no, or minimal, operating capital required. The cash flow of the business is already in place, and the business is up and running, so not as much capital is required when purchasing a stock sale.

- Leases are in place. It is much easier to acquire the rights to leases of the business, such as a premises lease and equipment lease, if applicable, since the credit for these leases have already been established by the seller. If a below-market premises lease is being transferred to the buyer, this can be a big advantage because it could save him a lot of money in decreased rent payments.

- Contracts are in place. Vendor, premises lease, and equipment lease contracts (as discussed above) are already in place, and in many cases, the cost of these contracts will be less expensive to the buyer than new contracts, as a result of the seller's prior good credit history.

- Employees are in place with worker's compensation rate established. If the seller had a favorable workers compensation rating as a result of a history of low workers compensation claims, this low rating will transfer to the buyer, who will enjoy lower workers compensation insurance costs.

- Licenses are in place. This will save the buyer money because he will not have to pay new license fees.

- No public notification of the sale. In California, you don' have to do a bulk sales publication to notify vendors, taxing authorities and others regarding a pending sale. This notification allows these entities to put claims in escrow against the seller prior to the close of escrow.

- No sales tax on the fixtures, fixtures and equipment.

- No deposits required.

- Corporation, tax, and employment numbers and documentation are in place.

Stock Sale–Disadvantages

- Legal liability for the corporation prior to the purchase. As a buyer of a corporation, you are at risk for all the liabilities of the corporation. Although the balance sheet of the business, as of the date you take over ownership of the corporation, is part of the sales documents, it is possible some liabilities are not included on the attached balance sheet. You need to get an indemnification and hold-harmless agreement from the seller, which says that you will be responsible only for those liabilities indicated on the attached balance sheet, as of the date of the sale. An indemnification and hold-harmless agreement is a document executed by the seller stating that the seller will be responsible for any liability that he does not represent to the buyer prior to the close of the deal. If necessary, after the sale, if some unknown creditors come after you, it might be necessary to press legal action against the seller to protect yourself. This is why you need an indemnification and hold-harmless agreement from the seller.

- Assets are normally fully depreciated. When you buy the corporation, you inherit the seller's depreciable base. There is a real disadvantage to the seller in not being able to set up a new depreciable base based on the new purchase price you are paying for the business. One of the major reasons someone buys a business is to set up a meaningful depreciable base so they can shelter their income from taxes, which results in increasing the non-taxable cash flow of the business. This, and the unknown liabilities of the corporation (as discussed in number one above), are the two major reasons sellers don't generally want to buy the stock of the corporation, and would rather do an asset sale.

Sometimes stock sale is a hard sell to accountants and lawyers (as shown by the reasons above), and make it hard to recommend stock sales to their clients.

Is Franchising for You?

Chapter 47

THE ADVANTAGES AND DISADVANTAGES OF BUYING A FRANCHISED BUSINESS vs. BUYING AN INDEPENDENT, NON-FRANCHISED BUSINESS

Success Rate of Independents Versus Franchised Operators

In a well-run franchise operation, the success rate is 80%, much higher than for non-franchised independent operations. In a well-seasoned franchise operation, all the operating procedures of the business are spelled out precisely by the franchisor. These operating procedures include:

    a. service procedures,

    b. food preparation and handling procedures,

    c. bookkeeping, accounting and administrative procedures, and

    d. marketing and advertising procedures.

If these procedures are not adhered to by the franchisee, the franchisor has the right to pull the franchise license from the franchisee, which means the franchisee cannot continue to run the franchise.

Customers trust a well-known franchise operation. Why is that? The customer experiences consistently good food and service in a clean, well-maintained environment that provides a strong price-value experience. This motivates them to frequent the franchise business. Another reason a customer may choose a franchise operation over an independent operation is safety. The chances of a customer getting food poisoning in a franchise operation are far less than a customer getting food poisoning in an independent, non-franchised operation. This is true because the franchisor is very concerned about the reputation of their entire system (which could be thousands of restaurants). If something goes wrong in one of their locations, this could have a negative spillover effect on their entire chain. A number of years ago in one incident, a customer found a finger in their chili at Wendy's Restaurant. In the financial quarter immediately following this incident, sales through the chain decreased materially. Customers frequent franchise restaurants because they know exactly what they will be getting, with little variation, if any, in the level of service and food quality.

To better understand, it is appropriate to discuss the terms indicated below:

- Franchise – An authorization to sell a company's goods or services in a particular place, using the company's marketing system, trademark, name, logo, and advertising. The company grants a franchise to an individual for fees as indicated below.

- Franchising – Methods of practicing and using another person's philosophy of business, which is memorialized in a written contract or agreement between two or more persons.

- Franchisor – Owns the rights and trademarks of the company, and allows its franchisees to use these rights and trademarks to do business. The franchisor sells the right to do business under a trademark to franchise.

- Franchisee – An independent person who is granted by the franchisor the right to use the franchisor's system of business— including the name, menu, concept, trademark, and other marketing, operating and administrative systems—at a particular location, and for a specified period, under terms and conditions set forth in the franchise agreement.

- Franchise Agreement – A written contract detailing the mutual responsibilities of franchisors and franchisees. It is usually for a several-year term, and when the term in up, the contract expires and must be renewed. Some states' laws require the contract to be renewable at the franchisee's option. Usually a franchise agreement may not be sold, transferred, or otherwise assigned without the franchisor's permission.

- Franchise Fees – The normal franchise fees paid to the franchisor consist of the following:

  1. Franchise Fee – A fixed amount a franchisee pays for the right to operate one or more franchise businesses.

  2. Royalty Fee – A percentage of the businesses sales the franchisee must pay to the franchisor on a regular ongoing basis.

  3. Advertising and Marketing Fee – A percentage of the business sales the franchisee must pay to the franchisor on a regular ongoing basis.

  4. Transfer Fee –A fee that is paid by either the buyer and/or seller of a franchise in transferring ownership of a franchise between the buyer and seller.

Buyers interested in finding franchise opportunities can locate such listings in various websites, franchise publications, and through franchise associations. Here are some things you need to know.

The Disadvantages of Buying a Franchise Business Versus Buying an Independent Non-Franchise Business

- If something goes wrong in another franchise store unrelated to your franchise store, this experience could have a negative impact on your business.
- If the franchise procedures are not adhered to by the franchisee, the franchisor has the right to pull the franchises license, which means the franchisee cannot continue to run the franchise.
- As a franchisee you have no control over the menu, service procedures, décor requirements, etc.
- You must keep the store up to the franchisor's physical standards, and must remodel the store on a regular basis per the franchisor's remodeling schedule.
- A material part of your sales goes toward paying a royalty fee for use of the franchise system, as well as an advertising and marketing fee. These royalty fees will vary depending on what franchise system you are part of, and will range from 4–12% of weekly and/or monthly sales, and advertising fees will range from 1–3% of weekly and/or monthly sales.
- You have little control over where the franchisor will decide to open another store. In Northern California, the majority of the Quizno's Sub Franchises I've encountered are either going out of business or have gone out of business. This has largely been a result of the franchisor's poor judgment in over-saturating the area with too many stores, thereby eroding the sales base of existing stores in the area.
- If you are a creative person, you won't be able to satisfy your creative desires as a franchisee since you must adhere to all the operational, marketing, and administrative functions of the operation, and in most cases, cannot deviate from the franchisor's policies.
- Most good franchises are very expensive, and unless you pick a strong franchise in a strong location, you'll most likely be just buying yourself a job, and probably won't make any serious money.

Using a Restaurant Broker to Your Advantage

Chapter 48

HOW TO FIND RESTAURANTS, BARS, OR CLUBS FOR SALE

You've finally decided to get serious about your dream or desire to own a restaurant, bar, or club. Now the question is where to find places that are for sale. The following is a list of places I know buyers have used with success.

Specialty Websites

Go to search engines and enter restaurants, bar, and clubs for sale. Some of the most popular search engines include Google, Yahoo, Bing, MSN, AOL, AskJeeves, Lycos, Excite, and others. The most popular websites for locating restaurants, bar, and clubs for sale are indicated below:

1. **RestaurantRealty.com** – This website specializes primarily in the sales, acquisitions, and leasing of restaurants, bars, and nightclubs in the greater San Francisco Bay Area of Northern California. Restaurant Realty Company is owned by the author of this book, and it is one of the largest websites of restaurants, bars, and clubs for sale or lease in California.

2. **RestaurantsForSaleOnline.com and Restaurants-for-Sale.com** – These are national listing sites for restaurants, bars, and nightclubs for sale throughout the world. The majority of their 2,000 listings are in the United States.

3. **BizBuySell.com** – This national listing service has the largest directory with all types of main street businesses for sale, and close to 50,000 business listings. They also have a section dedicated to restaurants, bars and clubs.

4. **BusinessesForSale.com** – This is a national listing service with approximately 50,000 general businesses for sale, with a special section for restaurants, bars, and clubs.

5. **ibba.org** – The International Business Brokers Association (known as "IBBA") website has listings of all types of main street businesses from many of its members throughout the world, with a concentration of listings in the United States. They have a specialized section for restaurants, bars and clubs for sale. The IBBA is an educational organization of business brokers from throughout the world.

6. **cabb.org** – The California Association of Business Brokers (also known as "CABB") website has listings of all types of main-street businesses from many of its members in California. There is a specialized section for restaurants, bars, and clubs for sale. CABB is an educational organization of business brokers throughout the State of California.

7. **loopnet.com** – This is the country's largest commercial real estate website listing commercial real estate for sale, and for lease; as well as a section of businesses for sale. Most of the listings in this website are non-confidential.

8. **bizben.com** – This is a California listing service with approximately 8,000 listings of general businesses for sale in California. A special section is dedicated to restaurants, bars, and clubs for sale.

9. **businessbroker.net** – This national business listing website has approximately 30,000 general businesses for sale throughout the country. They do have a special section dedicated to restaurants, bars, and clubs for sale.

10. **bizquest.com** – This national business listing website has the largest broker directory with approximately 40,000 general businesses for sale, with a specialized section for restaurants, bars, and clubs for sale.

Hospitality Periodicals

At one time, it is was effective to look in the classified section of hospitality periodicals to find restaurant, bar, and club opportunities for sale and/or lease, but the Internet has made this form of advertising less effective. You may, however, want to look at the informative hospitality periodicals indicated below. On occasion, it might lead you to a restaurant, bar, or club opportunity for sale and/or lease. Some of these periodicals include: Nations Restaurant News, Restaurant Hospitality, Food & Beverage Magazine, Restaurant Business, etc.

Local Newspapers

If you are using the newspaper to find restaurant, bar, or club opportunities, look in the classified section, especially on Sunday papers, in the following categories: businesses for sale; business opportunities; and restaurants, bars, cafes and clubs for sale. Look for restaurants, bars, or clubs for sale; and call brokers selling these businesses. Tell them what you are looking for, and if they can't help you, ask them to give you a referral to a broker that specializes in the sale of restaurants, bars, or clubs in the area where you are looking. Most of these newspapers have websites as well, which will advertise these opportunities. Like restaurant periodicals, this was an effective tool to find restaurant, bars, or clubs for sale and/or for lease in the past, but the Internet has replaced the newspaper classified section.

Phone Book Yellow Pages

In the yellow pages of the phone book, look under Business Brokers where brokers sell businesses. Next look for brokers in this category who specialize in selling restaurants, bars, and clubs. If there are no restaurant, bar, or nightclub specialists, call the general business brokers listed, and ask them if they have sold these kinds of businesses. If they haven't, ask them for a referral to a specialized broker who does..

Approach Owners of Businesses You Are Interested in Purchasing.

Contact a reputable restaurant, bar, and club business broker specialist, and ask him to represent you in approaching the owner of a business you are interested in purchasing, to see if he is interested in selling his business. The broker will then contact the business owner and tell him that he has a qualified buyer who is interested in buying his business. If the owner is interested in selling the business, the broker will then try to get as much information as possible about the business—the physical condition of the premises, the terms of the premises lease, and the financial books and records, etc. Most brokers will require that the buyer executes a buyer's broker's representation agreement to protect the broker and assure he will get paid for putting together the transaction.

Contact For Lease Signs that Look of Interest to you

Drive by buildings that have for sale or for lease signs that look interesting, and contact a Restaurant Broker specialist to check out these opportunities.

Chapter 49

WHY YOU NEED TO WORK WITH A RESTAURANT BROKER

A professional restaurant broker should have a vast amount of restaurant, bar, and/or club experience, and understand the operations, marketing, and financial aspects of the business. Additionally, a competent restaurant broker should have successfully completed numerous sales transactions involving restaurants, bars and/or clubs. By having the above experience, a restaurant broker can be helpful to a potential buyer in completing a sales, and can specifically help the buyer with the items mentioned below:

1. **Evaluate the Value of the Business**. The broker will help the buyer evaluate the value of the business to help ensure the buyer doesn't overpay for the business. The two major methods of valuation of a business are the Assets-in-Place Method and the Going-Concern Method, (see Section V).

2. **Evaluate the Location**. The broker will help the buyer review the many factors involved in finding the right location. See Section VI for detailed information on finding the right location.

3. **Review the Financial Statements of the Business.** If the business being purchased is a Going-Concern Business, the broker should have prepared a Buyer's Adjusted Cash Flow Statement, which details the cash flow a buyer should realize from the business. Additionally, the broker will help the buyer evaluate several years of past tax returns and profit and loss statements, as well as the current year's year-to-date profit and loss statement and sales tax returns. See Section V for details.

4. **Review the Fixtures and Equipment List.** The seller will have prepared a list of all the fixtures and equipment to be included with the sale. Additionally, a separate list will be provided of any fixtures and equipment not included in the sale, such as personal items to be retained by the seller, and/or items that are rented and/or leased. If certain items are leased, the buyer usually has the option to continue the month-to-month rental agreement of these items, or he can cancel the rental agreement at the time he takes possession of the business. If some of the equipment is leased, it may be a condition of the sale for the buyer to formally assume this lease. See Chapter 43 for sample fixtures and equipment List.

5. **Review Seller's Disclosure Statement**. During the initial stages of the transaction, the buyer will be given a seller's disclosure statement (completed buy the seller) that discloses all the pertinent information regarding the business—business conditions, regulations and other considerations of the business. See Chapter 43 for a copy of a seller's disclosure statement.

6. **Review the Physical Assets.** Through the due-diligence period, the broker will arrange for the buyer to do a physical inspection of the premises. During the contingency period, the buyer is free to bring in any contractor he would like to inspect the premises; including the plumbing, electrical, refrigeration, heating, air conditioning and ventilating systems, and any other mechanical systems. All the equipment must be in good working condition at the close of escrow. The buyer does another inspection of all the equipment immediately before the close of escrow to assure that it is in good working condition. Any piece of equipment, unless disclosed otherwise, that is not in good working condition must be repaired and/or replaced by the seller, or the buyer will receive a credit in escrow from the

seller to have the item(s) repaired, and/or replaced. The exception is if the business is being sold "as is." When the buyer gets a contract to purchase the business, it is disclosed in writing that certain pieces of equipment are not working and will not be repaired at the close of escrow, and that the buyer has agreed to these conditions. If a business is being sold "as is," usually the price is adjusted accordingly.

7. **Review Contracts**. The broker will provide and review all the various contracts in the transaction with the buyer; including: the purchase contract, premises lease, and if applicable, any equipment leases, equipment rental agreements, franchise agreement, and any other contracts. One of the most important parts of the sale is the premises lease. It is the broker's responsibility to work closely with the buyer and landlord in negotiating either an assignment of the existing lease, an assignment and modification of the existing lease, or a new lease. For further information about the premises lease see Section VII.

8. **Review Licenses and Permits**. The broker will provide and review all the various licenses and permits needed to operate the business with the buyer —the food permit, alcohol license, entertainment license, fictitious business name license, fire department permit, business license, and health department license, etc. In most counties in California, before a buyer can apply for his business license, he must have a change-of-ownership health department inspection clearance from the health department.

9. **Transfer Various Contracts and Licenses.** It is the broker's responsibility with the buyer to assure that all licenses and contracts are transferred to the buyer before the close of escrow.

   The Assignment of the Premises Lease – If the lease is going to be assigned to the buyer, it must be executed by the buyer (also known as the assignee), the seller (also known as the assignor), and the landlord.

   a. Execution of a New Lease – If the buyer is negotiating a new lease, the lease must be signed by the buyer and landlord.

   b. Equipment Lease – If the buyer is assuming the equipment lease, this lease must be executed between buyer, seller, and the equipment lessor.

   c.   Franchise Agreement – If the business is a franchise, all the various franchise agreements must be signed by the buyer, seller and franchisor.

   d.   Department of Alcoholic Beverage Control License in California (ABC) – If the buyer is having an alcohol license transferred to him from the seller, the ABC license needs to be transferred before the close of escrow.

   e.   Entertainment Licenses – If the buyer is taking over an entertainment license, the buyer must get approval from the proper authorities before the close of escrow.

   f.   Conditional-Use Permit – The right to use the premises for a certain use not typically allowed for the property, per the zoning laws of the local government. If the buyer is assuming a conditional use permit, he should review the conditional-use agreement, and be aware of the proper procedures for renewing the conditional use permit when it expires.

10. **Other Licenses and Permits** – The broker will help direct the buyer to get all the following remaining licenses and permits in place before the close of escrow. This includes the items indicated below:

- Business License – required by local government to operate business.

- Employment Development Department Permit – required to set up the payroll account.

- Franchise Tax Permit – in California you need to set up this permit, which is a registration with the state to pay sales tax and file sales tax returns monthly.

- Fictitious Business Name Statement – required in California to legally register a business name so the buyer has exclusive use of the business name in the state.

11. **Saleable Inventory.** Saleable inventory are the food products, alcohol products, paper supplies, and cleaning supplies that the buyer will have on hand when the escrow closes. If the buyer is buying a going-concern business, the buyer will most likely want to keep the existing saleable inventory at the close of escrow. There will be a not-to-exceed amount for the saleable inventory agreed to when

the purchase contract is executed. Just before the close of escrow, the buyer and seller will take a physical count of the saleable inventory. Then the inventory is computed at the seller's cost, which is paid for at the close of escrow, in addition to the purchase price. In some cases, the saleable inventory is negotiated at a not-to-exceed amount, and is included in the purchase price. If the business is being sold as an assets-in-place transaction, there is a strong possibility that the buyer will not want the saleable inventory because he is putting a new menu in place, or perhaps he wants to purchase only a portion of the saleable inventory, which will most likely include the alcohol inventory. The broker will oversee this whole process to make sure the buyer and seller are handling the inventory on a reasonable basis.

Chapter 50

HOW TO FIND BROKERS IN YOUR AREA THAT SPECIALIZE IN SELLING, RESTAURANTS, BARS AND CLUBS

You can find brokers that specialize in selling these businesses in the many resources listed below. Experienced expertise is available. You just have to do your research.

1. **Website Searches**. Search for the brokers that are selling these types of businesses. In particular, try to seek out brokers that are not generalist business brokers, but specialize exclusively in selling restaurants, bars, and clubs.

2. **Contact Business Opportunity Escrow Companies**. Call these companies and talk to escrow officers for recommendations based on their experience in working with restaurant, bar, and club broker specialists.

3. **Contact Business Broker Associations for Business Broker Recommendations.** Call associations such as:

> Arizona Business Brokers Association,
> Business Brokers of Florida,
> California Association of Business Brokers,
> Colorado Association of Business Intermediaries,
> Carolina-Virginia Business Brokers Association,
> Florida Business Brokers Association,
> Georgia Association of Business Brokers,
> Mid-Atlantic Business Intermediary Association,
> Mid-Atlantic Business Brokers Association,
> Michigan Business Brokers Association,
> Midwest Association of Business Brokers,
> Ohio Business Brokers Association,
> Pennsylvania Business Brokers Association,
> Texas Association of Business Brokers
> International Association of Business Brokers.

4. **Contact Trade Associations.** Call your local or state restaurant association for recommendations or the National Restaurant Association for their recommendations.

5. **Look at Classified Ads for Businesses For Sale, Business Opportunities and/or Restaurants, Bars and Cafes for Sale.** Contact the brokers representing these advertised business opportunities, and screen them as prospective brokers to help you.

6. **Contact Attorneys and Accountants.** Frequently, attorneys and accountants know who the good restaurant, bar, and club specialists are from their experience in dealing with them. I receive a lot of seller referrals from attorneys and accountants who are familiar with my reputation.

7. **Contact Restaurant, Bar, and Club Owners.** If you are familiar with various restaurant, bar, and club owners, contact them and ask for the names of the best-known brokers in the area who specialize in the sales of restaurants, bars and clubs. Then contact these brokers.

8. **Contact BizBuySell.com.** This is a national listing service that has all types of main street businesses for sale, with close to 50,000 business listings. They also have a section dedicated to restaurants, bars, and clubs.

Chapter 51

HOW TO SCREEN BROKERS

If you are considering working with a particular broker to help you find restaurant, bar and club opportunities for sale, here is a list of questions you should ask before deciding to work with them.

- How long have you been a business broker?
- How many restaurants, bars or nightclubs have you sold in the past 12, 24 and 36 months?
- What percent of your offers made close escrow?
- How much experience do you have in negotiating leases with landlords?
- Do you understand how the escrow process works, including the transfer of all licenses, especially the transfer of the alcohol license?
- Are you familiar with all the things I need to do to set up a new business, such as setting up new tax accounts, getting insurance in place, changing utilities, getting a fictitious business name, etc.?

- Will you walk me through the entire buying process—all aspects of the due-diligence process, including physical inspections, review of books and records, and negotiating an assignment of the premises lease, and/or negotiating a new premises lease?
- How many listings are you working on, at any one time?
- What percent of your listings close escrow?
- How long does it take to close escrow on an average deal?
- What sets you apart from other business brokers who sell restaurants, bars, and clubs?
- What sources do you use for finding restaurant, bar, and club opportunities for sale and/or lease?
- If there is a particular restaurant, bar, or club opportunity that is not on the market, but I am interested in purchasing, can you approach the owner to see if I can purchase it?
- What support staff do you have, if any, to help you accomplish your job?
- What is your inventory of restaurants, bars and clubs for sale?

Chapter 52

THE ADVANTAGES OF WORKING WITH AN EXPERIENCED RESTAURANT BROKER

A professional restaurant broker should have vast restaurant experience so he/she, understands the operations, marketing, and financial aspects of the business. Additionally, a competent restaurant broker should have completed numerous and varied types of sales involving restaurants, bars, and clubs. By having the above skills, the restaurant broker can be effective doing the following: 1) realistically evaluating the value of the business, 2) attracting the real buyers, and 3) working through the business points to overcome the buyers and sellers objections and concerns.

By being diligent in the areas indicated below, the broker has a higher probability of selling the business and closing the deal.

1. **Evaluating the Business** – A seasoned restaurant broker knows how to evaluate the business's financial records, the general condition of the business's physical plant, including the equipment, the attractiveness of the premises lease, and the marketability of the location.

2. **Attracting the Real Buyers** – In order to successfully sell a restaurant, bar, or club business, many approaches should be taken to give maximum exposure to selling the business. Some of these approaches include targeted mailings, website marketing, utilization of a well-established buyer data base, and specifically designed telephone campaigns. These approaches, when utilized with careful screening of buyers, especially in confidential sale situations, can provide the best and broadest pool of potential buyers.

3. **Overcoming the Buyer's Objections and Concerns** – When working with a professional restaurant broker, his or her objectivity in handling sensitive business points becomes a key element in making a deal happen. For example, when trying to complete a transaction, a major stumbling block can be dealing with the landlord. A good broker works as an intermediary to assist both buyer and seller in negotiating terms and conditions acceptable to both parties. There is no substitute for working with experienced professionals to gain the desired result of any restaurant.

In Summary

I have tried to cover all the bases, both the specific and minute aspects of my business. If you follow each step, you will have a more successful process. Buying a business is not the time to skip important steps along the way—because the step that you skip, might just be the one that you trip over—and it could cost you money, time, or even cause failure. Ignorance is not bliss when buying a business, so I gave you everything you need to know in my "Restaurant Buying 101," presented in a way, I believe, is easy to find and follow.

I learned these things "at my father's knee," in the family business, and later while working as a restaurant broker working with over a 1,500 clients, helping them buy or sell a restaurant, bar, or nightclub.

I think my clients would tell you that if I didn't cover it, it's not important in this process. Like a lot of things, we don't often talk about "restaurant successes," but rather focus on the "failures." But, today, I have a long list of people who run successful restaurants, and enjoy doing it. They find their business is an answer to their dream and desire to serve the public.

So thank you for entrusting your learning process to my years of experience. Now get out there and find your perfect location. Do your due diligence, buy a place—and start realizing your dream.